The Open University

D103 SOCIETY AND SOCIAL SCIENCE: A FOUNDATION COURSE

BLOCK 2
SOCIAL STRUCTURES AND DIVISIONS

THE OPEN UNIVERSITY

D103 PRODUCTION TEAM

John Allen
James Anderson (Production Chair)
Robert Bocock (Maintenance Chair)
Peter Bradshaw
Vivienne Brown
Linda Clark (Course Secretary)
David Coates
Allan Cochrane
Jeremy Cooper (BBC)
Neil Costello
Clare Falkner (BBC)
Stuart Hall
Susan Himmelweit
Jack Leathem (BBC)
Richard Maidment
Doreen Massey
Gregor McLennan
Andrew Northedge
Kay Pole
Marilyn Ricci (Course Manager)
Paul Smith
Richard Stevens
Elaine Storkey
Kenneth Thompson
Diane Watson
Margaret Wetherell

External Consultants
Tom Burden
David Deacon
David Denver
Caroline Dumonteil
Owen Hartley
Tom Hulley
Robert Looker
Angela Phillips
Colm Regan
Richard Sanders
Neil Thompson
Patrick Wright

Tutor Assessors
Alan Brown
Lyn Brennan
Mona Clark
Ian Crosher
Donna Dickenson
Brian Graham
Philip Markey
Norma Sherratt
Jan Vance

Tom Hunter, Chris Wooldridge, David Wilson, Robert Cookson, Nigel Draper, David Scott-Macnab (Editors); Paul Smith (Librarian); Alison George (Graphic Artist); Jane Sheppard (Designer); Sue Rippon (Project Control); Robin Thornton (Summer School Manager); John Hunt (Summer School IT); John Bennett; and others.

External Academic Assessors
Professor Anthony Giddens, Cambridge University (Overall Assessor)
Dr Geoffrey Harcourt, Cambridge University (Block III)
Dr Patrick Dunleavy, London School of Economics (Block IV)
Dr Halla Beloff, Edinburgh University (Block V)
Professor Brian Robson Manchester, University (Block VI)

The Open University,
Walton Hall, Milton Keynes,
MK7 6AA

First published 1991. New edition 1993, Copyright © 1991, 1993. The Open University

All rights reserved. No part of this work may be reproduced, stored in a retrieval system or transmitted, in any form, or by any means, without written permission from the publisher.

Designed by the Graphic Design Group of the Open University.

Typeset by The Open University and printed in the United Kingdom by The Alden Press, Oxford.

ISBN 0 7492 0159 2

For general availability of supporting material referred to in this text, please write to Open University Educational Enterprises Limited, 12 Cofferidge Close, Stony Stratford, Milton Keynes, MK11 1BY, United Kingdom.

Further information on Open University Courses may be obtained from the Central Enquiry Office, The Open University, P. O. Box 200, Walton Hall, Milton Keynes, MK7 2YZ.

BLOCK INTRODUCTION AND STUDY GUIDE

Prepared for the Course Team by Stuart Hall

1 MOVING ON FROM BLOCK 1

Welcome to Block II. This block picks up many of the threads from your work on Block I — for example, such questions as how social science data are organized and explained, and the discussion in Unit 4 on 'doing social science'. But Block II also has its own distinct concerns. It starts by asking 'what do we mean by society?' What is distinctive about 'the social'? What gives society and 'the social' their distinctive shape and structure? In the course of introducing the question of social divisions, it addresses a number of key social science concepts and definitions — such as 'social class', 'gender', 'race' and 'ethnicity'; it discusses the theories associated with them; and it returns to the issue of how we use concepts to build up social science explanations.

One key argument running through Block II is that the way in which society is structured influences all social behaviour as well as how resources and opportunities are distributed across different groups in society. It is this knowledge of how society is structured which we are drawing on when we try to explain anything in terms of 'social factors' or when we describe any phenomenon or form of behaviour as distinctively 'social'. Take a problem which is discussed at some length in Unit 6 — the question of health and illness. Good health is valued by everyone, regardless of their class background, 'race' or gender; and everyone, sooner or later, will experience illness. However, health and illness are very unevenly distributed throughout the population; and people of different classes or genders, or from different 'racial' and ethnic backgrounds, have remarkably different rates and experiences of illness and death. In other words, the class, gender and ethnic structure of society helps us to understand and unravel an extremely important social problem and one which touches all our lives: inequalities in health.

Block II begins to ask the questions which we need to be able to answer in order to explain inequalities of this kind. How is society divided? How are these divisions conceptualized? How do we use them to provide social explanations? For example, what do we mean by a *social* explanation of health — isn't health a matter of the physical, not the social, body? The block introduces a sustained discussion of the three major principles of social organization which give society its underlying framework — the division of society by class, gender and 'race'/ethnicity — and then suggests how we might use these aspects of social structure to explain social phenomena.

1.1 SYNOPSIS OF THE BLOCK

The block contains four units. Unit 6 introduces the fundamental concepts of 'society' and 'the social'. It examines the distinction between the social world and the world of nature, and between the social and the individual. It discusses the difficult idea of *social structure* — a key term, deployed throughout the social sciences — and the social relations, social processes and social divisions which provide society with its anatomy. It briefly introduces the three main social divisions.

These are much more fully developed in the succeeding units. Unit 7 Part I focuses on the question of social class. It provides examples of the way social

3

class is represented in the contemporary UK and it reviews some of the major theories (and theorists) of social class. It outlines some of the most significant historical changes in the British class structure and discusses the theoretical attempts to explain these shifts. Unit 7 Part II analyses ethnic and 'racial' divisions in Britain today. It discusses how the key concepts of 'race' and 'ethnicity' are defined and considers various explanations of 'racial' division, using different theoretical frameworks. Unit 8 Part I deals with questions of gender divisions, looking at the changing position of women in paid employment and domestic labour and considers a number of theories of the division of labour between men and women. Unit 8 Part II then examines how all three of the social divisions discussed in the block combine or articulate together to influence the position and circumstances of particular groups or individuals.

The first three units of Block II thus introduce you to some fundamental theories and concepts in social science. They also use empirical data and concrete examples from everyday life in contemporary society to sustain and illustrate their arguments. In this way, they help to build up a picture of contemporary society, as well as relating theoretical questions to recognizable issues in the 'real world'.

There is a second strand running through Block II. The block addresses not only what a 'society' is like and how it is structured, but also how we study and explain it. It looks at social science itself, its theories and methods — and it does so by giving examples of the work of social scientists. Many of the activities in the units are specifically designed to give you some practice in developing skills of analysis and thinking so that, by working through them, you can begin to 'do' social science for yourself.

This more 'methodological' aspect of the block includes the need for clear definitions of concepts, the role of conceptualization itself in building up a social science explanation, the interdependence between evidence and data — facts and theories, and the role which the classification and organization of data play in explanation. It also includes a brief introduction to some guidelines which can help in the assessment of theories and explanations. This question of conceptualization and theory construction is the main focus of Unit 9 which completes the block.

1.2   OTHER COMPONENTS

THE READER

Anderson, J. and Ricci, M. (eds) (1990) *Society and Social Science: a Reader.*

Chapter 4, extracted from the Black Report and *The Health Divide*, examines how life style and social class position have been used to explain differences in the distribution of health and illness in the British population. It picks up many threads first introduced in Unit 6 and Unit 7 Part I.

At the end of Unit 7 Part II you can read an article by John Solomos on how discussions of 'race' and racism change over time; and in Unit 8 Part II you will be asked to read an article by Tariq Modood on how Indians, as an ethnic group within the UK, have challenged assumptions made about them. You will be guided in the units as to when the reading of these articles would be most appropriate.

THE TRADITIONS

Block II carries over from Block I — and develops — aspects of the four *Traditions* of social thought first introduced in Unit 5. The discussion of individualism in Unit 6 relates directly to Section 2.1 in Unit 5 on liberalism, and there is also material in the block relating to the other traditions. In Unit 7 you will be asked to read Section 2.2 of Chapter 22 of the Reader — the section on marxism — and there is also a brief discussion on social reformism at the end of Section 2.3 which deals with the work of Max Weber, again referring you to a short piece in the Reader.

TELEVISION

There are two television programmes associated with this block. The discussion of class in Unit 7 makes the point that the British class structure has changed significantly since the term was first used in the nineteenth century. The first television programme, TV03, underlines this point about continuity and change across historical time by examining two key periods in the historical formation of the English class structure — the agrarian revolution in the seventeenth century and the industrial revolution at the beginning of the nineteenth. Both periods have already been referred to in Chapter 1 of the Reader. TV03 aims to show how these changes in class formation, which reflected the rise to power of different social classes, shaped and moulded the English countryside itself, as well as the image of 'England' which the landscape is often used to represent. This is one place in the block where you will find a more historical treatment of block concerns. The second programme, TV04, deals with more contemporary features of the UK. It looks at the distinctive — and different — experiences of family life amongst the different ethnic groups who have migrated to Britain since the Second World War. There is supporting material relating to both these programmes in the *D103 Media Booklet*. Reading through these materials *before* you watch the programmes and doing the Activities will help you to get the most out of the programmes.

RADIO AND AUDIO-CASSETTE TAPE

There are two radio programmes associated with Block II. Radio 03 contains a discussion of social divisions with researchers in this field; and Radio 04 is a magazine programme which will help with TMA 02.

The Block II cassette tape will be used, early in the block, to introduce the block's main concerns and you will be directed to the cassette at other appropriate points in your study of the block.

STUDY SKILLS

During the course of your work on Block II, you will be asked to read some relevant sections of *The Good Study Guide*. It is important, as you work on the substantive issues raised in the units, to keep up your work on study skills. We would suggest that you read Chapter 3, Sections 1 and 2, of *The Good Study Guide* in Week 6; and Chapter 4, Sections 1–4 in Week 7. In Week 8 you should spend your 'study skills' time working on the 'Use and Abuse of Statistics' section at the end of Unit 8.

COURSE THEMES

Block II builds on the course-wide themes which were introduced to you in Block I. The theme of *Representation and Reality* is used in Unit 6, in dealing with people's representations of illness and the body; in Unit 7 Part I, for representations of class; and in Unit 7 Part II and Unit 8 Part I for representations of 'race' and gender. The theme of *Public and Private* surfaces, especially in relation to issues of gender and the family, since the domestic world is so often misrepresented as exclusively the 'feminine' domain of social life, and thus — in one definition of the theme — *par excellence* the sphere of the *Private*. Both Unit 6 (in its discussion of 'slave societies' and the 'desert island' example) and Unit 7 Part II (in the discussion of the impact of migration on 'race' and ethnic relations) advance the theme of *Local and Global*.

RESOURCE FILE

Compiling a Resource File is optional, but Block II does provide many rich ideas for collecting your own materials and you would certainly benefit by following these up. Questions of inequality in health and illness in Unit 6, for example, are given extensive, almost daily coverage in the media and there are frequent reports and debates on this issue which will be reported in the press. Unit 7 Part I opens with an intriguing set of 'documents' from the press which tell us a great deal about how social class is represented in the media and experienced in everyday life. Questions about the position of women, of sex discrimination and equal opportunities, and debates about 'race' and ethnic discrimination are constantly in the news and it may help you to keep track of how these issues are being discussed and debated by collecting materials on them from newspapers and magazine articles and features.

2 STUDY TIME ALLOCATIONS

The basis of these time allocations is described in the Course Guide, Section 3.1. They will enable you to plan roughly what proportion of your available time to devote to each component.

Block components	Approximate study time (hours)
Block Introduction and *Study Guide*	$\frac{1}{2}$
Unit 6: The idea of 'the social' in social science	$6\frac{1}{2}$
Reader: Chapter 4	2
Audio-cassette — Tape 2	1
The Good Study Guide: Chapter 3, Sections 1 & 2	1
TV 03: Reading the landscape	2
Total	13
Unit 7: Class, 'race' and ethnicity	7
Reader: Chapter 22, Section 2.2 (marxism) and part of 2.3	2
The Good Study Guide, Chapter 4, Sections 1–4	2
Reader: Chapter 5 (Optional)	1
Radio 03	$\frac{1}{2}$
Total	$12\frac{1}{2}$
Unit 8: Gender divisions and the interacting dynamics of class, 'race'/ethnicity and gender	7
Audio-cassette — Tape 2	$\frac{1}{2}$
Study Skills Section: Uses and abuses of statistics	$1\frac{1}{2}$
Reader: Chapter 6	1
TV 04: Migration, prejudice and ethnicity	2
Total	12
Unit 9: The role of concepts in social science thinking	3
Radio 04	$\frac{1}{2}$
TMA 02	6
Total	$9\frac{1}{2}$

UNIT 6   THE IDEA OF THE 'SOCIAL'

Prepared for the Course Team by Stuart Hall

CONTENTS

1   MAKING SENSE OF 'THE SOCIAL'

Why do people die at a faster rate in the North of England or in Scotland than they do in the South-East? Why do children whose parents are bus conductors, cleaners or shop assistants have a much higher chance of being injured in the home than children whose parents are doctors or lawyers? Social scientists would say that the reasons have to do with 'society'. The factors which best explain these features of health and illness in Britain today are 'social'.

The concepts 'society' and 'social' are to be found throughout D103. They were used in Block I, for example, in the discussion of the social causes of world hunger. It is impossible to study the social sciences without using these concepts, yet they are very difficult ideas to define precisely. Social scientists don't always agree about them, and in the wider political world they have sometimes become what we call 'contested concepts' — ideas which are highly charged and about which people hold definite, but strongly opposing views. Since they are so fundamental to the whole social science enterprise, we need to explore them further, in order to discover what social scientists mean by them and how they put them to work in the business of 'doing' social science. That is what this unit is about.

The unit aims to do the following:

1   clarify exactly what we mean in social science by concepts like 'society' and 'social';

2   discuss, with examples, the relationship between 'society' and nature — between the 'social' and the 'natural' worlds;

3   discuss, with examples, the relationship between 'the social' and 'the individual';

4   examine the idea of society itself as a 'social structure';

5   show how we use our knowledge of society to make sense of social phenomena.

In common-sense language, 'society' refers to groups of people living together, in one community, and developing a common way of life. We also sometimes speak of 'a society'. This has a slightly different emphasis, meaning a particular society like Britain or the United States: a country with definite geographical and political boundaries, which also has a distinctive history, culture and pattern of development. 'Social' is the adjective from 'society', meaning 'deriving from or pertaining to society'.

Social science usage often seems to overlap with these common-sense usages. Thus a 'social relationship' is one that arises between individuals and groups as a result of how they organize and live their lives together in society. The family is a 'social institution' because it is formed in society, has a social function (organizing the sexual life of adults and providing the setting for the rearing of children) and is connected with the wider society around it. To explain any phenomenon 'socially' means relating it to society, showing that it arises as a result of the way the wider society is shaped and demonstrating which aspects of society have influenced or determined its shape or outcome.

However, it is necessary to identify and isolate the 'social' dimension from other aspects in order to describe and study it. We use the word 'social' as a marker, to distinguish it from other aspects of behaviour, other kinds of explanation. We really mean social rather than — as distinct from — physical, biological, mechanical or supernatural. The word 'social' marks off the 'sciences of society' from other sciences like anatomy, which is the science of the physical structure of the body, or astronomy, which is the science of the universe and of heavenly bodies. It also marks the difference between what is wholly the result of individual action and motivation and what has to be explained in terms of groups of individuals, or with reference to 'society' itself, as an object in its own right. We know what words mean, partly, by understanding what they are *not* — hot/cold, light/dark. In this unit we shall explore the social by trying to understand its difference from either the natural or the individual. This distinction is the key argument in the first half of the unit.

The need to differentiate the social aspect of behaviour from other aspects partly explains why social science needs to go beyond 'common sense'. In common-sense terms, we experience ourselves as both natural and individual. Like plants and animals in nature, we are born, develop and die. Our bodies are governed by physical and genetic principles. But where our bodies end, other people — the outside world — begin. We tend to identify our 'real self' with this unique entity — the individual. We don't experience the world exactly like other people. This is precisely what the word 'individual' means: distinct from others, whole, self-sufficient, that which cannot be divided.

The notion that we are not just individuals but also social, that our differences are determined not only by nature but also by culture, runs sharply counter to common-sense experience. The same is true when social scientists claim that our bodies and physical characteristics are 'socially constructed'. On the face of it, this seems neither plausible nor obvious. And yet this *is* what social scientists are saying.

In the rest of this unit I try to relate the discussion of 'the social' to these two adjacent and overlapping areas — the natural world and the world of the individual. Many of my examples will relate to the *body*, precisely because it seems to function as such a concrete, unquestionable guarantee of our physical nature and our individuality. I have chosen to do this in part because a lot of exciting work in social science is being done in this area, but mainly because it represents such a challenge to common-sense thinking, and runs against the grain of how everyday knowledge is organized in our culture. *If* I can show that the body is *also* social, then I will have gone a long way towards proving my point about the significance of 'the social' in general. The tougher the opposition, the stronger the case …

Let me give three common-sense examples to highlight the difficulty in arriving at a satisfactory definition of 'society' and 'the social'.

ACTIVITY 1

As you read each example, try to answer for yourself the question printed in italics at the end. I won't provide you with answers immediately; that is really what the rest of the unit is about. However, it will be helpful to have tried the exercise for yourself.

1 Take the example of a party, where several people are standing around, drinking and talking. We think of this as a 'social occasion'; we might even say that 'these people are socializing'. Now suppose someone came along and said, 'I don't see anything particularly "social" about this. It looks to me like a lot of individuals, standing around, having a good time', how would you reply? Is 'social' just another, rather loose way of referring to a random collection of individuals, or is there something additional, special and distinctive, which is the social aspect? In other words, *can you really separate the social from the individual?*

2 Consider a second example — the famous 'desert island' or Robinson Crusoe case. (We shall develop this example in Section 2.3 of the unit, but for the moment I want to use it simply to illustrate a point.) A person is stranded,

alone, on a desert island. He/she manages to build a shelter, to plant enough food to eat, to hunt, fish and generally live a reasonable existence until, years later, a rescue ship arrives. *While this person was on the desert island, would you describe his/her splendid isolation as living in a 'society'? Can you have a society composed of one individual?*

3   Consider a third example. We are in a hospital ward. A group of doctors and nurses are standing around a patient's bed. The patient is quite ill, and the hospital staff are urgently discussing what is the most effective treatment to use to prevent her heart shutting off for good. They are looking for the best medical answer to a physical problem. *Would you describe this scene as a 'social' situation and, if so, why?*

1.1   THE SOCIAL AND THE NATURAL: NO SMOKE WITHOUT FIRE

We can begin to develop an answer to this question of the distinction between the social and the natural by looking at a more detailed example of how a social scientist goes about 'working with the social' to construct an explanation.

ACTIVITY 2

As you read through the following example, treat it as an activity. Work through the example as you read. I will try to point out the steps the researcher is making. You should pay attention both to *how* it is being done — questions of method and approach — and of *what* this tells us about social trends in British society today.

The social scientist, Lesley Doyal, has done pioneering work on the health and medical problems of women. These problems have received much greater attention in recent years, partly because feminist researchers have directed our attention to the way such aspects of health have been neglected in the past by medical researchers. Social problems themselves have changing social visibility — and these shifts in attention can themselves be explained in sociological terms.

In her popular pamphlet, *Picture of Health*, Doyal (1983) made the following, startling observation: 'A great deal of money has been spent on trying to persuade people to give up smoking but in general the emphasis has been on men ... Smoking has been thought of as a predominantly male problem. In reality, smoking is increasingly a women's problem too'. Is this really the case? And if so, why? The published statistics suggest that the proportion of male smokers in the British population fell from nearly 60 per cent in 1961 to about 42 per cent in 1980, but the population of women smokers remained steady at around 40 per cent. It is certainly still the case that more men smoke than women; and the overall trend for this period is 'downwards'. But the gap between men and women is narrowing; men seem to be giving up smoking faster than women. It is even more dramatic when you look at numbers of cigarettes smoked, which has risen more among women (15 per cent between 1972 and 1980) than among men (about 3 per cent over the same period). This is influencing the pattern of health among women in Britain. Between 1969 and 1978 lung cancer rates rose by about 8 per cent in men but by an alarming 50 per cent in women. This *trend* — by which we mean the pattern over the period of time from 1948 to 1980 — can be seen at a glance from Figure 1, which summarizes the information in visual terms.

Let us follow how Lesley Doyal goes about 'working with the social'. She conceptualizes a problem and collects some data herself, or examines the available information from reliable sources. The data relate to a physical or medical problem — a matter of the body, of health and illness; but there is a *social pattern* to the way this is distributed in the population, when you compare one social group, defined by gender — women — with another — men; and it is *this* uneven distribution which, as a social scientist, she is trying to understand and explain.

Of course, we must never take data for granted. As Block I argued, gathering data is essential to the practice of doing social science, but we must always question the evidence. What do the data leave out? Who gathered them? What part of the country, section of the population or period of time do they cover? You can't just use data. You also have to interrogate them. For example, if you only look at the unemployment statistics for the latter half of the 1980s, they appear to be falling; but if you take the figures for the whole of the decade, you will see that they rose very sharply in the first half of the period and though they are going down in the second half, they were still much higher at the end of the 1980s than they were in the 1960s and 1970s. Politicians have a particularly sharp eye for how you can create a favourable impression by starting and stopping your statistics at particular dates!

In this case, more recent statistics about smoking suggest that the pattern has shifted again since Doyal's data were collected. According to the 1988 issue of the government publication *Social Trends*, smoking is going up again for *both* men and women. You also have to be careful about how things are defined. The data on smoking don't seem to include pipes and cigars, and this skews

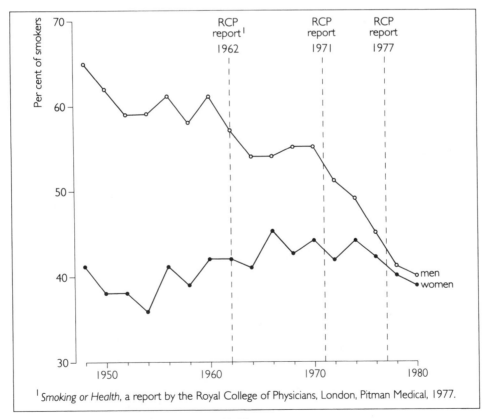

Figure 1   Percentage of cigarette smokers, 1948–79

Source: Doyal, 1983, p.8; based on statistics from the Tobacco Research Council and the Tobacco Advisory Committee

the figures somewhat. Men who are trying to give up cigarette smoking find it easier than women to move to a pipe or to small cigars — a fact which in itself requires a social explanation, since it points to differences in behaviour and social convention between men and women. Pipes and cigars seem to have a more 'masculine' image in our culture than cigarettes. In general, then, the gap between the total numbers of men and women who smoke may not be quite as small as is often suggested.

Now that we are clear about what the figures mean, let us stick with the data we have for the moment for the purposes of the exercise. Notice that the researcher has arranged or classified the data according to male and female smokers in order to bring out certain significant patterns and relationships which interest her. Classifying the data in this way highlights the contrast between smoking trends among men and women and therefore focuses our minds on the relationship between smoking and gender differences in society. Classification is a way of making sense of data; the data can't 'arrange' themselves! We need facts, information; but the facts don't speak for themselves. You may remember the discussions in Unit 4 of the two-way relationship between 'facts' and 'theories'. Where do you think Lesley Doyal got the notion that looking at smoking in terms of gender differences might reveal something important about smoking patterns? The short answer is that she knew this might be the case because of *her understanding of society itself and how it is organized.* Male/female differences are one of the principal ways in which human behaviour is differentiated, and arise from one of the fundamental divisions between groups in society. We will return to this question when we look at 'society' and its structures and divisions in Section 4 of the unit.

Having generated and classified the information, the next question is *why*? Supposing the figures to be roughly correct, how can we *explain* the trends and patterns we have discovered?

We could look for a purely physical or biological explanation of the data. Perhaps women have a special gene or something else in their biological make-up which makes it harder for them to give up nicotine addiction than men. This seems very unlikely. We do not know of any such factor in the biological

Is smoking a feminist issue?

constitution of men and women and, on the face of it, it seems unlikely that this should be the explanation. For one thing, the pattern of smoking among women has changed significantly over a period of thirty years, whilst changes in genetic or biological constitution only occur over a much longer period of time. There *is* a physical component to smoking — we can become physically habituated to or dependent on a particular drug. But that alone does not explain the distribution between men and women we have discovered here. So the researcher looked for a *social* explanation; that is, she looked for features of the society, or social causes, which might help to explain why the trends are as they appear to be. She related the phenomenon — the narrowing gap between male and female smokers in a certain period — to social conditions or to certain features of the way men and women live in society.

Bobby Jacobson, who has studied the same phenomenon in her book, *The Ladykillers: Why Smoking Is A Feminist Issue* (1981), suggests three social factors which might help to explain the trend:

(1) as men have given up smoking in large numbers, the tobacco manufacturers have increasingly concentrated their marketing efforts on women;

(2) once hooked, women seem to have their own particular problems in giving up — problems that have to be understood in the wider context of women's lives;

(3) health professionals have shown very little interest in these problems, and have offered women little support in their efforts to give up smoking.

(Jacobson, 1981, p.25)

Explanation is a critical part of social science (some would say the goal of the whole enterprise), so you might like now to read for yourself Lesley Doyal's own account of how she makes sense of the problem she identified. She drew on further research with women smokers and this helped her to provide a more developed and connected account which makes the relationship between women smoking and the wider context of women's lives in society more plausible and convincing.

Why do so many women smoke and why do they find it difficult to stop?

A simple answer might be that they enjoy it but discussion with women about their habit reveals that things are often more complicated. One of the most striking facts to emerge is that more women than men seem to smoke to reduce their negative feelings. That is to say, they smoke in order to suppress the frustration and anger for which they have no other socially acceptable outlet. Women at home, for instance, who are looking after small children, often use cigarettes to keep control of themselves and to avoid expressing the hostility they will sometimes feel towards their husband and children. For many women a cigarette also represents 'time for herself' — one of the only respites she may get from the demands of others. The mother is expected to hold the family together, to absorb other people's frustrations, and many women have said they smoke to relieve the tension. Men can come home and explode or go drinking 'with the boys' but most women have only their cigarettes to keep them 'on their best behaviour'.

Women who work outside the home smoke even more than full-time housewives. Discussion with women suggests that this is often a way of coping with the double burden of waged work and housework. Many women also relate their smoking to the kinds of jobs they do. Professional women often have to compete in what is effectively a man's world and smoking can be a means of hiding their fear or acquiring confidence. Women doctors, for instance, are more likely to smoke than their male colleagues. But nurses as a group are much more likely to smoke than doctors and this has been attributed to the high levels of frustration and boredom that are experienced particularly by those at the lower end of the nursing hierarchy. Hospital nurses are trapped on the ward, often with very little control over their own activities. At night especially they may have sudden crises punctuating long periods of boredom which many relieve with a cigarette. The same pattern is found in many other jobs typically done by women, where low wages, low status and repetitive work may drive them to cigarettes. Interestingly, then, the distribution of women smokers within society is different from that of men. Men are much more likely to smoke if they are manual workers than if they are professionals. However, among women, rates are high in both upper and lower social classes and there seem to be pressures that keep them smoking at both ends of the social scale.

So, women often smoke to suppress their emotions in situations where they are afraid of the consequences of showing their real feelings. This makes smoking an extremely important prop in their lives and one which most find it very difficult to give up. These difficulties are often compounded by women's lack of self-esteem and their lack of confidence in their own abilities. Research has shown that most men who want to give up smoking start off believing they can do it. Women on the other hand will admit to being 'addicted' and will say that they haven't the will-power to quit. This is an important point because it reflects other aspects of women's lives. They lack power in so many spheres — whether at home or at work — and many develop a self-image of 'powerlessness', believing themselves incapable of changing their own lives. So they go on smoking, though research has shown that a large proportion of women smokers would actually like to give up. In general, women are only about half as successful as men in giving up smoking and this applies across most age groups and social classes.

(Doyal, 1983, p.10)

1.2   DEATH IS A SOCIAL PROCESS

The Lesley Doyal example was concerned with how social factors — i.e. gender divisions — influence patterns of smoking. She could have organized and classified her data so as to highlight other significant social factors. Look, for example, at the data summarized in Table 1.

Table 1   Death rates by sex and social (occupational) class (15–64 years, rates per 1,000 population, England and Wales, 1971)

Social (occupational class)	Males	Females[1]	Ratio M/F
I (Professional)	3.98	2.15	1.85
II (Intermediate)	5.54	2.85	1.94
IIIN (Skilled non-manual)	5.80	2.76	1.96
IIIM (Skilled manual)	6.08	3.41	1.78
IV (Partly skilled)	7.96	4.27	1.87
V (Unskilled)	9.88	5.31	1.86
Ratio V/I	2.5	2.5	

[1] In this table women with husbands have been classified by their husband's occupation, women of other marital statuses are attributed to their *own* occupational class.

Source: *Occupational Mortality 1970–2*; reprinted in Townsend and Davidson, 1988, p.59

Table 1 sets out the rates at which people die according to their gender and occupational class position. (The death rate compares the speed at which people are dying in one group with another group.)

Think, first, about the evidence. This table is for 1971 and was included in *Occupational Mortality 1970–72*, published for the Office of Population Censuses and Surveys by Her Majesty's Stationery Office. Data of this kind take a long time to assemble and are usually somewhat out of date by the time they are published. The table covers England and Wales only (not, that is, Scotland or Northern Ireland, where trends might be different — we can't tell from this table). It would have been possible to find more recent data for the whole of the UK, but I wanted to underline the point that you must always be critical about the data you are using.

The data are classified according to social class and gender. Gender is defined in terms of sex (male and female). Class position is more complicated. This table defines social class position primarily in terms of a person's occupation. It doesn't tell us the death rates for every occupation but sorts occupations into six broad groupings (see the brackets in column 1):

Professional

Intermediate

Skilled non-manual

Skilled manual

Partly skilled

Unskilled

Not all statistics define 'occupational class' in the same way. In fact, as you may remember from Block I, the most common way of defining 'occupational class' in official statistics is according to the Registrar General's system of classification, which identifies five classes:

I Professional	(e.g. accountant, doctor, lawyer)
II Intermediate	(e.g. nurse, school teacher)
III Skilled Non-manual	(e.g. clerical worker, secretary, shop assistant)
IV Partly skilled	(e.g. bus conductor, postman)
V Unskilled	(e.g. cleaner, dock worker, labourer)

These rough-and-ready groupings contain a lot of anomalies. Where, for example, would you put managers? Or housewives? The statisticians constantly change their minds as to exactly where each occupation fits in the rank. Most confusing, and most dubious, of all, Table 1 tells us that, women with husbands have been given the 'occupational class' of their husbands, but women with other kinds of marital status are given their own occupational class!

However, now at least we know how the data are classified, their limitations and what the classifications mean. What does the evidence tell us about the different rates at which different groups in the population die?

1.3   INTERPRETING THE DATA

Answering the above question depends on making comparisons, and the most important clues to look for are similarities and contrasts. Look at column 2 and compare the top and the bottom figures. For every 1,000 people in the population, professional men, like doctors and lawyers, die at the rate of 3.98, while unskilled men, like cleaners, die at the rate of 9.88. The same class patterning is true for women, shown in column 3 (with the slight anomaly in the figures for class II (2.85) and class III (2.76)). But the rates in each group are higher for men than for women. You can see this by comparing men with women, for each class group, now reading across the table. In the Professional class (I) the rate for men is 3.98, for women 2.15. In the unskilled class, the rate for men is 9.88, for women 5.31.

What significant patterns do these comparisons and contrasts suggest? How do we interpret them? The table suggests that death rates are strongly related to occupational class position. As *The Health Divide* summarized the figures for the 1980s, which showed the same trends: 'the risk of death for lower occupational classes was much higher than that of the highest occupational classes at every stage of life' (p.236). This is not substantially affected by age. Though you can't see it from Table 1, if these statistics were broken down by age, the class differences for different occupational groups remain. 'At any age people in occupational class V have a higher rate of death than their better-off counterparts' (Black Report, p.43).

There are some significant differences related to gender. The risk of death for men in each occupational class is almost twice that for women. Men tend to have a higher death rate, throughout the population, than women. You may be interested to know that women seem to experience more illness, but die on average later than men. So, the Black Report says, 'the gap in life expectancy between men and women is one of the most distinctive features of human health in advanced societies'.

Summing up these two major patterns, the Report concludes that 'gender and class exert highly significant but different influences on the quality and duration of life in modern society' (p.49).

Now comes the most important question of all. *Why* do class and gender have this kind of effect on the rate at which different sorts of people die? How can the patterns be explained?

Ah! This the table cannot answer. For this we need ideas, concepts, hunches, but above all knowledge about how society is structured, how 'class' and 'gender' divisions work and relate to one another. We need theories and explanatory frameworks about how social divisions influence social behaviour in order to make sense of the relationships we have discovered empirically, between illness, death, class and gender.

1.4   THE BODY AS A SOCIAL CONSTRUCTION

You may by now have gained the impression that there is really only one kind of evidence, one kind of method or approach, one kind of work, which social scientists do in order to explain social phenomena. They deal with statistical data or data which can be quantitatively expressed. They collect this information, classify it according to some standard system, and see which of a variety of factors, drawn from an understanding of social structure and processes, best explains what they have discovered.

This is certainly *one* approach to empirical social science. But it is not the only one. Social scientists also use qualitative data — information which cannot be easily expressed quantitatively, but which is nevertheless rich in the detailed evidence and insight it provides into social processes and relationships. Quantitative information is a necessary part of mapping patterns across a wide sample of the population. Qualitative evidence compensates, in depth, for what statistical evidence offers in terms of breadth.

There are many different, but equally valid and useful, methods and procedures for isolating the *social* dimension of a problem, or for studying social processes at work. Historical analysis, for example, or setting a single event or a small-scale activity in the context of wider relationships or more long-term processes, or getting at the underlying dynamics of social development and changes over time, are all equally valid approaches and a necessary part of the interpretative procedures of social understanding.

This helps us to underline a point that we made at the end of both the Lesley Doyal and the *Health Divide* examples. Understanding — which is our ultimate objective — is not achieved by any technical research procedure alone. It isn't enough to isolate a number of factors that influence the pattern or shape of some social activity, like smoking, and quantify them. Our ultimate aim must be to provide an account of the phenomenon *which 'makes sense' of it, in social terms*.

I want to conclude this discussion of the social and the natural with an example of this second kind, by looking now at a piece of *qualitative* evidence. What follows is not statistical evidence about a social group but an account by a single individual. It is about the body itself, which is a physical object. Yet it tells us a great deal about the relationship between the social and the natural and shows how the body itself, and the way we experience our bodies, can be socially interpreted and explained.

Here is an account of what it feels like to be ill and undergoing treatment, by a woman whom I shall call Barbara. The passage is not a description of physical effects but rather Barbara's own observations of the way a physical illness altered her perception of her body and herself:

> What is it like to live in a body that keeps on changing? It's frightening, terrifying, and confusing. It generates a feeling of helplessness; it produces a slavish attention to the body; it creates an unnatural hypervigilance toward any and all sensations that occur within the landscape of the body. One becomes a prisoner to any perceptible change in the body, any cough, any difference in sensation. One loses one's sense of stability and predictability, as well as a sense of control over the body. It forces you to give up the idea that you can will the body to behave in ways you would like. Grieving over the loss of that predictability complicates the process of adjustment to an unstable body. Time becomes shortened and is marked by the space between symptoms.
>
> In our culture, it is very common to rely on the body as the ultimate arbiter of truth. We consult our bodies like an oracle. While every emotion may not be consciously available to be experienced, the body knows the truth. We cannot conceal the truth from the body.
>
> We turn to the body to decipher its coded language, to apprehend its grammar and syntax. By noticing the body's responses to situations, we have an idea about how we 'really feel about things'. For example, if you get knots in your stomach every time a certain person walks into the room, you have an important body clue to investigate. Or if you weep excessively during a yawn, you might suspect that you may be experiencing some deep and underlying sadness that has not yet come to the surface or, as Wordsworth put it, 'a thought too deep for tears'.
>
> We trust that the body will tell us the truth about emotions that are hidden from consciousness. We trust that the body knows things before the mind does. Our job is to mind the body, to mine the body, to interpret its language.
>
> I was thrown into a crisis of meaning. I could no longer assess and evaluate what sensations meant. I could no longer measure the

intensity of sensations. I was no longer fluent in the language of my
body, its signs, and symbols, and I felt lost.

(Rosenblum, 1988)

This is a very moving and powerful account of the experience of being ill and
under treatment. I stress *experience*. The body is a physical thing, part of
nature, and its processes are biologically, chemically and genetically determined. But it is also a social object — something that can be felt and experienced by us. However, in order to experience our own bodies, we have somehow
to give its physical sensations meaning; these meanings are not provided by
nature but drawn from the imagery and language that we find in society and in
the many representations of our bodies that are available to us through our
culture. In different cultures the body is experienced very differently from the
way Barbara makes sense of it. This is exactly what Barbara is commenting on
— how a physical process is interpreted meaningfully by herself; how she
'reads' the language of her body in order to 'make sense' of it; and the imagery
and language she then uses to convey or represent these changes in the meaning of illness to us, her readers.

Illness, she argues, turns our minds to the body's material and biological
character. We become preoccupied with its physicality, its fragility and vulnerability. She also reminds us of how individual an experience illness can be. It
isolates us from the community of other 'normal' people who are healthy. In the
end, we must go through an illness on our own. Other people may sympathise
with us, but they cannot be ill on our behalf. Yet Barbara's physical symptoms
only make sense to her if they can be culturally interpreted as a meaningful
experience; once communicated in language to other people, they can become,
in that way, part of a wider, shared social experience.

Thus, the body itself, though a part of nature and subject to its laws, is also
socially and culturally constructed. It can therefore be approached from many
different angles. For example, like Barbara, we can try to understand the body
in terms of how an individual makes sense of his or her body. Another approach
might be to study how illness, which affects our bodies, thereby influences the
'life chances' of people in different social groups (classes, occupational groups,
gender or ethnic groups). Or we could look at relationships between those who
care for the body — doctors and patients, the hospital or the health clinic as
social institutions. We could trace the patterns of health, illness and mortality
for different regions of the country or different occupational groups. We could
study how the routines of health, illness and death are organized in everyday
life, and so on.

One way of 'mapping' the body is to set it in a wider social context and study it
from the point of view of wider social processes.

From this point of view, we would study the body as the focal point of a variety
of different social activities. We have to reproduce it, feed it, look after it when
it is hungry or cold, groom and present it, train it, discipline it, use it to produce
and consume things, and so on. Each of these is a social process, involving
socially organized activities within institutions. Each connects our bodies to
wider social processes. 'Reproduction' relates our bodies to our sexual relationships, the forms of the family through which in our culture so much of the daily
life that keeps us alive is organized, as well as the medical and social services
which are concerned with pregnancy, birth and early life. 'Feeding' connects
the body to all the systems by which we produce, acquire, buy, prepare and
consume food. 'Discipline' relates the body to practices within the family and
home, as well as schooling and education. 'Grooming', a practice which takes up
a lot of time, money and effort in our society, covers the practices of choosing

and buying clothes, of dressing in different styles, as well as of cosmetics, diet and the arts of making the body desirable — the whole complex business of the adornment and presentation of the body.

These activities can also be studied at different levels. We can look at the body in terms of daily life: working, cooking, dressing, washing, resting and presenting the body. It can also be studied at a more 'macro' level: the way any society controls the body in space and time, by regulation, training and disciplining it for work, or city life.

Alternatively, we can look at the body in terms of long-term historical change. Compared with, say, two hundred years ago, some social scientists have argued that the body has become more like a commodity and more standardized. A hundred years ago no one would have approached the pursuit of exercise and fitness as part of an organized regime of 'body maintenance' in the way joggers and health fans do today. We have a much more 'rational' conception of how to look after and present our bodies. You have only to go into any large department store like C & A or Marks and Spencer and look at the sizes and shapes into which all their clothes are classified (30 waist, 32 length, slim cut) to see how the body has become 'standardized' as it has entered more and more into the mass production and mass consumption systems.

Another way of studying the body is as the subject of different forms of representation in cultural imagery and an object which is constructed in the different branches of knowledge. You will recognize here a connection with one of the main course themes — that of *representation and reality*. The body is represented in one way in medical language and in a quite different way in the imagery of fashion or advertising. Anatomists represent the body as held together by the scaffolding of our skeletal structure. Leonardo da Vinci made anatomical sketches but, as a sculptor, he saw the body as composed of sensuous curves. Advertisers use the body as a sign or symbol of the desirable object. We, too, handle our own bodies within these different codes of meaning. When we dress in a certain style of clothes, we are 'presenting' or representing our bodies in public or social space. We are using them to express or symbolize certain attitudes or feelings (we are happy, sad, feeling reflective, sophisticated or daring). We hope others will 'read' them according to the same codes of meaning. Our styles of dress are thus a sort of public language. Our bodies 'say' that we are street-wise, fashion conscious, confident about holding down an important job, don't care a damn about appearance provided we are comfortable, and so on.

"STOP THE TRAFFIC HONEY, DON'T GET STUCK IN IT"

Panda FROM £3,298

The body is represented through different codes of meaning. Advertisers often use the body as a sign or symbol of the desirable object

When we 'experience' our own bodies, like Barbara, we are also really representing them to ourselves. We perceive them (and others perceive and classify us) according to these different frameworks of meaning and social perception. They are measured against some culturally defined ideal or norm — they are 'beautiful', or 'ugly' or 'thin'. In some societies the body is marked in highly elaborate and ornate ways, and sometimes defaced, to signify that the person has made the transition from one social status to another: from child to adult, girl to woman, boy to man. The elevation of individuals to high public office is marked, in every culture, by rituals and ceremonials which involve 'dressing up' — the symbolic use of bodies.

SUMMARY

Let us pause for a moment and summarize the argument so far. The first task was to isolate the social aspect of a phenomenon from the natural. Lesley Doyal used gender differences, between the social position of men and women, to account for variations in smoking patterns. *The Health Divide* used both gender and occupational class to explain differences in death rates. Both smoking and dying are very physical, with clear biological and physiological characteristics and effects. But, the evidence suggests, their distribution across the population is significantly influenced by social factors. The social divisions of class and gender give smoking and death a distinctive shape, as social facts.

The second task was to see how one actually goes about using social factors to provide an explanation of something. These are the basic steps taken in both these pieces of research:

1 Identify and conceptualize a social problem.
2 Collect or consult some information about it.
3 Classify the data so as to highlight certain significant patterns, relationships, trends.
4 Summarize the data in a diagram or table.
5 Use social science concepts and theories to explain the patterns and relationships discovered.
6 Set the problem within a wider social framework.
7 Offer an account which explains and 'makes sense' of (3) in terms of (5) and (6).

Finally, we looked at a different sort of evidence — a more qualitative, personal account of the body and illness. We tried to show here that the body is a focal point for a range of different social processes. Its meanings vary from one social context to another, and between different cultures. How we experience and represent the body in our culture is also a social process that can be socially understood and interpreted. Contrary to common sense, the body itself is not just a *natural* entity. It can be said to be *socially constructed*.

2 THE INDIVIDUAL AND SOCIETY

The distinction that we have been pursuing in Section 1 between the natural or physical world and the social world — between 'the social' and 'the natural' — is a fundamental one in social science. It is also central to the social sciences as a body of knowledge and indeed to our culture. The social sciences became a separate and distinct body of knowledge towards the end of the nineteenth century, and one of the key moments in their self-determination was when they felt able to distinguish themselves from the natural and physical sciences. In sociology in particular, this moment is associated with the name of the French sociologist Emile Durkheim (1858–1917), one of its 'founding fathers'. Durkheim attempted to theorize about this difference, and one example he wrote about at length was *Suicide*, the title of the book he published in French in 1897. However, what mainly concerns us here about Durkheim and suicide is the second of the distinctions we introduced at the beginning of the unit — that between the social and the individual.

2.1   THE CASE FOR SUICIDE

Durkheim used the example of suicide to explore and clarify this social/individual distinction. He took up the question of suicide because it had been the subject of widespread debate during his lifetime. It was assumed (as it often still is) that the number of people committing suicide was an index of the moral health of his society. Data on the suicide rate were therefore part of what were called the 'moral statistics' of his society. However, Durkheim also took up the question because suicide is the result of a highly individual decision to end one's own life: it is both an individual and physical act. Durkheim therefore figured that, if he could show that, nevertheless, the rate at which people committed suicide in different countries had a *social* explanation, then he would have proved his point about the distinctiveness of 'the social' and the social sciences. Accordingly, he first considered and rejected the main non-social explanations — such as that suicide arose from the organic or psychic dispositions of the individual, or was attributable to the physical environment.

Emile Durkheim, French sociologist and author of the famous study, *Suicide*

In order to move from the individual to the social level, Durkheim studied not individual suicides, but the *rate* at which groups in different countries committed suicide. His object of study was the suicide rate. (You may remember that, in the smoking example, Lesley Doyal also looked at rates.)

What Durkheim claimed to discover from the data is that:

1 Suicide rates are very stable and regular. Within any one country, people tend to commit suicide at about the same rate, over long periods.

2 However, the rates differ significantly between countries. 'In purely Catholic countries like Spain, Portugal, Italy, suicide is very little developed [on average, 58 per million inhabitants], while it is at its maximum [190 per million inhabitants] in Protestant countries like Prussia, Saxony and Denmark' (Durkheim, 1952, p.152).

3 Even within one country, the suicide rates differ from one group to another. People in different social classes, or who belong to different religions, commit suicide at different rates.

Two main conclusions seem to follow. First, though each suicide may be highly individual and unique, suicide as a *social* (group or collective) phenomenon exhibits a range of very distinctive and surprisingly regular patterns. Second, though successful suicides end in physical death for the individual, the variations in the suicide *rate* can only be explained in terms of social factors.

In fact, Durkheim's statistics were not at all reliable. The recording of data has improved enormously since his time and his statistics have therefore come into serious question. This throws doubt on some of his arguments. However, on some of the main points his argument has remained more durable. Suicide rates for different countries, for whatever reason, *are* both different as between countries, and remarkably stable over long periods within countries. Anthony Giddens (1989, p.14) has shown that 'The suicide rate of the UK is four times as high as that of Spain but only a third of the rate in Hungary'. (The same, you may be interested to know, is true of murder rates. In good times and bad, the British murder one another at roughly the same rate from one year to the next.) It is this regularity in the pattern over time that marks the presence of what Durkheim called 'a social fact'. Regularity in the pattern, variations within a pattern, or things which stand out as strikingly different from the normal pattern are all clues about what the social scientist needs to interpret or explain.

Durkheim had many different ways of trying to explain the regularities he claimed to have found. One was to distinguish between different kinds of suicide. He grouped or classified suicide into different types: for example *anomic* suicide, where an individual feels isolated from the bonds which unite him or her to other people, or *altruistic* suicide, where people have a very high and rigid sense of disciplined belongingness to a group — for instance, Japanese kamikaze pilots who undertook suicide raids during the war. You needn't concern yourself with these distinctions, though you may want to note that, again, classifying something into groups is an essential part of making sense of it. A second approach Durkheim used was to identify the main social factors which the data suggested were associated with high suicide rates. One, which you can see from points (2) and (3) above, was religious affiliation.

—————————— ACTIVITY 3 ——————————

Why do you think a group's religion might influence their propensity to commit or not to commit suicide? For example, why did Durkheim think Protestants committed suicide at a higher rate than Jews? Jot down your reasons on a sheet of paper before reading on.

Durkheim attributed the difference in suicide rates to differences in the character of beliefs and organization between the two religions. Protestants, he argued, had to face God individually and account for their actions to Him directly, without the mediation of the Church. Protestantism also allowed greater freedom of thought and judgement to the individual, but Protestants were less integrated, collectively, as a community. Judaism, on the other hand, consisted 'of a body of practices minutely governing all details of life and leaving little room to individual judgement', and Jews had a strong community sense. Durkheim's reasoning went as follows. Protestants, left alone without clear detailed guidance as to how to live their daily life and without the support of a church and community around them, were *more* likely to take the suicidal path when something went badly wrong in their lives. In terms of his type classification, they were more prone to commit *anomic* suicide.

——————————— ACTIVITY 3 *(continued)* ———————————

1 Did Durkheim get this explanation directly from his data?

2 If not, where did it come from?

Try to answer the questions before proceeding.

The statistics helped Durkheim to identify the patterns, but the figures themselves did not produce the explanations. In fact, he probably *started* with the 'hunch' that religion might be a relevant social factor. He classified his data according to religious belief to test this hypothesis. Then he looked at the differences in suicide rate between Protestants and Jews which showed up in his data and this *confirmed* his hypothesis. But in order to *explain* it, Durkheim then drew on his deep and considerable historical knowledge of world religions and of what meanings these different religious traditions carried for followers. In other words, he had to use his historical and contextual knowledge about society to 'make sense' of the variations he found in his data.

Durkheim believed that social science should be 'scientific' and he tried to make his procedures as quantitative, objective and as much like the procedures of the natural sciences as possible. Social scientists who proceed in this way are sometimes called *positivists*, and Durkheim is considered to be a leading positivist. However, as we have seen, Durkheim also worked interpretatively. He tried to make sense of what he found. His explanation drew heavily on his *historical knowledge* and his *theoretical understanding of how society and social processes work*.

In terms of the more general argument we have been pursuing here, Durkheim's work makes us look at the society/individual question in a new way. He suggests that something like suicide, which looks essentially like a physical act, is also really a *social* process; and to understand or explain its occurrence in different societies, we need to draw on social and historical causes, not just individual ones.

2.2 THE INDIVIDUAL AND SOCIETY

The distinction we have been pursuing in this section between the social and the individual is a much more difficult one to argue through than that between the social and the natural, because it is much less clear-cut. Individuals, after all, *are* part of society and social science must be concerned, at least in part, to explain individual behaviour. In the end, you may feel, we are all individuals, so what is wrong with explaining social phenomena in terms of the individual alone?

In fact, there is considerable variation on this question, both between and within the different social science disciplines, and these differences have led to considerable tension and debate. Some social scientists would argue that, in terms of method, all social explanations *are* in the end reducible to the characteristics of individuals. Many classical economists argue in this way about economic behaviour. The German sociologist, Max Weber, believed that we must make sense of any social action in terms of the motives and meanings that people give to their actions, and, in the end, this means tracing them back to the individual. If you see a man in the distance chopping down a tree, you can only understand what he is doing if you know, or can guess, the meaning which he, as an individual, gives to his actions. However, this does not take sufficient account of *shared* meanings, which are not only individual and about which (e.g. Protestantism) Weber wrote so insightfully! In practice, Weber was far less strict than this theoretical position suggests. He used many 'collective' concepts in his work, such as class, group, sect, party, church, enterprise, capitalism, bureaucracy, and so on. The way he got round this apparent contradiction in his work was to argue that these collective concepts were merely necessary abstractions — useful counters to think and debate with, but which could all, if necessary, be translated into individual terms. Weber's own work did not attempt to follow this approach very consistently, and very few sociologists would adopt such an extreme 'methodological individualism' today. They would argue that, even if societies *are* collections of individuals, as they undoubtedly are, it does not follow that *all* explanations of the social world are reducible to individual factors. Many individual characteristics derive from society itself or arise through the interaction *between* individuals, so not all explanations are reducible to the single individual.

Max Weber, the German sociologist, argued that we must study the meanings and motives that people give to their actions

These considerations have brought many social scientists closer to the opposite position — the one advanced in a very strong form by Durkheim. Durkheim argued that 'the social' cannot be explained in wholly individual terms. 'The social' has a separate existence, in its own right, over and above the individual. Society is formed as the result of the social interaction or relationship *between* individuals, and acquires a reality of its own, irreducible to the individual, which needs to be studied in its own terms. 'Society', said Durkheim, 'is not a mere sum of individuals; rather, the system formed by their association represents a specific reality which has its own characteristics' (Durkheim, 1938, p.103).

This is a strong statement of the case and, in some ways, it runs counter to common sense. It may help to make Durkheim's argument clearer if we use an example. Take the case of *marriage*. Our common-sense image of marriage is that it is a very private affair, mainly concerning the two people involved. The domestic world, formed by marriage and the family, is the centre of what, in our culture, symbolizes the private rather than the public sphere. A 'methodological individualist' would say that we can only explain what is going on in the marriage in terms of what these two individuals think and do. However, the 'Durkheimian' would point out that a marriage is more than an individual man and woman who happen to live together under one roof. It is an institution. It has very clear rules (such as the prohibition against extra-marital sex). These rules are publicly established, legally and morally sanctioned. A marriage persists over a reasonably long space of time. Marriages between very different sorts of individuals in the same society tend to conform to the same type — for example, the nuclear family in advanced industrial societies. People *tend* to marry others of roughly the same social status. In these ways a marriage acquires a reality, a continuity of existence, a public character, a binding force of its own, separate from, and not reducible to, the lives of the two individuals who enter into it.

Durkheim believed that social institutions, like marriage, acquire an independent existence and exert an influence on individuals from the 'outside'. Those in the marriage feel constrained to behave in certain ways by the very fact that the marriage exists. You cannot enter and leave a marriage as a matter of pure free choice. You have to go through certain legal procedures, certain prescribed rituals or, in earlier times, certain religious procedures. These mark a marriage — which *seems* to belong to the private world — as belonging to the public social sphere. You may recognize, in this example, one aspect of the major course theme, *the public and the private*.

As an institution, marriage carries certain legal, financial, moral and sentimental obligations in the wider society. It has a wider social function — for example, in regulating the sexual behaviour of adults. It defines the roles which we, as individuals, play in it. There are also certain ideas or images (representations) which we have of 'marriage' — the 'good' marriage, a 'proper' marriage, the marriage that is 'falling apart'. This 'ideology' of marriage is part of our culture and influences the way marital partners behave. The imagery of marriage is fundamental to the culture of romantic love in Western societies. The roles of 'husband' and 'wife' are made — and abandoned — in society, not in nature. Nobody is *born* a 'wife'. So marriage belongs to the social, not just the individual, sphere.

In the marriage example we have emphasized the *social* aspect — to make a point. However, you may feel that it makes society appear to be, exclusively, the active force: a sort of 'actor' in its own right, doing things, bringing pressure to bear, making individuals conform, writing the scripts which the marriage partners are obliged to perform. If we take the argument too far in this direction, the individual becomes a mere cypher — a pawn or robot, a marionette whose strings 'society' is manipulating. This is a critique which some social scientists have levelled at Durkheim's argument, when it is advanced in its strong form. They call it an 'over-socialized' conception of society.

A better approach may be to try to get behind or underneath this society vs individual distinction and dissolve the hard-and-fast opposition between the two positions by looking at (a) *the way individuals help to create and construct society*, and (b) *the way society shapes and forms the individual*. In other words, we can try to study the individual socially and at the same time see how the actions of individuals are, in part, the means by which society is produced and constructed.

We will try to bring these two threads of the argument together, and explore the problems of a wholly individualist approach to explanation, by discussing the well-known example of the man on the desert island.

2.3   THE CASE OF ROBINSON CRUSOE

In 1719 the novelist Daniel Defoe published a classic story about a man on his own, called *Robinson Crusoe*. Crusoe, as you know, went out from England to make his fortune and had many adventures before being shipwrecked on a desert island. He was the only survivor of the wreck, and though he managed to salvage many things from it and to make himself some sort of life on the island, he survived entirely alone until he discovered a single footprint in the sand. This was the mark of a native whom he discovered, named 'Friday' (after the day on which he found him) and made his servant. Crusoe was finally rescued and taken home.

The story was set in the eighteenth century, at the height of Europe's early commercial expansion. The shipwreck occurred in the New World, the principal theatre of the struggle for mastery between France, Spain and Britain. It was modelled on the many tales of exploration, hurricane, disaster, shipwreck and encounters between white European and non-white 'natives' which crop up in the colonizing literature of the time. It has something of the mythic quality of a Utopia, so often associated with European voyages to the New World. But, in the story of Man Friday, and the fear of cannibalism that haunts Crusoe throughout, it is also part of that myth of an 'original' encounter between European civilization and primitive savagery, which fascinated many writers of the time; you may remember that Shakespeare's *The Tempest* is also set in the Caribbean, with a shipwreck, hurricane and desert island and the master/ slave relationship between Prospero and Caliban (i.e. 'cannibal'). In his classic study, *The Rise of the Novel,* Ian Watt offers one interpretation of the novel. *Robinson Crusoe*, he argues, is a representative tale, based on the new philosophy of *individualism* current in the early eighteenth century. Crusoe stands for the primacy and self-sufficiency of the individual and his/her capacity to survive as an autonomous being, outside of society. His adventures are a prototype of early capitalism in the period when countries like Britain and France were accumulating capital through commerce overseas which was later to fund economic development at home.

In *Robinson Crusoe*, the new capitalist entrepreneur is shown to be incessantly moving into new worlds to conquer them, taming and harnessing nature and people to his needs across the globe.

─────────────────────────── ACTIVITY 4 ───────────────────────────

Before reading further, ask yourself whether Robinson Crusoe really *is* a good example of the self-sufficient individual.

Robinson Crusoe arrives on his island fully formed and kitted out by eighteenth-century British society and is therefore sustained by the fruits of other people's labour

For much of the novel Crusoe is certainly depicted as the heroic but lonely individual — solitary man surviving on his own. It seems much less clear whether we could make sense of, or account for, Crusoe in wholly 'individualist' terms. He arrives on the desert island fully formed by and kitted out by eighteenth-century British society, of which he was a member. Who he is, what he does, what he has around him and how he thinks are all unimaginable without this process of being *socially formed*. He winds up shipwrecked in the mouth of the River Orinoco because of the whole historical process of 'discovery', colonization and settlement which laid the basis for European commercial expansion and economic power for the next two or three centuries. Crusoe brings on shore all the products of eighteenth-century trade, manufacture and technology: 'bread, rice, Dutch cheeses ... a carpenter's chest, two pistols, powder horns, barrels of shot, swords, saws, an axe, a hammer', and so on — the fruits of the labour of many other people who don't figure in the book at all.

Let us try to identify the different social processes and institutions which form and position 'Crusoe', the individual.

1 *Class position*. He comes originally from an impeccable merchant middle-class background. In the opening of the novel he locates himself very precisely in the class system — 'the middle state, or what might be called the upper station of low life' — because he rightly understands that it *places* him socially, and tells us a great deal about who he really is. It greatly influences what sorts of opportunities and life-chances are open to him. Had Crusoe been an aristo-

crat, he would probably not have been involved in commerce and trade or held the economic and religious views with which Defoe endows him. Had he been one of the labouring poor, he could only have come to the West Indies as an indentured servant, and thus would not have been free to travel but would have been tied for a period of years, by contract, to work for his master. Many white indentured servants went in this way to the West Indies before African slavery to the colonies began.

2   *Family.* Crusoe was a representative example of the merchant family in the eighteenth century: 'Born in the city of York, of a good family, though not of that country, my father being a foreigner of Bremen, who first settled at Hull. He got a good estate by merchandise, and leaving off his trade lived afterwards at York, from whence he married my mother ... from a very good family in that country'. Crusoe's father was an instance of the classic text-book merchant's family career: a fortune made in trade, a 'good marriage' with a large property settlement, enabling him to retire into the life of a gentleman.

3   *Education.* Robinson Crusoe had the classic middle-class education. He was destined for a career in one of the 'old' professions: 'My father had given me a competent share of learning, as far as house education and a county free-school generally goes, and designed me for the law'. However, 'Being the third son of the family [i.e. not being the first son who, according to the property relations and inheritance system of the period, inherits the bulk of the father's property] and not bred to any trade, my head began to be filled with very early rambling thoughts'. Like many second and third sons, who ended up as plantation slave-owners in the West Indies, Crusoe set off to make his fortune.

4   *Culture.* Crusoe carries in his head the whole mental baggage and culture of a true eighteenth-century merchant's son. He believes in the primacy of trade and of the risk-taking involved at that time in commercial projects and enterprises (many of them, like the South Sea Bubble, destined to collapse in financial ruins and scandal); this took him voyaging to the new worlds in Asia and the Americas only recently opened up by the era of exploration. In terms of his economic ideology, he belongs firmly to the mercantile rather than the manufacturing stage of capitalist development. He is the world's most committed accountant. He is always making lists, reckoning up how much he has, how many things he has acquired and whether he has made any profit on an exchange. At one point he spends £40 on trinkets and toys, which he manages to exchange for £300 of gold dust, £200 of which is banked with the captain's widow for safe-keeping against his return to England, and the rest of which is converted to trading goods, unfortunately lost when the ship is captured by pirates. On the island he makes use of the fruits of the labour of others in terms of all the things he rescues from the wreck. But he is not into the business of making and manufacturing. It is the lure of fortune and treasure to be made or found abroad, the opening up of new worlds to trade, and the bringing of this accumulated wealth back to England as the basis of a personal or business fortune that drives Crusoe on. We could call him an 'adventure' (rather than a venture) capitalist. He does not sit at home and speculate on the newly created stock-market. He risks his capital, his body and his life in search of profit.

5   *Religion.* In ways that were characteristic of the rising merchant classes of his time, many of whom were also Puritans, Crusoe's very worldly, secular and materialist outlook was combined with deep religious sentiment. He is constantly invoking God; but the principal way in which God figures in the story is in terms of God's providence to him. It is God who saves him from the wreck, God who puts good things his way, God who looks down with benevolence on his efforts: 'I frequently sat down ... with thankfulness and admired the hand of God's providence, which had thus spread my table in the wilderness ... These reflections made me very sensible of the goodness of Providence to me and very

thankful for my present condition.' Fortunately for Crusoe, God's will for him, and his own will to survive, succeed and prosper, turn out to be one and the same thing. This 'providential' aspect is as strong as the economic side of the story.

6 *Gender.* It is doubtful whether the same opportunities to rise in the world and succeed, or the same heroic achievements as a 'self-made man', would have been open to Crusoe if he had been born a woman. His fate and fortunes are profoundly shaped by his gender. Opportunities for women of the same class to establish a career in this manner were severely restricted, since at this time they were not allowed to own property in their own right; marriage was more a part of the property inheritance system and its arrangements than a matter of love and romance, and it was the women, not the men, who were exchanged. Very few women of Crusoe's class travelled to the New World in the way he did, though many poor English women went as indentured servants, and thousands of black ones were forcibly transported as slaves.

7 *Race and Ethnicity.* Crusoe was also typical of eighteenth-century European explorers in terms of his attitudes towards the native, non-European, non-white people he encountered. He treats Friday with an unquestioned assumption about his own natural superiority.

To sum up, Robinson Crusoe was indeed a unique individual, making his way in the world by his own efforts, 'master of all he surveys', as the poem puts it. But this is very different from saying that he can be understood and explained *in individualistic terms*. We can't fully explain who he is, where he comes from, what he thinks and does, how he behaves, by looking at him simply as an individual. This is the problem with individualist types of explanation. The problem arises when social scientists try to explain things that are social in wholly individual terms. The objection is really to descriptions, accounts and explanations which *reduce* social phenomena to individual causes. This distinction between 'the individual' and 'individualism' as an approach is a fundamental one in the social sciences, and a source of constant confusion. We need to explore it further before being able to grasp the relation between 'the social' and 'the individual'.

2.4   INDIVIDUALS AND INDIVIDUALISM

One thing you may be wondering is, where does this 'individualism' come from? Haven't there always been individuals throughout history and in every society? Of course, there have been 'individuals' in the sense of individual human beings. But there is a great deal of evidence to suggest that, in Europe until the end of the Middle Ages, and in other cultures up to the present day, individuals have not always been regarded as separate and unique in the modern or even the 'Robinson Crusoe' sense — self-sufficient and self-contained entities. This is a very modern conception of the individual and, to judge from the evidence, a philosophy founded on this conception of the individual (what we call *individualism*) doesn't really take hold in English thought or language until the eighteenth century — at just around the time when *Robinson Crusoe* was written! In feudal times, for example, the individual was thought of much more in terms of his or her membership of a particular social group or 'estate' which defined the status of each individual; this status tended to remain fixed throughout life and determined much of the individual's destiny. Once a serf in feudal society, you tended to remain one all your life. In religious terms, the individual was linked to others and ultimately to God in a great social pyramid or hierarchy — what medieval philosophers called 'the great chain of being' — and it was not considered a specially heroic thing to step outside of one's appointed place in the chain and start to carve out one's destiny for oneself. For many people in feudal times, this 'heroic' individual career, which is so celebrated in *Robinson Crusoe*, would have been regarded as incipient rebellion against the natural order of things.

So the philosophy of individualism — the idea that the individual is the centre of the universe, that all things can be traced back to the individual, that the individual sets things in motion, makes the world go round and is the motor of social action and change — was a new idea which only gradually emerged and slowly became the dominant conception.

Why individualism arose at that particular moment is a complex historical question which has been the subject of intense debate for many years. But among the principal causes of this shift, which the great majority of modern historians would accept, are 'the break-up of the medieval social, economic and religious order', the rise of Protestantism (about which Max Weber wrote, and

Robinson Crusoe was often represented as the lonely, self-sufficient, autonomous individual

which was very much an individually centred religion) and the early forms of capitalist commerce, which put such a high premium on individual enterprise and risk-taking. These are all central themes of Defoe's novel.

Raymond Williams, the literary historian, who has made a study of certain 'keywords' in the English language whose changes of meaning reflect changes in social, economic and cultural organization, sums up these themes in his brief account of the emergence of modern conceptions of the individual and of individualism

ACTIVITY 5

Read carefully the passage from Williams quoted below. It summarizes much of the foregoing argument about 'individualism' in this section of the unit. It might help if you break the passage down into a list of separate points.

> In the general movement against feudalism, there was a new stress on man's personal existence over and above his place or function in a rigidly hierarchal society. There was a related stress in Protestantism on man's direct and individual relation to God. But it was not until the late seventeenth and eighteenth centuries that a new mode of analysis, in logic and mathematics, postulated the entity, individual … from which other categories and especially collective categories were derived. The political thought of the Enlightenment followed this model. Argument began from individuals who had an initial and primary existence, and laws and forms of society were derived from them … In classical economics, trade was described in a model [based on] separate individuals who decided at some starting point, to enter into economic or commercial relations … In ethics, separate individuals calculated the consequences of this or that action … liberal thought based on 'the individual' as a starting point was criticized from conservative positions, but also, in the nineteenth century, from socialist positions, most thoroughly in Marx who … argued that the individual is a social creation born into relationships and determined by them.
>
> (Williams, 1983, p.136)

This may at first seem a very dense passage, because it brings together so many ideas, but if you read it a second time you will see that you are already familiar with most of the ideas from our earlier discussion of *Robinson Crusoe*. I don't want to pursue this point any further here, but before we leave it and sum up the general thrust of the discussion, you might like to note the following points:

1 Williams suggests that the rise of modern individualism is the result of both changes in social organization — 'the break-up of the medieval social, economic and religious order' — and ways of thinking — 'a new mode of analysis'. This point will be more substantially developed later in the course, in Unit 17 in Block IV, which discusses the question of ideology.

2 The final part of Williams' discussion relates to the four Traditions, introduced in Unit 5 and expanded on in Part 2 of the Course Reader, which you will be asked to read later in the course. The rise of individualism, he argues, is associated with the birth of *liberalism* as a political philosophy and social theory. It is opposed by both *conservatism* and *marxism*. Liberalism has clearly influenced the social sciences, as it has, according to Williams' account, every other branch of thought.

3   Most important for our argument here — and a way of returning to the main themes of the section — individualism has also influenced our common-sense ways of thinking about and making sense of the world. This is one reason, perhaps, why we fall so easily into an 'individual versus society' way of thinking, and why starting every explanation with the individual appears such a 'natural' way of thinking to many of us. We tend to work with these boxes already fixed in our heads — individual/society — and we use them as a way of classifying and representing the social world to ourselves and to others.

SUMMARY

In this section we have been following up the relationship between the individual and society. The two are even more closely interrelated than the distinction discussed in Section 1 between society and nature. The individual is clearly part of society and thus a legitimate object of study by social scientists. Looked at in this way — at what is sometimes called the 'social individual' — we can see that 'the individual' is thoroughly shaped and constructed by society, as the example of Robinson Crusoe amply demonstrates. *The real objection arises when we try to explain social phenomena in entirely individualist terms and reduce 'the social' to 'the individual'.* This was identified as a particular kind of social philosophy and a specific approach in social thought — individualism. Individualism itself has a history, as Raymond Williams suggests; and its pervasive hold on our common-sense ways of thinking can itself be historically and socially understood.

The case of Durkheim and suicide was also instructive. Suicide is, or appears to be, a very individual act, yet Durkheim went a long way towards showing that it can also be examined as a social phenomenon. In his method, Durkheim used many of the same procedures as Lesley Doyal did in Section 1. But, as in Doyal's case, gathering data and working with them statistically did not, in itself, provide an explanation of the phenomenon of suicide. Durkheim had to draw on his broader historical and theoretical understanding of society in order to provide an account of the problem which made sense of it.

3   SOCIETY AS A 'THING IN ITSELF'

In this section we turn to a consideration of the term 'society' itself. What is this 'society' that is used in the explanation of social phenomena and which gives rise to 'the social' as a distinct entity? Remember Durkheim's injunction: study society as something that is separate and 'has its own characteristics'. Treat it as a 'thing in itself'. But what exactly does Durkheim mean by this latter phrase? What is this 'thing' that has its own reality, not reducible to the individuals who make it up? I think the Robinson Crusoe example can help us here too. As we saw there, the individual can only be properly understood once he or she is set in the context of a whole society. Crusoe was born into a system of social relations which he did not create but which shaped him. He was formed by a history which he inherited. He was the beneficiary of systems of economic relations, forms of production and a particular set of technologies without which he could not have survived on his desert island. He was positioned through his family within the class structure of his society. He was educated into the culture and customs of his time. His thoughts, ideas, attitudes and ambitions were formed through his intercourse with society. Far from being a unique and self-sufficient individual outside society, Robinson Crusoe seems more to be what Marx once called 'a résumé' or summary of all the social relations of his time and place.

But if Robinson Crusoe was a 'social construction', what about the other way around? Does the novel also help us to see how the individual constructs society? We cannot answer this question without bringing in Friday, because society can only exist *where individuals are in relationship with one another.*

Until Friday appears, Crusoe is only participating in society through the past — in the way he was formed and the material goods from his society that are available to him from the wreck. But as soon as Friday appears, the two individuals form a relationship and begin to construct a rudimentary form of society together. We can learn something about what 'society' is, as a 'thing in itself', to use Durkhheim's phrase, by looking at what this 'thing' is that they construct together on the desert island.

The first thing that happens — the beginning of 'society', so to speak — is that relationships develop between individuals. Crusoe and Friday need to communicate with one another: there is no relationship — and no society — without a system of communications. So the teaching and learning of language is a key feature of society. Interestingly, there is no dialogue in the book until Friday arrives because language is always a medium of *social* intercourse and exchange. For there to be 'society' there also has to be 'education' in a broad sense. Crusoe needs to teach Friday about his way of life, how things are done in *his* society, before he can get Friday to conform to his way of life. Friday has a culture too, and Crusoe's culture is entirely alien to that of the Carib Indians of whom Friday was a member. Crusoe cannot get Friday to work or labour in the way he wants until Friday has learnt Western skills and technology. He has to be taught how to build a house, what food to grow, how to use the tools Crusoe has saved from the wreck. But technology and skills are also forms of power which those who have them can sometimes use against their masters. So it is noticeable that Crusoe waits a long time before he teaches Friday how to use the means of violence, the ultimate source of power — firearms and gunpowder! As a common way of life develops, the two men share out the daily tasks, one doing one thing while the other does something else: a simple form of the division of labour. In short, they begin to construct a set of relationships.

This is a simple or rudimentary form of 'society', and meets one of Durkheim's criteria — that there must be forms of 'association' between individuals. But you will also remember Durkheim's second, and more difficult, requirement. These relationships should acquire an existence independent of the individuals concerned — that 'something else' which arises as a result of the relations between individuals, and which can be studied in its own right by the social scientist.

3.1   SOCIAL RELATIONS

Notice that in the previous sentence we have made a distinction between two terms — relationships and relations — which are sometimes confused. The words sound much the same but they really mean different things. When individuals associate with one another they form relationships (family relationships, work relationships, sexual relationships, and so on). But when these relationships persist over time, they lose their immediate connection to the particular individuals and groups which first formed them, and acquire an independent existence or 'thing-like' quality of their own. Then social scientists tend to call them *relations* (economic relations, social relations, sexual relations). 'Relations' are relationships that have persisted for so long and become so regular and institutionalized that they have lost all apparent connection to the particular individuals and groups who first created them and seem to function almost on their own. They become, in their own right, the 'building blocks' of society, the 'motor' of social change and development.

Notice also that we are no longer talking about 'relationships' in general, but about very specific sets of relations — relations specific to a particular society or type of society at a particular historical moment and at a particular stage of social development. You may recognize here a distinction that we made right at the beginning between 'society' and 'a society'. So, as we saw in the Williams passage on individualism and in the Crusoe discussion, we can speak, without any reference to individuals, of different types of society, characterized by different kinds of social relations: 'feudal' society, 'early capitalist' society, 'primitive' society, 'modern' society, 'Third World' society, and so on.

What Crusoe and Friday construct together is not just any old 'relationship' or just any form of 'society'. It is relations of a specific kind, in a society, however simple, of a particular type.

 ACTIVITY 6

Before reading any further, you might like to glance back over the 'Robinson Crusoe' section and try to decide for yourself what sort of 'society' it was that Crusoe and Friday constructed together. How would you characterize it? What name would you give it? Is it a 'capitalist' society, a 'primitive' society, an 'underdeveloped' society?

To answer this question you must think of what type of relations prevailed *between* Crusoe and Friday. The relations that developed between them were those of master and slave. They were typical of the social and economic relations that were emerging throughout the New World at the end of the seventeenth century, in the wake of European expansion: first, between the colonizers and the native Indian peoples, who the Europeans put into forced labour and who died out in the Caribbean within a hundred years; second, between the colonizers and the black slaves who were brought by force from Africa to work the plantations. Crusoe and Friday do not therefore just 'associate' as individuals. They are defined as individuals, by the relations of 'civilized' European to 'primitive' savage, colonizer to colonized, master to slave. Their behaviour as individuals is therefore constrained by these relations, which *position them*, whatever their personal, individual feelings are for one another.

We say 'master and slave' because though Crusoe benefits from Friday's labour and appropriates some of what he does, he does not pay him a wage. So Crusoe's desert island, in terms of its labour relations, is a pre-capitalist society. Does that mean that *Robinson Crusoe* is not, as Ian Watt suggested, a book set in the conditions of early capitalism? Not necessarily. For just as New World slavery existed as a sort of enclave within the wider, more global system of early European capitalism, so Crusoe's desert island is an enclave within the wider, more global system of England's mercantile and commercial overseas expansion. The parallel is perfect.

But Crusoe and Friday don't only 'relate' to each other through relations of economic exploitation. Not only does Crusoe make use of Friday's labour; he also stands in a relation of power and authority over him. By power, we mean that Friday is obliged to conform to Crusoe's wishes and commands — Crusoe can get Friday to do his bidding, whether Friday wishes to obey or not. Authority means that, in addition, Crusoe requires Friday to acknowledge that his power is rightfully and properly exercised. These relations of power are beautifully captured in the key scene where Crusoe in effect gives or bestows a new social identity on Friday, and baptizes him into a position of subordination: 'In a little time I began to speak to him and teach him how to speak to me; and first I made him know his name should be Friday, which was the day I saved his life … I likewise taught him to say Master, and then let him know that was to be my name.' So far as Friday is concerned, Crusoe's name is synonymous with his position of power — 'master'. These relations of domination and subordination are then sealed in the key scene where Friday kneels in homage at Crusoe's feet, acknowledging subjection to Crusoe's authority.

What in fact Defoe depicts in the novel is a model of early mercantile and commercial capitalist society, not simply as a type of society peculiar to England but in its *global* setting — that is, complete with its dependent colonial regions. We can really only understand what happens on the island within the framework of Crusoe's wider career, his whole life history before and after the 'colonizing' episode, and the society from which he came — seventeenth-century England. You will recognize here an idea discussed earlier in Block I, that local forms of society (the New world slave plantations) are dependent on the wider global network of relations (commercial capitalism) in which they are set. This is one aspect of the course theme of *the local and the global,* which was introduced in Block I and which is developed more fully elsewhere.

Just as a way of pulling these ideas together, you might like to reflect back on the question of society as a 'thing in itself' and the Robinson Crusoe case, in the light of an observation by Karl Marx which, whether you subscribe to Marx's general theories of society or not, represents a very powerful statement of one position in the social sciences. Writing in 1857–8, Marx argued that:

The social relations between Crusoe and Friday are sealed in an act of homage which also represents the exercise of power

> Society is not merely an aggregate of individuals; it is the sum of the relations in which these individuals stand to one another. It is as though some were to say that, from the point of view of society, slaves and citizens do not exist; they are all men. In fact, this is rather what they are outside society. Being a slave or a citizen is a socially determined relation between an individual A and an individual B. Individual A is not as such a slave. He is only a slave in and through society.
>
> (Marx, 1973, p.75)

What Marx meant by being a slave 'only in and through society' is that an individual can only play the role of slave-master or slave in a society where slavery *as a system* had become the dominant way of organizing the economy, harnessing labour, producing goods and accumulating wealth. In other words, 'being' a slave-owner or a slave, as an individual, depends on the prior existence of a set of relations which position the individual within a group and prescribe how the various actors must behave in relation to other actors. There is nothing universal or 'natural' about this. Indeed, New World slavery was such an unnatural form of production for Western societies, and so contrary to the religious outlook of Christian Europe, that there were fierce debates about it, and lengthy justifications had to be developed to prove that Indians like Friday and later the African slaves were 'not really human beings' — that is to say, not true individuals at all!

What the discussion of Crusoe and Friday suggests is that society *can* be studied as a 'thing in itself'. To study it in this way means studying the *social relations* which place and constrain the actions of all the individuals who belong to it. We can study them, to some degree, separately from the individuals who are organized by these relations.

4 THE STRUCTURE OF SOCIETY

We can now look at the structure of this 'society' and at what gives it its distinctive shape. But first, let me briefly remind you of how far we have come in the argument. The Lesley Doyal example in Section 1 helped us to see how the social scientist uses her understanding of 'society' to try to explain a social problem. In the course of that, we identified some difficulties with the definition of the word 'social' and with the distinction between 'society' and nature or the physical world, which we explored. The suicide and Robinson Crusoe examples helped us to explore further the differences and interrelationships between 'society' and the individual. In particular, they suggested ways in which, as social scientists, we can understand individual behaviour and individuals themselves as socially constructed — formed in and by society. In other words, we need 'society' and a sense of what is distinctive about 'the social' to understand and explain social phenomena. But this still left us with Durkheim's question: what makes society a 'thing in itself', which can be studied independently? What do we really mean when we say that 'society' can be the cause of some social problem, like smoking or ill-health? This is the question that we shall be pursuing in this final section.

4.1 SOCIAL RELATIONS

One point which gives society its distinctive structure is the fact that it is made up of specific *social relations*. We should think of these as *relations* in their own right. The important thing about them is *not* the individuals who are placed and positioned within them, but the way the relations themselves constrain individuals and groups to behave in certain ways, whatever their individual feelings and inclinations. According to this way of looking at things, the obedient and the rebellious slave are both *slaves*. The paternalistic and the oppressive slave-owner are both *slave-owners*. Both are positioned by a particular system or structure of relations that exists independently of them. The slave society depended on these relations being in place, no matter which particular individuals actually performed the specific roles of 'slave' and 'slave-owner' in it.

4.2   SOCIAL PROCESSES

A second factor is that a society needs activities which reproduce it over time and keep it going. We call these *social processes*. All societies, of whatever type, have strong, persistent, regular sets of activities of this kind, and these processes must be sustained, in a regular way, across time. Particular societies (be it eighteenth-century England or twentieth-century England) could not exist without an economic process which produces and distributes goods, and reproduces the material basis of life; or a reproduction process which produces and socializes the next generation; or a legal process which punishes those who deviate too far from what is considered the norm, and so on.

─────────────────────── ACTIVITY 7 ───────────────────────

Using the social processes identified in Section 2.3, make a short list of the main differences between Crusoe's England and contemporary society. (They referred to such questions as class, family, education, culture, religion, gender, 'race' and ethnicity.)

Contemporary western societies are, of course, advanced, industrial capitalist economies, not early mercantile capitalist ones. People are hired to work for a wage; their labour is not forced, as it was under the colonial slave system. Our legal systems of property ownership and inheritance are different too. We are not allowed to 'own' people, though we do hire their labour. Married women are no longer debarred from owning property and a person's estate is no longer necessarily inherited by the eldest son. In a more secular world, fewer people might be inclined to regard a shipwreck as, by definition, a sign of God's providence. Contemporary society is multi-racial. And so on.

The first point we can draw from this comparison, then, is the point about historical specificity. Social processes in general may be 'the same' (every society has an economy), but in each society in different historical periods they are structured and organized differently (a slave economy differs from an advanced industrial capitalist one).

4.3   SOCIAL DIVISIONS

Another thing to notice is that, though individuals must relate and associate together in order to keep a social process going, the positions they occupy within that process are *different*. Crusoe and Friday work together. But Crusoe is 'boss', Friday his slave. The Caribbean plantation economy created one economic 'system', but the groups and individuals had very different positions within that system. Each had different degrees of power. The slave-owner's power was absolute. He exercised powers of life and death over his slaves. Technically, the slave had no power at all and was subject to the master's will and whim. The plantation-owner took all the profits made from his estate after the costs were paid. The slave received enough food and shelter to keep him or her alive and working, but had no share in the rewards of his/her labour. We call these differences between them *social divisions,* and can see now that these divisions form an essential part of the basic *structure* of slave society.

We have now identified *three* fundamental dimensions of 'society' — *social relations*, *social processes* and *social divisions*. Along these three dimensions we can begin to make sense of society (or perhaps, since we are giving particular attention now to differences between one type of society and another, we had better start saying it in the plural — 'societies'). Of course, social processes take place somewhere. Social processes are sustained within different institutions which keep the processes going. Institutions connect the different parts of a process together and regulate the behaviour of individuals and groups within it. In the economy we can identify institutions like factories which produce goods, markets and shops where goods are bought and sold, industrial enterprises or multinational corporations which own and co-ordinate the different activities that make up the economy, banks and other institutions which accumulate capital and invest, and so on.

Another fundamental aspect of all societies is power, how it operates and how it is distributed. Power is also exercised within social relations, and through very different institutions, in our society. The state, for example, has considerable power in the political process. Those who own a great deal of wealth wield economic power: they can command a larger share of the resources and goods in society deriving from the economic process. The law exerts a different kind of power — legal power, the power to require the citizen to obey the law and to deprive a person of his/her liberty if the law is infringed. To exert that particular kind of power, a number of different legal institutions are linked within the legal processes: the legislature, which frames the laws; the police, who apply them on the ground; the courts, which decide whether or not an individual has broken the law; the judges, who have the power to impose a sentence; and the penal system, which supervises confinement. Each of these particular institutions functions differently. It is the connections between them that sustain what we call 'the legal process'. It is this process which not only decides, on the basis of the law, who is guilty and innocent, but also delivers, in practice, different legal outcomes for different social groups — the poor and the rich, men and women, black and white. One of the key points where power operates in society is across such social divisions — not only in law but between employers and employees, the well and the poorly educated, the governors and the governed and so on.

If we were trying to build a model of society, then in terms of what gives it its shape and structure, and reproduces its pattern over time and space, the following would be our key building blocks: *relations, processes, divisions.*

4.4   THE SOCIAL DIVISIONS OF AGE, CLASS, 'RACE'/ETHNICITY AND GENDER

So far we have briefly discussed social processes and the sets of relations and institutions that give society a distinctive shape and structure. These processes are more fully discussed later in the course — for example in Block III on the economy, Block IV on power and the political system, and Block V which concentrates on the individual in his or her social context. In this section we look specifically at the other dimension of social structure: social divisions.

One such division is age. Age is a significant line of division in modern societies. The old have very different social experiences from the young, as well as different — and sometimes conflicting — interests. Misunderstanding between the generations has frequently been a source of social tension. If we divided the population of the UK into age groups of about ten or fifteen years each, and counted the numbers in each group, it would give us a broad picture of the 'age structure' of the society. This has real social consequences for society. A society with large numbers in the younger age groups has a 'youthful' population, but it will have to provide schools for them. A society with a larger percentage of its population in the older age groups has an 'ageing' population, and therefore needs to provide forms of care for the aged. The latter is now the case in Britain: the proportion of people in the over-65 age group rose from 5 per cent in 1901 to 16 per cent by the end of the 1980s.

You might be aware, from newspaper articles or comment in the media, of the growing importance of the older sections of society. As they have increased in relative size in the population, they have become more organized as a group and have attracted more attention as a target audience for advertisers and a focus for policy-makers.

However, the kinds of social division that have preoccupied social scientists are those where power and inequality are very strongly linked. The social divisions which social scientists believe exert the greatest influence and carry the most explanatory power are those associated with *class, gender* and *'race'/ethnicity*. Inequalities of class arise from the differential access of different groups to economic goods, resources and opportunities. Inequalities of gender are associated with the differential position of and opportunities for women and men to participate in social life and the differences of power and influence between them in shaping the world. Inequalities associated with 'race' or ethnicity are where one group is disadvantaged *vis-à-vis* another because of its 'racial' or ethnic characteristics.

You should bear in mind that, for the moment, we are not making a very sharp distinction between power and inequality: we are using them more or less interchangeably as a way of defining social divisions. The different social classes, the different gender groups (men and women) and the different 'racial' groups (black and white) all have different degrees of *power*, influence and authority in the society. They also have unequal access to wealth, goods and material resources — and consequently there are significant degrees of *inequalities* between them. Both power and material goods are unequally distributed throughout the society and there is a pattern to this structure of inequalities. There are certainly debates as to how and why these two things — power and inequality — are linked, but we do not need to go into those here. For our purposes, I am accepting the well-documented fact that they do appear to be closely associated. The powerful are able to amass wealth, have higher incomes, own a greater share of the property and can purchase more of the available goods and resources than those with less power. By the same token, those who come low in the 'equality' stakes also tend to wield less power, authority and influence.

The social divisions based on class, 'race' and gender have a wide-reaching impact on society. Class divisions, especially, figure in the analysis and explanation of a very wide range of social phenomena. Until recently, class was the privileged explanation in social science — the one which, most social scientists believed, explained, or was in some way essential for explaining, all aspects of society. You can see this 'privileging' of class explanations even in so simple a thing as the way social statistics are organized. Most of the official statistics issued by government and research agencies automatically and routinely classify their data by social class. Agencies like the UK Tobacco Research Council quoted in Section 1 of this unit now regularly classify their data by both class and gender. However, this was not always the case. It is only relatively recently that social scientists have come to understand the significance of gender divisions in society and to give them comparable weight in the way they organize and present their information.

It is doubtful whether, even today, you could find much data on smoking organized according to 'racial' or ethnic groups, since 'race' is a form of social division that is still not taken with equal seriousness either by those who gather and arrange data or by social scientists who are trying to explain social behaviour. So the social divisions we have been discussing do not have 'equal weight' in the work and thinking of social scientists. In the past, class was widely considered the 'master category' — the one that affects everything else and influences all the other divisions and relations, and thus the one which best explained the patterning of social phenomena. You may appreciate the irony of calling this category of explanation, which has so often failed to include issues of gender or 'race', the 'master' category, with all the connotations of masculine authority and colonial dominance that the word 'master' carries. Try, for example, describing 'class' as the 'mistress' category! This example reminds us that the way meanings are constructed through language in our culture has always been influenced by gender and ethnic divisions.

It may be of no surprise to you to learn, then, that the privileged position of 'class-based' explanations has come under increasing challenge in social science, as people have become more aware of the growing importance in our society of gender and 'race'/ethnicity and as the new social movements have begun, once again, to organize. The 'privileging' of (i.e. the granting of special explanatory importance to) class has been effectively contested; many social scientists have moved towards a more 'interactive' model of social divisions where each is considered to have an impact on the other (you will explore this more fully in Unit 8). In general terms, however, these critical questions of theory and research in social science remain ultimately unresolved.

This issue, and many other related questions, will be developed in the next two units in the block, where we turn from the general discussion (above) of how social relations, processes and divisions give a definite structure and shape to the social, to look more substantively at the major social divisions which structure our society — social class, gender and 'racial'/ethnic divisions. As you will have seen from the previous discussion, these divisions shape the societies in which we live, determine how wealth, opportunities, resources (material and cultural) and 'life-chances' are distributed, unevenly, between different groups in society and position or place individuals within the social structure. The next two units will be concerned with three major issues: first, the complex patterns of social inequalities which these divisions produce and how they affect the experiences and 'life-chances' of different groups; second, how and why these divisions arise, how they function and how social scientists have set about theorizing and conceptualizing them, and explaining their effects; and thirdly, using examples to pose a number of questions about social divisions and how they relate to one another in shaping the position, opportunities and identities of particular individuals and groups.

Of course, even the interaction of these different social divisions has itself to be 'theorized' — theoretically analysed and explained. Is the impact of these divisions on individuals, groups, society as a whole, *autonomous*? That is to say, does each of these factors have its own, separate way of working, its own dynamic, its own causes, requiring its own explanatory theories? Or is this taking the reaction against the 'privileging' of class explanations too far? Are each of these divisions of equal weight in explaining the patterns of inequality and disadvantage we find in society? Are there over-arching theoretical concepts, models and explanations — like patriarchy or 'race' or marxism or liberalism, for example — which can account for *all* the divisions, without reducing one to, or explaining it in terms of, another? Or is there something still to be said for thinking that, despite the danger of reductionism, one of these divisions — say, gender — really *is* the one which can explain or encompass all the others, and which therefore deserves a privileged position in social science explanations? These are some of the underlying questions which organize the discussion of the major social divisions which follows in the later units in this block.

4.5 IS 'STRUCTURE' THE RIGHT WORD?

I want to end this discussion of social relations, processes and divisions with a word of caution. We have been pursuing what might be called the 'Durkheimian' path to some extent, trying to discover what it is that gives society and 'the social' a distinctive structure. Social relations, social processes and social divisions are three key dimensions which provide a society with its anatomy. In general, this seems the right direction in which to go, for without it, it seems impossible to distinguish what is distinctively 'social' from anything else. If that were the case, there would be nothing studied by the social sciences that was distinctively their own. Social science would lose its character as a distinctive body of knowledge. Moreover, Durkheim seemed to be correct in stressing that society does acquire a 'thing-like' character over time, and thus becomes a sort of force which constrains us to behave in certain ways, apparently from 'outside' us. These three dimensions therefore help us to see more clearly what gives 'society' its separate and distinctive structure and makes 'the social' an object of study in its own right.

The word 'structure' is therefore an essential concept in filling out and giving 'body' to this idea of 'the social'. The relations, processes and divisions we have been looking at are not a random assortment of activities. They occur in the central areas of life. They give regularity to what happens and help us to predict the ways in which people are likely to behave. They constrain the activities of large numbers of people. They create patterns in the distribution of resources, cultural and material, which remain remarkably stable across time. Regularity and predictability are key features of a 'structure'. Another key feature is continuity through time. The processes and divisions of society are the means by which a society reproduces itself across historical time. The concept of 'process' is important, because it calls to mind the notion of an activity that is continuous and sustained over long periods. Processes and divisions are also organized spatially (this is discussed more fully in Block VI). This spatial network of processes and institutions and the cleavages or lines of division that they produce are yet another dimension along which a society acquires a structure.

However, one problem with the concept of 'structure' is that it can also sound very static. Where have these processes, relations and divisions come from? In one sense they are nothing but the organized activities of men and women living, producing and associating together. The metaphor of a 'structure' makes a lot of sense when thought of in terms of a building. But what it sometimes leaves out is the activity of construction itself: people doing things, activity, practice. Relations, processes and structures don't seem to have an active subject. They just exist. They confront us with their brute existence. We forget who built them, who keeps them going. We can't use these concepts in an active way — it's difficult, for example, to say that a social process or a structure 'does something'! Like Topsy, they seem to 'just grow' and work by themselves.

This is one aspect of the problem which social scientists sometimes call *'agency versus structure'*. This refers to the argument between those who stress how individuals and groups *produce* society, and those who put greater stress on how they are shaped and 'produced' *by* society. The great advantage of taking a more individualist perspective is that it helps you to see agency, activity, people wanting things, doing things. There is a sort of parallel between those who take a more individualistic view of society and those who emphasize the agency or 'active' side of social processes — men and women actively making the social world what it is. On the other hand, there is a similar parallel between those who emphasize structures and those who view society more in terms of how structures limit and constrain the group's or individual's freedom of action, from the outside. However, it is dangerous to push these parallels too far: groups (classes, gender or ethnic or age groups) can be seen as active agents too — collective social actors.

There is no immediate solution in sight to this 'agency versus structure' dilemma. It would be nice to be able to square the circle and to have both agency and structure. And it may be that both things are operative at the same time. Men and women do actively construct the world, but they do so under conditions and constraints, built into the structures they inhabit, which limit their freedom to act. Moreover, the processes and institutions they actively construct are 'experienced' by the next generation, not as a set of active relationships, but as a set of already fixed relations, within whose limits they, in their turn, must act. We were making a very similar point earlier when we said that relationships (active), when sustained over long periods, come to be experienced and function as relations (passive). The argument is also similar to that advanced by the contemporary social theorist, Anthony Giddens, with his idea of 'structuration'. It is worth bearing it in mind, as a sort of corrective against a too-structural view of what society is:

> Social structures are made up of human actions and relationships: what gives these their patterning is their repetition across periods of time and distances of space. Thus the ideas of social reproduction and social structure are very closely related to one another ... The actions of all of us are influenced by the structural characteristics of the societies in which we are brought up and live; at the same time, we recreate (and to some extent alter) those structural characteristics in our actions.
>
> (Giddens, 1989, p.19)

5   CONCLUSION

We have covered a lot of ground in this unit. Let me help you to pull the threads together by reminding you of the different stages in the argument.

We started by taking two key concepts in social science — 'society' and the 'social'. The social sciences study society. They deal with the specifically social aspect of human behaviour and they use their knowledge of society to offer an explanation of why 'social' phenomena are as they are and which social factors give these phenomena their distinctive shape and structure. However, we can only use these concepts of 'society' and 'the social' if we know precisely what they mean and how to work with them. This is not as simple or as commonsensical an activity as it seems at first sight.

I suggested that we can identify and isolate 'the social' by distinguishing it from other things, in particular:

1   from the world of nature and explanations based on natural, physical, genetic or biological factors alone;

2   from the world of the individual and explanations which reduce everything to the individual level.

These distinctions (social/natural, social/individual) were then pursued and developed through a series of examples. The Lesley Doyal example showed how gender differences influence the pattern of smoking. *The Health Divide* showed how the death rate varies according to both occupational class and gender. The Barbara example showed that the body itself is a social and cultural construction. The 'suicide' example showed how social and historical factors (i.e. differences in the organization and meanings of different religious practices and beliefs) affect the suicide rate. The *Robinson Crusoe* example showed how the individual is always socially and culturally formed or 'constructed' by society. The Crusoe case also helped to advance the argument about the individual and 'individualism'. We used it to highlight the distinction between social relationships and social relations, between different types of society or social structure, and between inequality and power. This brought us to the final step in the argument. What *is* a society? What gives it its distinctive shape or structure? How, as Durkheim asked, can we conceptualize society as a 'thing in itself'? We answered this in terms, mainly, of social relations, social processes and social divisions. We ended with a warning: don't push the metaphor of social 'structure' *too* far. Remember that the social structure is really only social relations and activities, sustained over space and time (structuration).

There was a second story or sub-plot to the unit, running alongside the main argument. This was about method: *how* do we develop a social explanation? There were important points to note here about data, how to use them, and their gaps and limitations.

Alexander Selkirk, often considered the model or prototype of Crusoe, stranded on the island of Juan Fernandes. His shipwreck was the result of European expansion and colonization, but the picture represents him as the individual, alone and at one with nature.

There was a lot, following up on Block I, about what a 'social science explanation' is about and how to construct one — how to *do* social science. Here we concentrated on (a) being clear about definitions of terms (society, social, class, etc.); (b) the importance of how we classify data; and (c) the move from manipulating the data to constructing an explanation. The 'Barbara' example was particularly important here. It reminded us of the importance in social science of both qualitative and quantitive data. It showed that social science must attend to questions of *meaning and representation*, as well as questions of so-called 'fact'. It also helped us to highlight the key point: that social science uses different techniques to get at the evidence, but that giving an explanation is *not* a technical exercise alone. We must provide an account which puts the phenomenon into its *wider* social context and gives it meaning or makes sense of it. This took us full circle to the beginning of the unit — making sense of 'the social'.

In revising the unit you should keep in mind these two threads — the substance of the argument about the social, and the methodological questions about *how* social scientists go about building an explanation.

The main social divisions introduced towards the end of the unit, when we were looking at society and structure, were principally concerned with class, 'race'/ethnicity and gender. These are now taken up in far greater detail in the next two units. Unit 7 Part I looks at the different theories of class and the ways in which social scientists use them in analysing society. Unit 7 Part II looks at divisions based on 'race' and ethnic identity. Unit 8 Part I examines in detail the impact of gender and recent attempts to theorize and explain gender divisions and Unit 8 Part II attempts to pull together the theoretical material around all three divisions primarily through an examination of the notion of the existence of an 'underclass' in contemporary society. Unit 9 looks back across the block as a whole and focuses particularly on the role of concepts and the nature of social science explanations.

READER and TAPE 2

You should now look at the extract from the Black Report and *The Health Divide* in Chapter 4 of the Course Reader, 'Inequalities in health'. The extract takes up and develops many of the arguments contained in this unit . It is also relevant to some of the themes of Unit 7. The extract is fully discussed, and teaching points are identified, in the Block II cassette, Tape 2. You should listen to the first two sections of the tape after reading Chapter 4.

GOOD STUDY GUIDE

When you have finished reading Chapter 4 of the Course Reader and have listened to the cassette, turn to Chapter 3 of *The Good Study Guide* and read Sections 1 and 2 on 'Learning in groups' which relate to the benefits of tutorial discussion.

REFERENCES

Armstrong, D. (1984) *The Political Anatomy of the Body: Medical Knowledge in the Twentieth Century*, Oxford, Blackwell.

Defoe, D. (1965) *Robinson Crusoe*, Harmondsworth, Penguin (first published, 1719–20).

Doyal, L. (1983) *Picture of Health*, London, Channel 4 TV.

Doyal, L. (1979) *The Political Economy of Health*, London, Pluto.

Durkheim, E. (1952) *Suicide*, London, Routledge and Kegan Paul.

Durkheim, E. (1938) *The Rules of Sociological Method*, Glencoe, Ill., Free Press.

Giddens, A. (1989) *Sociology*, Cambridge, Polity Press.

Jacobson, B. (1981) *The Ladykillers: Why Smoking is a Feminist Issue*, London, Pluto.

Marx, K. (1973) *Grundrisse*, Harmondsworth, Penguin (written 1857–8).

Rosenblum, B. (1988) 'My body myself...', *The New Statesman*, 12 February.

Showalter, E. (1987) *The Female Malady*, London, Virago.

Townsend, P. and Davidson, N. (1988) *Inequalities In Health*, Harmondsworth, Penguin (includes *Report of the Working Group on Inequalities in Health* (the Black Report), chaired by Sir Douglas Black, first published 1980 by HMSO; and *The Health Divide* by Margaret Whitehead, first published 1987 by the Health Education Council).

Turner, B. (1984) *The Body and Society*, Oxford, Blackwell.

Turner, B. (1989) *Medical Power and Social Knowledge*, London, Sage.

Watt, I. (1963) *The Rise of the Novel*, London, Peregrine.

Weber, M. (1965) *The Protestant Ethic and the Spirit of Capitalism*, London, Unwin Hyman.

Wilson, E. (1985) *Adorned In Dreams: Fashion and Modernity*, London, Virago.

Williams, R. (1983) *Keywords*, London, Fontana.

Wright, P. and Treacher, A. (eds) (1982) *The Problem of Medical Knowledge*, Edinburgh, Edinburgh University Press.

ACKNOWLEDGEMENTS

Grateful acknowledgment is made to the following sources for permission to reproduce material in this unit:

Text

L. Doyal (1983) *Picture of Health*, Channel 4 Television.

Figure

Figure 1: L. Doyal (1983) *Picture of Health*, Channel 4 Television.

Table

Table 1: OPCS (1978) *Occupational Mortality* 1970–72, reproduced with the permission of the Controller of Her Majesty's Stationery Office.

Illustrations

p.12: Michael Pearson; *p.19*: Jenny Matthews/Format; *p.21*: Photographie Giraudon; *p.24*: Bildarchiv Preussischer Kulturbesitz; *pp.27, 30, 35 and 43*: Mary Evans Picture Library.

UNIT 7   CLASS, 'RACE' AND ETHNICITY

Prepared for the Course Team by Kenneth Thompson (Part I) and Andrew Pilkington (Part II)

CONTENTS

PART I: SOCIAL CLASS

PART II: 'RACE' AND ETHNICITY

PART I: SOCIAL CLASS

1   INTRODUCTION

In the first part of this unit we will look more closely at what is meant by 'social class' and consider whether class divisions are changing in our society. Some writers consider that class is becoming less important in Britain, because economic and social changes are reducing class divisions. They maintain that most people are better off than their parents' generation was and feel that they have risen in the social scale. Others insist that economic progress has not reduced the divisions between classes (as illustrated by 'The Black Report' from *Inequalities and Health,* Chapter 4 in the Course Reader). Class divisions are still thought to be the cause of many social problems, ranging from ill-health to hooliganism and economic inefficiency. In order to judge these various claims we need to clarify the ideas of class that people use and examine some of the evidence of change.

The strategy of Part I is as follows:

1   First, we will look at some popular views or representations of class divisions. This relates to one of the course themes — *representation and reality.*

2   Next, we will examine two theories of social class that have been most widely used and developed by social scientists — those deriving from Karl Marx and from Max Weber (you will be asked to read the short accounts of these two theorists in Chapter 22 of the Course Reader).

3   We then turn to an examination of some of the theories and evidence about changes in social class divisions with regard to wealth, work, social mobility and inequality.

2   REPRESENTATIONS OF CLASS

It is perhaps symptomatic of the importance of class in British society that any debate in the mass media about a British social crisis or a disaster is likely to lead to a discussion of class divisions. The Hillsborough tragedy of 1989, in which ninety-five Liverpool supporters were crushed to death whilst attending a football match, was no exception. Although subsequent investigation made clear that organizational mistakes by the police and others were the main cause of the tragedy, in some of the early press comments it was assumed to be just another case of football hooliganism, and these reports contain revealing ideas about perceptions of social class. The three that I have selected for your consideration typically feature a variety of ideas drawn from several traditions of thought. As you read each account, I would like you to think about the ideas of class that seem to emerge from them.

> Going to football is now the recreation of what Marx called the lumpenproletariat, what sociologists call the underclass, and what the rest of us are content to call the yobs ... From about 1918 to about 1960 it was that of the respectable working class ... The respectable working class now spends its Saturday afternoons at the DIY centre, the garden centre, strolling around National Trust properties and theme parks and going out in the car — the proof being the advertisements that now appear in the tabloids.
>
> (Frank Johnson, *The Sunday Telegraph*, 23 April 1989)

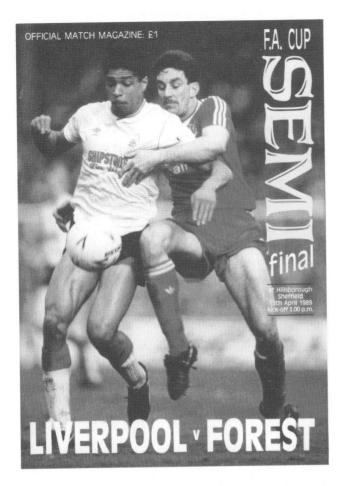

Programme cover for the ill-fated Forest v Liverpool match at Hillsborough

It is a myth that hooliganism in British football is a recent problem. Claims that it is rest upon familiarity with that remarkable period from about 1920 to about 1965 when, for some reason which has never been satisfactorily explained, the working class was exceptionally orderly, and not only at football matches ... Intelligent observers have known the real lure of soccer throughout its modern history. One Midland critic in 1913 summed up the matter in a way that is just as relevant in 1989. 'Soccer is the religion of the male masses and their patriotism too. It is an escape from discipline and restraint into the frenzy of a crowd. It offers a release for the unsatisfied instincts of toilers that nothing else in our culture provides.' When Britain wrestles with its soccer problems it has to battle to exclude the worst features of British society ... Above all, we are a society dominated by producers. Traditionally, British consumers are used to being treated like dirt.

(Brian Walden, *The Sunday Times*, 23 April 1989)

The French press shows none of the reluctance of its British counterparts to link Hillsborough with Thatcherism. Like many French commentators, *Le Monde's* Alan Giraudo stressed that soccer is a working-class sport: 'The behaviour of this proletariat has undoubtedly become tougher during Mrs Thatcher's ten years. One sign has been the growth of hooliganism.' ... *Liberation's* coverage has been even more committed. 'Working-class drama in the land of the Iron Lady', said one headline, and *Liberation's* editorial went one better, arguing that the working class was not yet caught in 'the iron net of the Iron Housewife'. According to the paper's Jean-Francois Fogel, 'the fatal stampede was a reminder of the limits of the Thatcherite revolution'. Britain's economy is prosperous again, he argued, but 'the impact on society is very diverse'. Merely to see and listen to the spectators at Sheffield, Fogel wrote, was to be reminded of 'the eternal English working class, the one class in English society which Thatcherism has not touched, and the one working class in Europe to remain a thing apart'.

(Martin Kettle, *The Guardian*, 20 April 1989)

———————————— ACTIVITY I ————————————

What were the main ideas of class in these accounts and what view did each of the commentators take about changes in the British class system?

The interesting feature that these different comments have in common is an anxiety about what is happening to the working class and speculation about whether it is losing or maintaining its separate, and seemingly threatening, 'class' character. In the view of the conservative columnist Frank Johnson, the majority of the working class have become respectable 'consumers' although Johnson expresses fears about what he calls the 'yobs' (a derogatory term he equates with Marx's 'lumpenproletariat', and the sociologists' 'underclass'). Walden quotes fears about the 'unsatisfied instincts' of the working class, and the fact that British society is still dominated by the vested interests of producers and treats working-class consumers like dirt. The French commentators, particularly the socialist newspaper *Liberation*, are struck by how relatively little the British working class has been assimilated into consumer society — if anything, becoming more separate and angry during a period of increasing economic prosperity. The implicit suggestion is that Britain lags behind other Western European countries in this respect.

In summary, the main difference between these commentators is about the extent to which the working class has maintained its collective identity rather than being assimilated with other groups into a society of individual consumers. Of course, football may not be a good test-case, as it has always been regarded as a sport appealing mainly to working-class males, whereas consumer activities are frequently family-based and include both sexes more evenly.

We will mention one more example of representations of class and class changes before turning to social science theories and evaluation of the evidence of change. One of the most common propositions about class changes is that universal education is steadily dissolving class divisions. When *The Independent* newspaper devoted its 'Free Speech' column on 28 January 1989 to debating the question 'Is social class still the most divisive force in Britain?', the Headmaster of Eton College, Eric Anderson, answered in the negative as follows:

> The class system has never recovered from Rab Butler's Education Act of 1944, and its condition is now terminal. By establishing secondary education for all and opening the grammar-schools to clever pupils, irrespective of wealth or home background, Butler laid the foundations of meritocracy. After the war the expansion of the universities, the founding of the polytechnics, and in particular the provision of mandatory student grants made higher education also freely available to merit. The result is that this year more than six times as many people will graduate as in 1939, and they will nearly all fill what used to be thought of as 'middle-class' jobs.
>
> The grammar-school allowed the boy or girl from the meanest streets of the town to climb up and out. Those previously imprisoned by lack of money, parental pressure to get a job, or a bad neighbourhood school,

now had their chance — if they were clever and hard-working. A university education beckoned, and its glittering prizes were open to merit. More than anything else, the chance to get an education and the sort of job that educated people do has made social class increasingly unimportant. Our universities, where people from all backgrounds mingle, study (and often meet their future husbands and wives), have proved a powerful unifying force. Class can't survive universal education.

Today people are more concerned about money, status and life-style than class. We hardly even use the word any more. Only old-fashioned trade union leaders ever talk of 'the working class' and you wait a long time to hear anyone say 'the upper class'. Only 'middle class' is in common use — usually in the context that we are all middle class now.

(Anderson, 1989)

─────────────── ACTIVITY 2 ───────────────

We will examine the statistical evidence about education in a later section on 'Social mobility and inequality'. However, what are your first impressions about the accuracy of Anderson's picture in the light of your own experience?

───────────────────────────────────────

Clearly the headteacher, Eric Anderson, like the commentators on Hillsborough, has a complicated mixture of ideas about class positions and the relations between classes. If we take all these sets of representations together, we can see that there are many ideas about what is happening to social classes in Britain. The Hillsborough commentators suggested that the working class might be becoming assimilated into the middle class as they become more affluent, or simply losing their class characteristics altogether and taking on the identity of individual consumers. However, one of the commentators, Johnson, worried about an 'underclass' remaining unassimilated, whilst Walden feared that Britain was still too much a society of producer classes rather than individual consumers. The French saw the British working class as remaining relatively distinct from other classes. Anderson insisted that the system of class divisions was in terminal decline.

How can we ascertain the reality behind these different representations of class changes in Britain? Of course, in half a unit we cannot hope to reach final conclusions about all the real changes that may be taking place, but it should be possible to clarify some of the issues. An essential first step is to become more aware of the criteria we tend to use in forming judgements about such matters.

─────────────── ACTIVITY 3 ───────────────

You might find it useful to jot down your own impressions about changes in the class structure of contemporary Britain and compare them with those in the representations. Do you think such social divisions are widening or narrowing? What kind of criteria influenced your decisions?

───────────────────────────────────────

What kind of impressions did you find you have about class changes? Did you decide that class divisions were reducing, increasing, or staying the same? And what were the main criteria you used — were they concerned with fundamental economic changes or were they spread across a range of social factors affecting inequalities and opportunities?

There is an immense amount of social science research and analysis on these topics because they relate to so many questions about the effects of economic and social trends and policies. In this introduction to class analysis we will concentrate on two sets of issues. The first set of issues is concerned with whether *economic changes* are reducing class divisions or polarizing them further. The second set of issues concerns changes in *social inequalities*, and opportunities for social mobility.

In tackling the first set of issues we will examine ideas about class derived from Karl Marx's work. The reason for giving prominence to this approach is that it has argued that capitalism, by its very nature, will *always* produce class divisions. Against the suggestion that class divisions may be disappearing and the working class becoming more like the middle class, this tradition argues the opposite thesis of a fundamental class division and widespread 'proletarianization'. This could apply to other capitalist societies, not just to Britain.

The second set of issues will be examined from different viewpoints, but giving greater prominence to ideas about social stratification associated with the work of Max Weber and the social reformist tradition of thought. This approach takes a more pluralistic view of the sources of social divisions than does the class theory of Marx. Consequently, it looks for changes in social stratification resulting from the actions of sectional interest groups and professional groups, or piecemeal social reforms reducing inequalities or increasing opportunities for social mobility, as for example do educational policies.

3   MODELS AND THEORIES OF CLASS

The kind of criteria which we have come across so far in making distinctions between classes has yielded a list along the following lines:

- Material resources — both in terms of the amount and source of wealth (e.g. wages, or rent, dividends and profits)
- Education and qualifications
- Occupation and type of work
- Social standing and prestige
- Power and influence
- Life-style and behavioural patterns.

Each of these sets of criteria refers to specific characteristics that, in principle, can be treated in isolation. We can even draw on statistics that attempt to measure them — income levels, educational qualifications, skill and prestige ranking of occupations, social background of those in powerful positions (e.g. cabinet ministers), health statistics and living conditions (e.g. diet and housing). However, when we speak about class and make judgements about it, we tend to have a broader image in mind than just factors such as income, occupation, education and so on. Experience teaches us that these specific factors are usually linked together in a patterned way. We have in mind a social 'map' of classes in which social groupings are distinguished from each other not only by factors such as income and occupation, but also by their way of life and, possibly, a common awareness of their position. (This view features in the definition of *social class* that appears in 'The Black Report' in 'Inequalities in health', Chapter 4 of the Course Reader: 'segments of the population sharing broadly similar types and levels of resources, with broadly similar styles of living and (for some sociologists) some shared perception of their collective condition'.)

The various representations of class and class changes all employ social 'maps'. In constructing and using such 'maps', we know that they are not completely accurate — they are only a rough guide, and we accept that there are bound to be exceptions to our generalizations. For example, the Hillsborough commentator, Frank Johnson, would probably not insist that *none* of the 'respectable working class' goes to football matches. In making a generalization he is performing an exercise that we all engage in (not only social scientists). *That is the process of abstraction. We build models of generalities, things that seem generally true, even though we may be aware of particular exceptions.*

This process of 'mapping' the world through the use of abstractions enables us to make sense of it by highlighting what we conceive of as important differences and similarities, and excluding less significant ones. The various representations of class and class changes that we examined, each produced a different 'mapping' of class differences because they differed over what they took to be the most significant criteria. This is sometimes evident in the terminology: lumpenproletariat, underclass, yobs, respectable working class (Johnson); working class, toilers, producers, consumers (Walden); English working class (the French Press); upper class, middle class (Anderson). Clearly, when people talk about 'social class', they usually have more in mind than simply someone's 'occupation' or even a set of occupations. The variety of terminology suggests they may be referring to *different sorts of classes,* and using *different sorts of criteria* for drawing the lines or boundaries between classes. These different mappings or *models* are also related to different sorts of explanations about why classes exist and what causes them to change. In other words, they relate to different *theories* about what causes class divisions.

There are a number of social science theories about class, some of which have been developed and refined to a greater degree than others. In everyday speech and popular representations of class, people draw on the various models and implicit theories without bothering about how they differ. However, it is one of the tasks of social science to introduce greater precision and clarity in descriptions of patterned social differences and explanations of their causes. To achieve this end we will focus on the two models of class mentioned above, one derived from Marx, the other from Weber.

The first is essentially a two-class model, with a theory of class divisions which is organized around the identification of one primary factor — *wealth,* and its accumulation through the relations between an exploiting class and an exploited class.

The second is a multi-class model, with a theory of social divisions (or 'social stratification') which focuses on the interaction of several factors giving rise to patterns of *inequality* between social classes or strata. We will call the first the 'two-class' model, and the second the 'multi-class' or 'inequalities' model.

3.1 THE TWO-CLASS MODEL AND MARX'S THEORY OF CLASS

=== READER ===

Now read Section 2.2 on marxism in Chapter 22 of the Course Reader, paying particular attention to the subsection on 'Economy and society'. It might be a good idea to make a list of the key points that emerge about how Marx constructed his two-class model and his theory explaining how classes originated and developed.

I want to pick up and develop just a few of the points made in Chapter 22, Section 2.2 and then move on to discuss some later developments in this theory and give an indication of the kinds of evidence that relate to them.

1   Marx distinguished historical epochs — Antiquity, Feudalism, Capitalism and, eventually, Socialism — in terms of their predominant *mode of production*.

2   Each mode of production was distinguished from the others according to the way in which a small class of non-producers, who owned and controlled the means of production, extracted their wealth from the labour of the majority class of producers. It was in this sense, for Marx, that classes were *relational* (i.e. defined by the way in which they were related in the mode of production). The relation entailed *exploitation* and *domination* of one class by another. ('Exploitation' means that the majority class of producers lose part of what they produce to the small class of non-producers.) The major classes were: slaves and slave owners in Antiquity; lords and serfs in Feudal Europe; capitalists and workers (bourgeoisie and proletarians) under Capitalism.

3   The distinguishing characteristics of capitalism are: production of commodities for sale in the market and the reliance on 'free wage labour'. The workers are free to sell their labour, but they are never free of the need to find some capitalist to employ them.

4   The basic inequality in capitalist society is between those who are obliged to sell their labour and those who have sufficient resources (capital) to be able to live off the labour of others.

5   People in the same class have more in common with each other, in the form of shared experiences and interests, than they have with people in the other class.

6   Marx argued that the productive achievements of capitalism would eventually be outweighed by the increasing severity of its recurrent crises. There would be a growing tendency towards the polarization of the two major classes as capital became concentrated into larger units and as smaller capitalists and partly independent workers were forced down into the ranks of the proletariat.

7   Workers would become more conscious of their common interests and this class consciousness would drown out other divisions that separated them. The radicalization of the workers would eventually lead to the overthrow of the capitalist mode of production and to the emergence of Socialism.

A summary of the defining features of Marx's two-class model and his theory of the origins and development of classes would be on the following lines: *classes are based on the relations of production; these relations involve exploitation and domination; in the capitalist mode of production the two major classes will conflict and polarize, leading to the development of a radicalized class consciousness in the working class.*

Although Marx used a two-class model and constructed his theory in terms of the relationships between the two main classes, he was aware of some complicating factors. Most importantly, he acknowledged the persistence of classes from an earlier mode of production, such as landlords and peasants, within capitalist societies. He also recognized the existence of a class of people who owned capital but did not employ labour, such as small shopkeepers or self-employed family business owners — the so-called *petit bourgeoisie*. Towards the end of his life he became aware of a growing class of white-collar workers, a 'middle class' who stood between the manual workers on the one hand and the capitalists and landlords on the other. However, he never incorporated these developments fully into his theory, which emphasized polarization of the two major classes. Recently, social scientists working in the Marxist tradition have attempted to remedy this deficiency by distinguishing between the various intermediate strata or 'middle classes' in terms of the different positions they occupy in the social relations of production.

Erik Olin Wright, who has developed this aspect of Marx's class theory, agrees with Marx that the main social relations of production involve exploitation and domination of one class by another. Exploitation and domination can be expressed as 'control' — control through ownership of the means of production (capital investment); control over workers (labour power or the labour process). The two major classes in the capitalist mode of production — the bourgeoisie and the proletariat — are located at opposite ends of each of these processes. The owner of a factory, for example, can be contrasted on both these dimensions with a worker on the production-line in that factory. However, Wright argues, some intermediate strata occupy *contradictory class locations*. To varying degrees they are both controllers and controlled. Many white-collar and managerial staff occupy contradictory locations between the bourgeoisie and the proletariat. A manager, for example, may control the work of others but she/he is also subject to the control of the owner. Some small business people are located between the bourgeoisie and the kind of position occupied by the traditional petit bourgeoisie (e.g. the small, family-shop owner), who had control over their own productive means (including their own labour power) but not over that of others. Other strata of skilled crafts workers and lower professionals (e.g. some laboratory researchers), who retain some degree of autonomy and control over their own labour process, are located between the petit bourgeoisie and the proletariat. (This is illustrated in Figure 1.)

What situates each of these strata is the 'structural ambiguity' of their position, their partial involvement in one or more of the three processes of control (control of labour power, control of the physical means of production, and control of investment and resources), and their partial exposure to those control processes at the hands of others. In each case, their contradictory location can be estimated as variable rather than an all-or-nothing characteristic. In other words, for research measurement purposes, they can be translated into concrete activities such as participation in decisions dealing with budgets and investments, the ability to design and execute work-tasks, possession of authority to impose sanctions upon subordinates, and so forth. This is useful for mapping the class structure according to economic criteria and for investigating the processes facilitating or retarding class polarization.

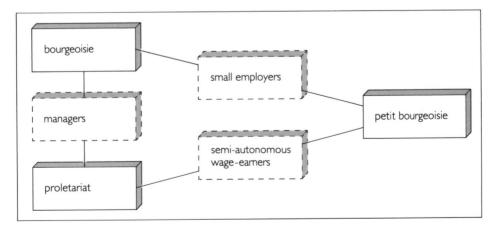

Figure 1   Contradictory class locations for key sections of the intermediate strata

Source: Wright, 1985

At first glance it might seem that this development of Marx's theory takes it away from the two-class model and so sacrifices its distinctiveness. However, this is not necessarily the case because the focus is still on the relations of exploitation and domination between the two polar-opposite classes, and most of the new intermediate strata are located in terms of this main axis:

bourgeoisie————proletariat

For example, foremen and supervisors are nearer to the working class than are middle managers, and senior managers shade into the propertied bourgeoisie itself. Middle managers and technicians are the most contradictory in their location here, controlling various bits of the labour process while being themselves wage-earners excluded from any control over investment and resources. Many of the most severe economic class conflicts are concerned with struggles over control — efforts to tighten or resist control, which can move strata closer to the position of the working class or align them more closely with the capitalists. Whereas the traditional petit bourgeoisie largely stood outside this polar class structure, as do some independent professionals and self-employed people, many white-collar workers are involved in the processes of control. They provide services that assist employers to exercise control and they enjoy some privileges, but they remain employees and so are subject to control. Even white-collar workers in the public sector are frequently involved in similar struggles over control, due to the fact that their employment contract shares many of the same characteristics as employment in the private sector. In marxist theory, public employees are paid out of the 'surplus' wealth generated by the production of 'commodities', much of which derives from the private sector, and when that declines the same pressures to tighten control and reduce labour costs are experienced in the public sector In both the private and the public sectors in capitalist society there is a conflict of interests between workers, who press for higher wages, and employers, who have an interest in keeping down wage costs. Another marxist argument for aligning public employment with class divisions is that the state functions to support the capitalist *system's* interests, even if state agencies are not themselves capitalists.

Finally, Marx's theory of class has been developed to explain changes in the ways in which the processes of exploitation and domination are built into the organization of the labour process. It has been suggested, for example, that efforts by employers to automate jobs are frequently aimed at tightening control over labour by dividing it into smaller tasks, which deskills or narrows the skills of workers and reduces their autonomy (Braverman, 1974). This is taken to be further evidence of the polarization of the two main classes, despite the apparent growth of intermediate strata.

In conclusion, the class theory derived from Marx represents the strongest and most highly-developed version of a two-class model. It focuses on control processes: the ownership and control of wealth invested in the production of goods and services to yield a profit (*capital*/wealth), and control over the *labour process* — design of work systems and rewards. In its origins, the theory dates from the nineteenth-century period of capitalism when class divisions and class conflict were most starkly evident, with a small class of owner–manager capitalists directly controlling a large class of manual workers. Since that time it has been adapted to deal with developments that have complicated that picture — developments in the capitalist class and the working class, as well as developments in various intermediate strata. In a later section we will examine its capacity to explain these class issues, particularly developments concerning the ownership and control of wealth and changes in the labour process.

SUMMARY

- Marx's theory of class focuses on the relations of production, involving exploitation and domination (control), between a class of owners of the means of production and a class of non-owner workers.

- The theory posits a long-term trend towards increasing polarization of the two major classes and radicalization of the working class.

- The theory has been adapted to take account of the growth of occupations that seem to occupy an intermediate and contradictory position between capital and labour.

- According to the revised marxist theory of class, the growth of intermediate or contradictory class positions need not count against the thesis of long-term polarization of the two major classes in modern capitalism for two reasons: capital is becoming more concentrated in large, global units, managed by professional managers on behalf of the capitalist class; whilst the work process in advanced capitalist society is designed to control workers more effectively through automation, which narrows the skills of workers and reduces their autonomy, resulting in further proletarianization of formerly semi-autonomous workers.

3.2 THE MULTI-CLASS MODEL AND WEBER'S THEORY OF SOCIAL STRATIFICATION

In contrast to the two-class model, a multi-class model of social stratification provides a more complicated 'mapping' of social divisions. It starts from the premise that the patterns of social inequality that constitute a hierarchy of social classes are not determined by a single factor or relationship, such as that between owners of capital and non-owners. It attempts to trace the interaction of a combination of factors, accepting the fact that those combinations are fluid and may change from one period or situation to another.

The hierarchy of *occupational classes,* ranked according to prestige or skill, as in the Registrar-General's list of occupational classes, is one of the most widely used examples of a 'multi-class' model. However, as 'The Black Report' points out, occupational class is only a convenient or pragmatic guide to a person's social class 'and as such has its limitations. It is only an approximate indicator of family living standards or social position' (Course Reader, Chapter 4). As it stands, such a single-indicator approach does not provide an adequate theoretical basis for a multi-class model of *social* classes. Consequently we need to look at a theory of class that builds up a multi-class model. It is generally agreed among social scientists that the most influential attempt to provide an adequate theoretical basis for a multi-class model was made by the German sociologist, Max Weber writing in the early twentieth century.

=== READER ===

You should now read the short passage on Max Weber (at the end of Section 2.3 of Chapter 22, pp. 276–7) in the Course Reader. As you read, keep in mind the need to see how Weber's ideas on social stratification emerge from his general approach, which emphasized the multiplicity of causal factors involved in *stratification* rather than giving pre-eminence to the economic factor as in Marx's theory.

Whereas Marx's class theory was primarily concerned with relations between owners and non-owners of the means of production, Weber's theory focused on distinguishing classes in terms of how they gained their income. For Weber, class position was determined by *'market situation'* — what people could offer in order to gain an income (Weber, 1968). The market might be for particular skills and labour, or for property to rent or capital to invest. Those who shared a similar class situation also had similar life-chances. In other words, their market situation directly affected their chances of securing the good things of life, such as a certain level of income, good health, access to higher education and good housing.

Weber agreed with Marx that a major social division was between those who owned the forces of production and those who did not. The minority class of those with substantial income-yielding property, or shares, enjoyed superior life-chances. However, Weber's theory of social stratification devoted consider-able attention to differences in market situation of particular groups *within* the two broad classes, particularly the various skills and services offered by differ-ent occupations. There were substantial differences in the *market situation* and *work situation* of managers, administrators and professionals, compared with those of routine clerical workers and manual workers in contemporary capitalist society. Not only did the higher occupational groupings tend to receive additional benefits, such as occupational pensions and better career prospects, they also enjoyed superior working conditions in matters like level of supervision and pleasant surroundings.

In his writings, Weber tended to refer to the following class groupings in capitalist societies:

1   A propertied upper class
2   Propertyless white-collar workers
3   Petit bourgeoisie (e.g. shopkeepers)
4   Manual working class.

Although in principle he agreed with Marx about the importance of the division in capitalist society between those living off property and those living off salaries or wages, in practice he went on to make finer distinctions between social classes in terms of different market position. Competition for rewards between occupational groups in the marketplace produces a complex hierarchy of class divisions. This is a far cry from Marx's picture of a society split between a dominant and a subordinate class in a relationship of exploitation. Weber never provided a single clear-cut means of identifying the boundaries between classes. This did not trouble him unduly because, unlike Marx, he did not believe that the system of production was the single main determinant of social stratification. We have already referred to the importance he gave to the structured inequalities derived from the distribution of rewards as a result of market position. There were two other major sources of division — prestige and political power. Differences in prestige gave rise to groups distinguished in terms of status. Access to power and influence through political organization in 'parties' or pressure groups was another major source of social stratification. Weber regarded status (prestige and entitlements) and political power groups ('parties') as potentially on a par with economic class in social stratification. Economic power need not bring status or political power, although it frequently does 'in the long run', he maintained.

Where Weber's theory begins to diverge more clearly from Marx's is with regard to the processes involved in social stratification. Although Weber agreed with Marx about the basic division of interests between capitalist and worker, and even spoke of the 'wage whip' that keeps the worker in line, he disagreed with Marx's prediction of increasing class polarization. Weber believed that as the division of labour became more complex, classes would become more rather than less heterogeneous. This was because divisions arose within classes as well as those which cut across classes. Weber pointed out that in contrast to classes, which were merely aggregates of individuals, status groups tended to have real group characteristics. They were much more likely to have a sense of group belonging and to engage in group action. Although Marx talked about class struggle giving rise to a class consciousness by which people in the same class situation (a *class-in-itself*) would act together (becoming a *class-for-itself*), Weber believed such a group character was much more likely to occur among people enjoying the same privileges and prestige (status groups) or sharing the same political aims and allegiance (political groups). For example, people in the same profession, such as doctors, are more likely to see themselves as a group and act in their common interest than they are to identify with the bourgeoisie or proletariat. They wish to preserve their prestige and pursue their political aims. In pursuit of their group interests, status groups practise policies of *closure.* Closure can take two forms: the first consists of *exclusion,* keeping out the unqualified so as not to dilute their prestige; the second is where aspiring groups practise *usurpation* — trying to gain access to the social prestige and privileges of higher ranking groups (Parkin, 1971, 1979).

However, Weber did not argue that status was of more fundamental importance than class. It depended on the circumstances, particularly the economic circumstances in each period and society. He suggested that, whilst status competition tended to predominate in periods of relative economic stability, class struggles came to the fore in periods of extensive technological or economic change. Political 'parties' became organized for the attainment of common goals and they seek to influence those in authority. By 'parties' Weber meant any pressure group or movement, even within clubs or other institutions, where people associate together to engage in planned action to exert pressure directed towards achieving goals. However, he was mainly interested in political parties as they related to the modern state, the actions of which he predicted would become increasingly important in the development of capitalist society, and even more important in socialist societies.

Thus we see that Weber's theory of stratification has three structural components: class, status and party. In the area of class divisions, these derive from the different economic resources people have to offer in the market. Like Marx, Weber believed that ownership or non-ownership of the means of production was the most fundamental economic division. However, he gave more attention than Marx to other resources, such as skills and qualifications, which affected people's marketability. For example, professionals or qualified skilled workers have more power in the labour market than unskilled workers.

The three sorts of processes, in relation to the three sorts of stratification — class, status and party — are:

- economic struggles over interests in the market;
- status group efforts at closure, either exclusion or usurpation, to maximize their prestige or social standing;
- political 'party-organized' efforts to wield power by influencing decision-makers.

Weber's purpose in making these analytical distinctions was to alert us to the possible variations in the patterns of inequality that occur in social stratification. Economic position does not always determine prestige and political influence throughout the whole social order. For example, manufacturing industrialists in Britain have often complained that they enjoy less prestige and political influence than their economic position would seem to warrant, while some of the older professions, such as the clergy, doctors and lawyers, probably enjoy more prestige and political influence than their economic position would lead us to expect. It is these sorts of variations that Weber's theory was meant to take account of, directing attention to the different processes of market struggle, status group closure, and political influence.

Weber's theory of social stratification has been developed in two respects for the purposes of social science research into changes in class structure:

1   The first is concerned with occupational classification and attempts to group occupations into categories, so that these can be used as an approximate indicator of social class structure. This has led to studies of *social mobility* — studying the extent to which there are opportunities for people in different occupational classes to move up or down the social scale, or whether there is social closure around some occupational class positions that reduces such opportunities (see Heath, 1981).

2   The second development concerns the concept of status and particularly the status of *citizen,* which entails *citizenship* rights — political–legal entitlements to health, education and other social benefits guaranteed by the state and to which all citizens have an equal claim, in the same way that they have an equal entitlement to justice and democratic representation. These citizenship rights are intended to cut across and reduce inequalities of class (see Marshall, 1977).

One classification used in studies of social mobility in Britain, developed by the Oxford sociologist John Goldthorpe, subdivides three main classes to give an eleven-category version. The theoretical justification for the categories derives from Weber's conception of class as defined by the market and work situations of particular occupations. It attempts to combine occupations into categories whose members appear to be similar in terms of their sources and levels of income, their degree of economic security and chances of economic advancement; their location within systems of authority and control governing the process of production, and hence their degree of autonomy in performing their work-tasks and roles. It then seeks to check these categories against empirical evidence to see to what extent they form bounded social groupings in terms of their life-chances, their life-styles and patterns of association, and their socio-political attitudes and modes of action. On the basis of his research, Goldthorpe arrives at the class categories outlined in Table 1.

Table I   Goldthorpe's class categories

Class			
Service	I		Higher-grade professionals, administrators and officials; managers in large establishments; large proprietors.
	II		Lower-grade professionals, administrators and officials; higher-grade technicians; managers in small businesses and industrial establishments; supervisors of non-manual employees.
Intermediate	IIIa		Routine non-manual employees in administration and commerce.
	IIIb		Personal service workers.
	IVa		Small proprietors, artisans etc., with employees.
	IVb		Small proprietors, artisans etc., without employees.
	IVc		Farmers and smallholders; self-employed fishermen.
	V		Lower-grade technicians, supervisors of manual workers.
Working	VI		Skilled manual workers.
	VIIa		Semi-skilled and unskilled manual workers (not in agriculture).
	VIIb		Agricultural workers.

Source: Goldthorpe and Payne, 1986

It was not only different positions in the economic market that led to social divisions, according to Weber, there were also differences of status and political power. In theory, in modern democratic societies the legal status and political standing of citizens is supposed to be equal. In practice there are persistent inequalities in the distribution of social benefits such as health and education. These inequalities often correlate with the hierarchy of occupational classes, as shown in 'The Black Report' in 'Inequalities in health' (Chapter 4 in the Course Reader). However, there are also status groups that cut across classes, such as those whose status derived from their ethnic background or their gender, and such people often have less status prestige and power than fellow members of the same economic class. Correspondingly, they also suffer greater inequalities with respect to their citizenship entitlements. At the bottom of the social hierarchy there exists a stratum or 'underclass' of citizens who seem to fall outside the lowest occupational class, because of unemployment or underemployment and, lacking prestige and influence, suffer multiple inequalities.

The Weberian approach to social stratification attempts to differentiate between these various stratifying factors and to investigate how they combine to produce a persistent social hierarchy.

SUMMARY

- Weber's approach to social divisions differed from that of Marx in that he did not assume that economic factors were the primary cause of the structure of social stratification. He favoured a multi-factor theory of stratification. Prestige (status) factors could also be important, as could political power factors.

- In the economic sphere, people's class positions were determined by their market situation — what they could offer so as to gain an income.

- The Weberian theory's multi-factor approach to social stratification suggests that the various factors may combine or diverge in different ways depending on particular circumstances. Unlike Marx's theory, it does not predict that social classes will develop in line with a historical trend common to all societies with the same economic mode of production.

- This approach to social stratification has been developed in two ways:

  (a) Occupations have been grouped into categories, on the basis of certain shared characteristics, and then checked against evidence about whether they form bounded social groupings, i.e. social classes. The extent to which these are closed off or open is also measured in terms of the extent of social mobility of individuals between them.

  (b) Whether class divisions are narrowing or widening can be tested by measuring evidence concerning inequalities between classes in their access to citizenship entitlements, e.g. health and education.

4   COMPARING THE TWO MODELS AND TESTING THE THEORIES

We will now test the theories against some evidence concerning specific class changes. Each of the theories is stronger on some issues than others. The first two issues are those most relevant to the marxist theory: (1) wealth, ownership and control; and (2) work and the working class. The next two issues are those which the Weberian theory has focused on: (3) social mobility, and (4) inequality and opportunity.

4.1   WEALTH, OWNERSHIP AND CONTROL

It is a central tenet of the marxist theory that control of capital remains concentrated in the hands of the minority capitalist class — the bourgeoisie. How far has this remained the case in Britain? Has there been sufficient redistribution of wealth to support the multi-class model of more gradually spaced rungs on the social ladder?

There can be no doubt that, in absolute terms, the wealth and income of the majority of the working class has increased fairly steadily over the last century in the UK. There has also been a decline in the proportion of marketable wealth (property that can be sold) owned by the top 1 per cent of the population over most of the last sixty years (see Table 2).

Table 2   The distribution of wealth, 1923 to 1989 — share of total wealth(%)

	1923	1938	1960	1971	1976	1980	1985	1987	1989
Top 1%	60.9	55.0	33.9	31	24	20	20	18	18
Next 4%	21.1	21.9	25.5	21	21	19	20	18	20
Next 5%	7.1	8.1	12.1	13	15	13	14	14	15
Top 10%	89.1	85.0	71.5	65	60	52	54	50	53
Next 10%	5.1	6.2	11.6	16.6					
Next 15%					21	24	23	22	22
Top 50%				97	95	94	93	93	94

Source: 1923 to 1960 figures are for England and Wales, after Atkinson and Harrison (1978). Figures for other years are for the adult population of the UK, from CSO, *Social Trends*, 1988, 1990 and 1993

However, there has been little further redistribution downwards of marketable wealth between the top and the bottom classes over the last quarter century, not since the shift that occurred following the Second World War. In 1989 the bottom half of the population still had only 6 per cent of the wealth. The top 5 per cent (about two million people) own 38 per cent of the total personal wealth, and the top 10 per cent own over half the nation's personal wealth. If we take marketable wealth excluding dwellings, we find that between 1976 and 1990 the most wealthy 5 per cent increased their share from 47 cent to 51 per cent and the most wealthy 10 per cent from 57 per cent to 63 per cent. Furthermore, in the 1980s, there was a widening of the *income* gap between the top 25 per cent and the rest of the population. The share of pre-tax income going to the top quarter of taxpayers increased to 50 per cent in 1989–90, whereas in 1978–79 it was 45 per cent. Conversely, the income share going to the bottom 70 per cent of taxpayers fell from 50 per cent to 45 per cent over the same period (figures given by the Financial Secretary to the Treasury in a written reply to a question in the House of Commons, *Hansard*, 13 February 1990).

Despite the changes that have taken place in the distribution of wealth in this century, there is evidence that ownership and control of the sort of wealth that yields further substantial income is still heavily concentrated in a relatively small section of the population and that inheritance plays an important role in perpetuating that concentration.

Marx's concept of the upper class, which he termed the bourgeoisie or capitalist class, did not rest solely on their ownership of personal wealth, but on their possession and control of 'capital'. The distinction between personal wealth and wealth as capital can be described as follows:

> Capital ... is different from other forms of wealth: shares in an industrial company, for example, will typically grow in value over time, produce a regular dividend, confer legal ownership over part of the company's material assets, and are, moreover, easily marketable when necessary. Other forms of wealth are quite different: consumer goods generally depreciate and have a low second hand value; the value of houses may in the main appreciate, but they are often difficult to sell and the owner generally needs to buy another as a replacement; pensions provide an entitlement to further income only as long as the pensioner lives, are not transferable, and often depreciate in value; and cash, although it confers immediate economic power through its purchasing power, generally depreciates. It is changes in the ownership and control of the means of production that need to be treated as the central criterion in assessing the distribution of wealth, for changes in other forms of wealth are intimately related to these.
>
> (Hird, 1979)

In other words, the upper class, or 'capitalist' class in Marx's terms, is composed of those whose wealth is in the form of capital that can be used to generate further income. The spread of home-ownership (except for inheritance) and consumer goods does not substantially affect the division between the upper class and other classes. Nor does ownership of a few shares take people into this upper class. An individual would need a very large number of shares in order to be sure of an investment income equivalent to average earned income. Despite the extension of 'popular' wealth (homes, pensions, savings) in the post-war period, the ownership of substantial power-conferring assets (capital) remained concentrated in the hands of a very few.

According to Inland Revenue statistics in 1986, one per cent of the population owned nearly two-thirds of the private land in Britain, while 5 per cent owned almost 90 per cent. While the richest one per cent owned only 5 per cent of residential buildings, their portfolios include one-sixth of all other privately owned buildings. The richest one per cent also owned two-thirds of unlisted company securities and foreign securities, almost half the listed company securities, and a third of the trade assets and shares in partnerships (Inland Revenue, 1986; Pond, 1989). The purchase of small quantities of shares in privatized companies by many individuals in the 1980s does not substantially alter this picture of wealth and power concentrated in the hands of an upper class. These small shareholdings, like pensions and home ownership, provide security for members of other classes, but they do not bring the same opportunities for exploitation and domination that capital provides for the upper class. Privatizations and the give-away of 5 million free shares by the Abbey National Building Society raised share-ownership from one adult in fourteen in the 1970s to one adult in five by 1990 — 9 million people, according to a Government statement (*Hansard*, 6 February 1990). However, the proportion of shares owned by individuals rather than institutions had fallen from a third in 1978 to below a fifth in 1992 — and compares to two-thirds of shares in private hands in 1957 (*The Sunday Correspondent,* 10 December 1989; *Social Trends,* 1993). For most people, the increase in their ownership of wealth was mainly in the form of home ownership, not shares: the proportion of personal wealth accounted for by stocks and shares in 1989 was 8.1 per cent, compared to 19.9 per cent in 1971 (*Social Trends,* 1992).

Although much of what has been called 'popular wealth' other than housing, is deposited in large financial institutions, such as building societies, banks and pension funds, where the power of control is wielded by directors and top executives, according to the marxist theory this does not make the managers themselves members of the capitalist class. Nor need it weaken the power of the capitalist class. It is only those managers, or directors, who themselves own large amounts of capital that the two-class model would place in the capitalist class. Managers dependent for most of their income on salaries would, however, be considered as agents of capital. On the other hand, there is evidence that members of the upper class do exercise a large amount of control even over companies where they are not themselves large shareholders. This can occur either through their involvement in interlocking directorships, or because of influence through personal networks of family, friendship or social background (e.g., school, university and club contacts). In fact, there is evidence that these two channels of influence and power coalesce: there is a core within the upper class made up of rich individuals who serve as directors on the boards of several large companies, and who are also integrated through ties of kinship ('kinter-lock'), friendship, or membership of exclusive social institutions — public schools, ancient universities, London clubs, etc. (Scott and Griff, 1984). At the core of this are the banks and other financial institutions. Furthermore, companies which have such core representatives of the upper class as directors on their boards are found to be more likely to make contributions to bodies with political-economic aims, such as the Economic League and British United Industrialists, which act as political pressure groups to promote the capitalist system and safeguard it against interference (Scott and Griff, 1984, p.145).

Those who uphold the continuing relevance of Marx's theory can point to the evidence about wealth holdings and interlocking directorships as showing that, whilst some senior managers do share in control of their own company as executive directors, it is the non-executive directors and company chairmen (sic) who continue to represent the wider interests of the propertied class. These non-executive directors are the core of the propertied class, which has its interests dispersed throughout the system which they manage. The end-result is that the interests of the class that lives off profits are safeguarded in the long run.

Whilst the evidence on wealth concentration and interlocking directorships would seem to support Marx's class theory, there are criticisms that can be made against the claim that this evidence supports the marxist model:

1   The evidence of wealth concentration and interlocking directorships may not in itself prove anything about class integration and control. It would need many case studies of decision-making and decision-makers on the boards of large corporations in order to show that there was collusion to promote the interests of a propertied upper class. Not surprisingly, companies are not very keen on allowing social scientists to carry out such research at their board meetings! Research has to be done from the outside looking in. We have noted that it is also argued that the increase in institutional ownership of shares (i.e. by pension funds and other financial institutions) reduces the importance of ownership by wealthy individuals and must reduce their control.

2   Another criticism that can be made is that the marxist class theory places too much emphasis on economic classes and does not give enough attention to

different sectional groupings — elites, status groups and political factions. This is the position of critics who prefer a Weberian theory. They would stress differences in background and values of leaders in various sectors of the economy (e.g., retailing, brewing, heavy industry, mining, transport, banking and insurance, etc.); managers as bureaucrats whose actions are determined by technical considerations rather than class interests; the differences between various elite groups, such as politicians, civil servants, landowners, the old professions, and the new technological specialists etc. In general, the Weberian theory promotes a scepticism towards the marxist claim that there is an integrated upper, or bourgeois, class bound together by shared interests. Weberians are more likely to point out the differences among the upper social strata and to focus on social mobility between the middle and upper strata.

SUMMARY

- Although certain kinds of personal wealth, such as home-ownership, have become more widely spread, there is evidence to support Marx's theory of increasing class polarization as it related to the capitalist class. Capital is increasingly concentrated in large global enterprises whose control is linked through interlocking directorships, and these key capitalist controllers have considerable political influence.

- However, Weberians would argue that, as large capitalist enterprises are increasingly owned and controlled by pension funds and other financial institutions on behalf of many individuals, so the class of pure capitalists is shrinking, whilst the intermediate classes of managers and skilled workers are taking a greater share of wealth and participating in control.

4.2   WORK AND THE WORKING CLASS

Having examined some of the arguments about class polarization as it relates to the capitalist, or bourgeois, class, we will now focus on the other side of the two-class model. Is the working class changing so much that it can no longer be considered as a single, majority class polarized against a controlling class of capitalist employers? Many of the adaptations that have been made to Marx's theory are a response to changes in the division of labour since the nineteenth century. Firstly, there have been changes in the division of labour between different sectors of the economy, particularly the decline in heavy industry and manufacturing, and the growth of service industries in both the private and public sectors (ranging from entertainment and retailing to central and local government administration). (See Table 3 overleaf.) Secondly, there have been changes in the division of labour in terms of the occupational or skill structure of the workforce, for example a decline in skilled manual occupations and an increase in white-collar occupations. Thirdly, there have been changes in the organization of tasks in the workplace, for example a decline in numbers of workers employed in assembly-line production, an increase in computerization, and the use of more part-time workers (the majority of whom are, in fact, women).

All of these changes affect the composition of the working class and have led some social scientists to talk about either a 'decline of the working class' or at least its 'recomposition'. The changes also present problems for those wishing to locate the boundaries of the working class, particularly in relation to various segments of the middle class. As we saw earlier in discussing recent adap-

Table 3   Employees in employment: by sex and industry, United Kingdom (thousands)

	SIC[1] (1980)	1971	1979	1981	1983	1986	1990	1991	1992
All industries	0–9	22,139	23,173	21,892	21,067	21,387	22,899	22,229	21,758
of which									
Males		13,726	13,487	12,562	11,940	11,744	12,069	11,592	11,253
Females		8,413	9,686	9,331	9,127	9,644	10,830	10,637	10,504
Manufacturing	2–4	8,065	7,253	6,222	5,525	5,227	5,138	4,793	4,589
Services	6–9	11,627	13,580	13,468	13,501	14,297	15,945	15,744	15,644
Other	0,1,5	2,447	2,340	2,203	2,042	1,863	1,817	1,692	1,524
Employees in employment by SIC division									
Agriculture, forestry and fishing	0	450	380	363	350	329	298	291	283
Energy and water supply	1	798	722	710	648	545	449	439	403
Other minerals and ore extraction etc.	2	1,282	1,147	939	817	729	721	657	635
Metal goods, engineering and vehicles	3	3,709	3,374	2,923	2,548	2,372	2,310	2,139	2,030
Other manufacturing industries	4	3,074	2,732	2,360	2,159	2,126	2,106	1,997	1,924
Construction	5	1,198	1,239	1,130	1,044	989	1,070	962	839
Distribution, catering and repairs	6	3,686	4,257	4,172	4,118	4,298	4,822	4,686	4,605
Transport and communication	7	1,556	1,479	1,425	1,345	1,298	1,382	1,349	1,324
Banking, finance, insurance, etc	8	1,336	1,647	1,739	1,875	2,166	2,744	2,687	2,639
Other services	9	5,049	6,197	6,132	6,163	6,536	6,996	7,022	7,076

[1] Standard Industrial Classification

Source: Employment Department, *Social Trends 23*, © Crown Copyright 1993

tations of Marx's theory, the swelling ranks of certain sections of the middle class seem to occupy 'contradictory' class locations between capital and labour.

In the affluent years of the 1960s — after Prime Minister Harold Macmillan told the British people in 1959 that 'You have never had it so good' — debates in class analysis revolved around the thesis of 'embourgeoisement'. According to this theory, the rising affluence of the working class seemed to herald the demise of the class system and the emergence of a mass consumer society in which workers would increasingly take on the characteristics associated with the middle class. It was not until the late 1960s that the theoretical foundations of the embourgeoisement thesis were clarified and its core propositions subjected to systematic empirical scrutiny, notably in the research by John Goldthorpe and his colleagues into the attitudes of Luton car-workers — *The Affluent Worker* (1968–9). They found that the relatively affluent section of the working class to which the Luton car workers belonged might differ from the more traditional working class in their attitudes towards unions and politics (being more 'instrumental' — only giving support when it served their own interests — rather than exhibiting blanket allegiance) and in life-style (being more 'privatized' — family-centred — and less communal), but there was still a clear boundary separating them from the middle class. This was borne out by the fact that the car workers became known for their trades union militancy in the 1970s.

After the economic recession of the late 1970s and early 1980s (which led to intensified efforts by employers to reduce labour costs as a way of increasing competitiveness and restoring profit levels), debate in class analysis centred on a revival of Marx's thesis of 'proletarianization'. Those social scientists who believe the evidence supports this thesis, have pointed to the so-called 'de-skilling' of particular jobs, either white-collar jobs previously thought of as non-proletarian (clerks and administrators), or formerly skilled craft jobs (Braverman, 1974; Crompton and Jones, 1984). The discussion of proletarianization is concerned with the twin processes of deskilling and increased control by management due to incorporation of skills into the machinery itself. In this way the capitalist labour process is said to withdraw the last vestiges of skill and control over work from the working class and puts the control necessary for exploitation firmly in the hands of management. It is argued that the expansion of administrative and professional occupations is probably more apparent than real because many of these involve the performance of increasingly routinized, and therefore 'degraded', labour. Moreover, routine clerical work has been deskilled because such employees commonly experience the same limited autonomy in the workplace as do unskilled manual workers. Since clerks often perform routine tasks under close supervision, they are effectively proletarians.

Critics of the proletarianization thesis argue that the evidence used to support it is based on case studies of only a few occupations (notably local authority, life assurance and banking clerks) and that these can easily be offset against others reporting an upgrading of occupational skills and tasks. Furthermore, some opponents maintain that there has been a real expansion of a relatively privileged 'service class' of professionals, administrators, managers and other skilled white-collar workers, drawing recruits from the working class (Goldthorpe *et al.*, 1980). They claim that the net result of organizational and technical changes over the whole economy is one of increasing both skill levels and the proportion of the workforce benefiting from service-class conditions of employment.

Furthermore, the situation is complicated by the fact that office workers are not a homogeneous group, but are differentiated by age, qualifications and

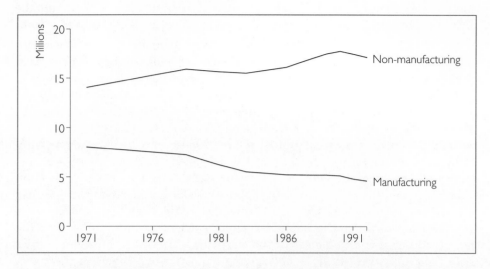

Figure 2   Manufacturing and non-manufacturing employees in employment, United Kingdom
Note: In March 1991 employment in manufacturing fell below 5 million for the first time since 1959, when records were first kept on this basis.
Source: Central Statistical Office, *Social Trends 21*, 1991, *Social Trends 23*, 1993

gender. Research shows that the majority of men who start their working lives as clerks will have been promoted by the age of 35; the bulk of clerical work is performed by women whose careers include routine non-manual and manual jobs alike; and a significant minority of clerical workers are male ex-manual workers who have been promoted from the shop-floor late in life. Critics of the proletarianization theory conclude:

> It is difficult, given this information, to see how clerical work has been in any sense proletarianized, since even if the associated tasks themselves are highly routinized, they are done by young credentialled employees (mostly men) *en route* to promoted service-class destinations; older men who are by past (as well as current) experience proletarian; and women of all ages whose occupational careers embrace 'proletarian' non-manual and manual work alike. There is actually no group of individuals here who have been proletarianized. Moreover, there are good grounds for arguing that clerical work has always involved routine and often trivial tasks, and that the introduction of automated office machinery is as likely to be perceived by clerical workers themselves as involving an extension (rather than diminution) of autonomy and skill in the office.

(Marshall and Rose, 1988, p.514)

Perhaps the best evidence concerning exploitation and domination in response to economic downturns in the early 1980s and again in the early 1990s, lies in the millions of workers cast out of their jobs or subjected to tightened managerial control and worsened working conditions. However, this is different from the proletarianization thesis, as many of these workers were already working class (although in the recession of the 1990s many non-manual workers have also been affected). On the other hand, it could still be argued that class polarization does take place in times of capitalism's periodic crises or slumps. Even Weber was prepared to concede that class divisions came to the fore at such times. What is more difficult to decide is whether such crises will become progressively worse as capital becomes more globally concentrated in large multinational enterprises.

We will return to discuss the deskilling thesis again in Unit 10. In the meantime, you might find it interesting to test the marxist thesis about proletarianization against your own experience of changes in occupational skills, levels of job autonomy, and the organization of tasks. Have you, or people of your acquaintance, experienced such a trend?

SUMMARY

- With regard to Marx's thesis of increasing class polarization, the discussion shows that, just as the theories derived from Marx and Weber produced different interpretations of trends in the ownership and control of capital, and so differed about what was happening to the capitalist class, so too they diverge in their interpretation of what is happening to the working class.

- There is evidence to support the proletarianization thesis on the grounds that some working-class occupations have been 'deskilled' and workers' autonomy reduced in order to keep up profits in conditions of increasing international competition. However, the extent of this trend is difficult to judge without many more case studies of different occupations. The Weberian approach would tend to stress the rivalry between different occupational groups and various social strata, each seeking to strengthen its position through closure or usurpation.

4.3   SOCIAL MOBILITY AND INEQUALITY

Whilst Marx's class theory has been the chief inspiration for many of the debates about class struggles over exploitation and control in the capitalist system of production, Weber's theory has influenced studies of many other aspects of social stratification. Two of the most important aspects, because they are central to arguments about 'fairness' in liberal-democratic societies, are *social mobility* and *inequality*. Whereas Marx regarded his concept of 'exploitation' of labour as a technical economic concept rather than a moral judgement (a controversial claim), the notion of 'fairness' is clearly a moral matter. The Weberian approach takes seriously the claim of liberal-democratic societies that they have a moral basis, and that one of their central values is 'fairness' of treatment of citizens. The next step for social scientists has been to investigate the existence of inequalities and their likely causes, with a view to allowing citizens to judge whether there is fairness. Is Britain becoming a fairer society and perhaps even a 'classless society'?

4.4   SOCIAL MOBILITY

Evidence about the extent of social mobility in Britain, or any capitalist society, is important because it allows us to make informed judgements about equality of opportunity. This is regarded by many as a crucial test of fairness in a liberal democracy where rewards and status are supposed to be based on personal merit.

The main conclusion drawn by researchers, about social mobility rates in the UK since the Second World War, is that there has been an increase, but the reason for this has less to do with equal opportunities and is more attributable to increases in the number of higher white-collar jobs relative to manual or blue-collar jobs. A major survey carried out in 1972, found that two-thirds of the sons of unskilled or semi-skilled manual workers were themselves in manual occupations. Whilst 4 per cent of men in blue-collar work were from professional or manual backgrounds, about 30 per cent of professionals and managers were of working-class origin (Goldthorpe *et al.*, 1980). In a follow-up study ten years later they found an increased number of males getting professional or managerial jobs, although once again most of this could be traced to a growth in such occupations and a decline in blue-collar jobs. Downward mobility had further declined. However, more men from working-class backgrounds were now unemployed (Goldthorpe and Payne, 1986).

A severe limitation of many of these social mobility studies is that they focus on men only. Men are often taken to be the chief 'breadwinners' and it is mobility in their occupational career ('intragenerational mobility'), or son's occupation compared with father's ('intergenerational mobility'), that is recorded. This neglect of gender differences leaves an important gap in the data on mobility. However, despite incomplete data, some effort has been made to calculate women's mobility. One study of social mobility calculated that over half the daughters of professional or managerial fathers were in routine office jobs, and no more than 8 per cent obtained positions comparable to those of their fathers. Only 1.5 per cent of women from blue-collar homes were in such occupations, whilst there were 48 per cent in routine office work (Heath, 1981; discussed in Giddens, 1989).

SUMMARY

- There is evidence of increasing upward social mobility in Britain since the Second World War.

- However, much of the upward social mobility is due to the growth of white-collar occupations and the decline in manual occupations.

- Social mobility studies often tend to neglect gender differences. Where women's social mobility is studied, the evidence suggests they have fewer opportunities for upward social mobility on the basis of their own occupational careers.

- Social mobility studies tend to use a Weberian model of social stratification, treating categories of occupations with similar incomes and work situations as classes, and tracking the movement of individuals between these, with a view to making judgements about whether, and why, social mobility rates are increasing or decreasing. This is relevant to issues of inequality and fairness. (The marxist theory of class is more concerned with the relations between classes, which it maintains are always based on exploitation and domination.)

ACTIVITY 4

Consider your own reaction to the evidence on social mobility, taking account of the different ways in which the evidence can be presented and evaluated depending on the values of the writer and your own values. For example, my presentation may have tended to accentuate the negative view, whereas others would accentuate the positive, laying emphasis on the fact that '*no fewer than 28 per cent of class 1 males ... had started life in the working class* and that only one quarter of men in class 1 had been born into this class' (Saunders, 1989, emphasis added).

Do you judge that society is becoming fairer in the light of such changes?

4.5   INEQUALITY AND OPPORTUNITY

In order to understand the link between studies of social mobility and issues of inequality and fairness, I would like you to consider the following statement made by the social mobility researchers Marshall and Rose in their defence against their critic Peter Saunders' criticisms that they give too negative a view of opportunities for social mobility in Britain:

> In sum, we conclude by observing that market societies are legitimized by the principle of equal opportunities; that equality of opportunity has been the explicitly stated objective of all post-war governments in Britain, Conservative and Labour alike; that relative mobility rates are a measure of equality of opportunity; these rates have not changed in this country since the 1920s; and, therefore, that 'the post-war project of creating in Britain a more open society through economic expansion, educational reform and egalitarian social policies has signally failed to secure its objectives'.
> (Marshall and Rose, 1989, p.5)

The issue they pose is: have inequalities of opportunity decreased and so made Britain a fairer society? This is a different question from that posed by Saunders, which was concerned with 'whether people's lives have improved over time'. His position is based upon the liberal tradition of thought. He quotes the argument put forward by the liberal thinker Hayek, that 'capitalism is a beneficial system precisely because it improves everybody's life-chances as time goes on', and criticizes the social mobility researchers for the focus on equality. Saunders argues that the social mobility researchers 'cannot admit of even the possibility that talents may be unevenly distributed through the class system, that the more talented tend to rise towards the upper positions, and that talented parents very often have talented children'. This poses the question: are patterned or structured inequalities due to inequalities of talent more than to unequal opportunities?

Certainly the evidence is clear that the inequalities are patterned or structured along class lines, and along other stratification lines such as 'race' and gender. (You examined some of those inequalities with regard to health in Unit 6.) I would like you to consider Figure 3 and Table 4 which illustrate inequalities in education, with a view to reaching a conclusion as to whether they are due to the distribution of natural talent or to class privilege.

Figure 3 is a graph based on information drawn from the various social mobility studies that have used education as one of the main indicators to determine whether there has been any reduction in inequalities of opportunity between classes in Britain. The various graphs do not coincide because there were slight differences in definitions of social class and of selective schooling, but nevertheless they do show that in the period studied there was no consistent trend towards either increasing or declining class inequality. Both with regard to entrance to selective schools (largely grammar and private schools) in the early period, and with respect to attainment of O level (or, earlier, school certificate) qualifications, the conclusion drawn is that: 'The socially and economically advantaged classes conferred on their children great educational advantage and the gap between the classes stayed more or less constant for their respective time spans.' It remains to be seen whether the succession of educational reforms since the 1970s will close the gaps between the classes.

Evidence of the effects of past inequalities can be seen in figures for highest qualification level attained, as shown in Table 4 from *Social Trends* (1993), where only 3 per cent of those whose fathers were in unskilled manual occu-

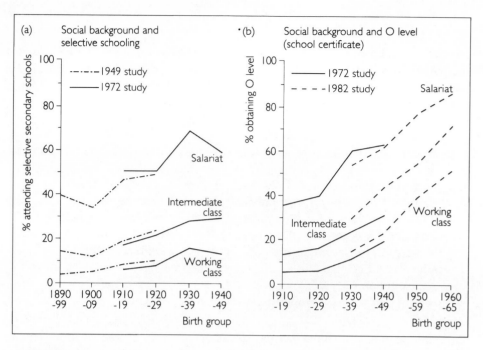

Figure 3   (a) Social background and selective schooling; (b) Social background and O level (school certificate)

Source: Heath, 1987, Figure 3.3.1

pations had a degree, compared with 32 per cent of those with fathers in professional occupations. Contrary to Saunders' suggestion, it is difficult to see how these differences of attainment between the classes could be accounted for by IQ differences, as the overall level of attainment of all classes has risen within a relatively short time, and it is not conceivable that the IQ of the whole population has risen. Furthermore, larger proportions of comparable populations in other countries succeed in higher education. The British Conservative government thinks that there is a large untapped pool of working-class children capable of succeeding in higher education in the 1990s and aims to double the total number of people in higher education between 1992 and the end of the decade.

Pupils at Eton learn how to handle computers

Table 4 Highest qualification level attained[1]: by socio-economic group of father, 1990–91, Great Britain (percentages and numbers)

	Professional	Employers and managers	Intermediate and Junior non-manual	Skilled manual and own account non-professional	Semi-skilled manual and personal service	Unskilled manual	Total
Degree	32	17	17	6	4	3	10
Higher education	19	15	18	10	7	5	11
A level	15	13	12	8	6	4	9
O level	19	24	24	21	19	15	21
CSE	4	9	7	12	12	10	10
Foreign	4	4	4	3	2	2	3
No qualifications	7	19	18	40	50	60	35
Sample size (= 100%) (numbers)	961	3,963	2,028	8,618	2,931	1,168	19,669

[1] Persons aged 25–59 not in full-time education. (See Appendix, Part 3: Education in *Social Trends* 23.)

Source: data from General Household Survey; table from *Social Trends* 23, © Crown Copyright 1993

With the increase in 'citizenship rights' to education as a result of 'social engineering' in the post-war welfare state, all classes have made gains. In Saunders' terms, 'the column moved forward'. But the gaps within the forward moving column, between the classes, stay wide; inequalities remain great. As the working class struggles to usurp or overcome barriers that deny it access to higher income opportunities, the qualification entrance levels to those jobs are raised. The opportunities are closed off. Furthermore, as with many other social benefits offered by the welfare state, it is the middle and upper classes which take more than their 'fair share'. In the case of education, better-off families can move to areas where the state schools are superior or they can more easily afford to send their children to private schools or to tutors. They have the social and organizational skills to exert influence and secure results. The same families then benefit most from state-subsidized higher education. Children from poorer families leave school earlier to supplement the family income and, with the decline in the value of the student support grant in the 1980s, higher education has become more expensive and they may be less inclined to take up student loans since they are less likely to have a potential safety-net.

SUMMARY

- Most social mobility researchers, who tend to use a Weberian multi-class model, conclude that inequalities of opportunity between classes have not decreased in Britain since the Second World War.

- Some critics from the 'liberal' tradition charge that this is because the social mobility researchers come from the 'social reformist' tradition, which emphasizes the value of equality, rather than acknowledging the general improvement in people's life chances.

- However, the evidence with regard to citizenship entitlements such as education and health suggests that the differences between classes remain wide.

- The marxist theory of class is less concerned with these issues of social mobility and relative inequality. Its main interest is in investigating the relations between the two major classes of capitalists and workers, hence its concentration on the processes of capital wealth accumulation and the labour process. It regards issues of social mobility and relative inequality as secondary matters.

---

5 CONCLUSIONS ON TESTING THE THEORIES

Marx's theory directs our attention to one of the most fundamental sources of inequality — the differences in social power between those who own and control the means of production and those who are in a more dependent position. Weber's theory focuses on processes that produce some of the finer distinctions between social strata, emphasizing not only ownership or non-ownership of wealth, but also prestige and influence. How well do our two theories of social class stand up to the test of explaining class issues? What can we say about their relative strengths, having examined a series of key issues in Section 4?

It seems to me that the strength of Marx's theory lies in its capacity to explain class issues involving conflicts between the two major classes of capitalist-employers and worker-employees. As we saw in Section 4, there is some evidence of polarization of these two classes. Capital is becoming more concentrated in massive (increasingly multinational) enterprises. Workers in some occupations find their position weakened by automation, which may deskill them or tighten control over their performance, or they face the threat of their jobs being transferred to cheaper countries or regions. Contrary tendencies, such as the expansion and higher remuneration of professions like salaried managers and accountants, may be harder to explain in terms of Marx's original theory of class polarization. However, the theory has been developed using the concept of 'contradictory' class locations. On the one hand these professionals are salary-earners, but on the other hand they act as agents of capital, carrying out capitalists' delegated functions.

Weber's theory focuses more attention on class issues that relate to subdivisions within the two major classes due to differences in market situation. These market situations are explained in terms of the relative capacities of the various occupational groups to keep their assets (e.g., qualifications and skills) scarce, either by closing off entry or by usurping the advantages of groups in higher positions. Status, prestige and political influence, although conceptually separate from class, based on economic position, are also assets that can combine with it to produce a category of occupations with a common group character (although they may also fragment a class into competing occupational groups). The Weberian theory is useful for the light it throws on these dynamics of coalition and subdivision of class fractions. It has been frequently used to explain class divisions such as those between skilled and unskilled manual workers, and professionals and other white-collar workers. Weber himself did not devote much attention to drawing up a list of classes because his theory of stratification attached more importance to the dynamics by which various social strata developed conscious group characteristics, and he thought ideas of prestige and shared political purpose were more important than economic position in many cases. However, some social scientists believe that classifications of occupations such as those carried out by the Registrar General, using notions of skill content to rank occupations into roughly six classes, are similar to what Weber had in mind. And, although the boundaries between these classes may be rather hard to define in theoretical terms, this kind of classification has the advantage of being widely used for the collection of official statistics. Just how useful this kind of data is depends on the problem being addressed. On the whole, it is most useful for answering questions about how people in different occupational groupings fare in terms of life-chances, such as illness and mortality rates, and access to citizenship entitlements, such as education. It is least useful in explaining why this occurs, whereas Marx's theory offers an explanation in terms of class relations and Weber's theory yields explanations involving market situation and social closure mechanisms.

Social class represents one social division but it is not the only one. Gender and 'race'/ethnicity are two other important divisions. We turn next to a consideration of 'race'/ethnicity in the second half of this unit and to gender in the first part of Unit 8.

REFERENCES

Anderson, E. (1989) 'Education is the great equalizer', *The Independent*, 28 January.

Anderson, J. and Ricci, M., (eds) (1990) *Society and Social Science: A Reader*, Milton Keynes, The Open University (Course Reader).

Atkinson, A.B., and Harrison, A.J. (1978) *Distribution of Personal Wealth in Britain*, Cambridge, Cambridge University Press.

Braverman, H. (1974) *Labour and Monopoly Capital: The Degradation of Work in the Twentieth Century*, New York, Monthly Review Press.

Coates, D. (1990) 'Traditions of thought and the rise of social sciences in the United Kingdom', Ch. 22 in J. Anderson and M. Ricci (eds).

Crompton, R. and Jones, G. (1984) *White-collar Proletariat*, London and Basingstoke, Macmillan.

Giddens, A. (1989) *Sociology*, Cambridge, Polity Press.

Goldthorpe, J.H., Lockwood, D., Bechhoffer, F. and Platt, J. (1968–9) *The Affluent Worker: Political Attitudes and Behaviour*, 3 vols, Cambridge, Cambridge University Press.

Goldthorpe, J.H., Lewellyn, C. and Payne, C. (1980) *Social Mobility and Class Structure in Modern Britain*, Oxford, Clarendon Press.

Goldthorpe, J.H., and Payne, C. (1986) 'Trends in intergenerational class mobility in England and Wales, 1972–1983', *Sociology*, vol.20, pp.1–24.

Heath, A. (1981) *Social Mobility*, London, Fontana.

Heath, A. (1987) 'Class in the classroom', in Cosin, B., Flude, M., and Hales, M. (eds) *School, Work and Equality*, pp.184–8, London, Hodder and Stoughton.

Hird, C. (1979) 'The poverty of wealth statistics', in Irvine, J. *et al.* (eds) *Demystifying Social Statistics*, London, Pluto Press.

Inland Revenue (1986) *Statistics*, London, HMSO.

Marshall, G. and Rose, D. (1989) 'Reply to Saunders', *Network* (Newsletter of the British Sociological Association), no.44, May, pp.4–5.

Marx, K. and Engels, F. (1959) *Manifesto of the Communist Party*, Moscow, Foreign Languages Publishing House. (First published 1848.)

Parkin, F. (1971) *Class Inequality and Political Order*, London, McGibbon and Kee.

Parkin, F. (1979) *Marxism and Class Theory: A Bourgeois Critique*, London, Tavistock.

Pond, C. (1989), 'The changing distribution of income, wealth and poverty', in Hamnett, C., McDowell, L. and Sarre, P. (eds) *The Changing Social Structure*, London, Sage Publications/The Open University.

Saunders, P. (1989) 'Left Write in Sociology', *Network* (Newsletter of the British Sociological Association), no.44, May, pp.3–4.

Scott, J. and Griff, C. (1984) *Directors of Industry*, Cambridge, Polity Press.

Townsend, P. and Davidson, N. (eds) (1988) *Inequalities in Health* (including *The Black Report* (1982), and Whitehead, M., *The Health Divide*), Harmondsworth, Penguin Books.

Weber, M. (1968) *Economy and Society*, New York, Bedminster Press. (Originally published in German in 1922.)

Wright, E.O. (1985) *Classes*, London, Verso.

PART II: 'RACE' AND ETHNICITY

1 INTRODUCTION

As we have seen in the first half of this unit, social scientists concerned with social divisions in Britain have tended to focus on class. Since the Second World War, and especially since the 1960s, however, increasing attention has been given to other divisions including the subject matter of this half-unit — 'race' and ethnicity.

In this part we shall firstly define our key terms; secondly, show how social scientists have come to recognize that 'racial' divisions are a major feature of modern societies; and, thirdly, examine three explanations of 'racial' divisions. It is when we move on to consider explanations that we shall return to the two major social theorists discussed in the first half of this unit — Marx and Weber.

2 DEFINING 'RACE' AND ETHNICITY

To help us to clarify the meaning of 'race' and ethnicity and why such divisions are now considered so significant, we would like you to look at two different sets of material. The first comes from a Policy Studies Institute survey and comprises statistical data on the job levels of different groups. The second comes from a recent newspaper article and depicts increasing violence in Britain faced by particular groups.

───────────────── ACTIVITY 5 ─────────────────

When you look at Table 5 you should note which kinds of social groups are distinguished and what it tells us about the job levels of different groups. It is probably advisable to begin by taking each row in turn and comparing the percentages at different job levels. Finally, you might ask yourself whether there is any important information which is *not* presented in this table.

Table 5 Job level: all employees by ethnic group and gender, 1982 (percentages)

Men	White	West Indian	Asian
Managerial and Professional	19	5	13
Other non-manual	23	10	13
Skilled manual	42	48	33
Semi-skilled manual	13	26	34
Unskilled manual	3	9	6
Women	White	West Indian	Asian
Managerial and Professional	7	1	6
Other non-manual	55	52	42
Skilled manual	5	4	6
Semi-skilled manual	21	36	44
Unskilled manual	11	7	2

Source: Brown, 1984

The title of the table gives us a good hint as to what to look for. The first part of the table looks at men, the second at women; and both involve a comparison of the job levels (which might be seen as a rough indicator of class) of distinct ethnic groups, among both men and women.

What the table reveals is that, relative to white people, both West Indians and Asians are less likely to be found in the higher level non-manual jobs and more likely to be found in the lower-level manual jobs. Thus, while 19 per cent of white men are classified as managerial and professional, only 5 per cent of West Indian men and 13 per cent of Asian men were in this category. And, at the other extreme, while 16 per cent of white men were found in semi- and unskilled manual work, 35 per cent of West Indian men and 40 per cent of Asian men were located here. You might note that the contrasts are less clear-cut among women, but this needs to be seen in the context where women generally are less likely to be found in managerial and professional jobs and more likely to be found in routine non-manual work.

There are, of course, a number of issues the table tells us nothing about. You may have noticed that no information is provided about those not in employment; you may be sceptical as to whether those classified as being at the same level are in an identical situation; and you've probably already realized that further information is needed before we can go on to explain the differences in job levels revealed by the table. Nonetheless, the statistical data we have examined do reveal that in an area of central importance to life-chances, West Indians and Asians are disadvantaged relative to white people. Indeed, the data underestimate the extent of disadvantage, as Table 6 reveals. Can you see how?

Table 6   Unemployment rates in Great Britain by highest qualification level, ethnic origin and sex, 1987–89 (percentages)

Level of highest qualification held	All origins*	White	Minority ethnic groups
All			
All*	9	9	14
Higher	3	3	16
Others	8	7	14
None	14	13	19
Males			
All*	9	9	15
Higher	3	3	–
Others	7	7	13
None	16	15	21
Females			
All*	9	8	13
Higher	4	4	–
Others	8	8	15
None	11	11	15

Higher = degree/BTEC higher level; others = any qualification; * includes 'not known'; – = sample too small.
Source: Skellington, 1992

This table derives from the annual Labour Force Survey and is based on averaging three years' data in order to increase reliability. What the table reveals is that relative to white people, minority ethnic groups (who mainly comprise West Indians and Asians) have a higher overall unemployment rate (14 per cent compared to 9 per cent). What is more, the unemployment rate is higher among minority ethnic groups than among the white population even when they have the same level of qualifications.

We need to clarify the meaning of 'ethnicity' and the rationale for distinguishing above three ethnic groups. The term, in fact, derives from the Greek word, *ethnos*,

> ... which refers to a people, a collectivity sharing certain common attributes. Ethnicity, in its modern usage, continues to imply the possession of some degree of coherence and solidarity among a group of people who have some awareness or conception of common origins, shared culture and experience and common interests.
>
> (Rattansi and Donald, 1992)

Given this definition of ethnicity, which emphasizes that groups can be distinguished in terms of cultural criteria, it is not surprising that West Indians and Asians were labelled ethnic groups above and distinguished from the majority ethnic group. There are still some further questions, however, we need to address. Are there any problems with the terms used to describe these three ethnic groups? Are there other ethnic groups in the UK to be distinguished? Are there any further sources of ethnic diversity?

You might have identified a number of problems in thinking about these questions. Perhaps you consider it misleading to label people West Indian or Asian when they are British citizens and may have been born in this country? Perhaps you find the term West Indian rather old-fashioned given the preference of many for the more accurate term Afro-Caribbean? Perhaps you find it odd that the majority ethnic group has been identified in terms of colour, while the two minority ethnic groups have been identified in terms of geographical origin? Perhaps you find all the terms too inclusive in that they fail to identify other sources of ethnic identity?

Integrated England: bowler David Lawrence gets congratulations from his white team-mates after taking a West Indian wicket

We can certainly identify more than three ethnic groups. The UK itself consists of different nationalities, all of which can be seen to comprise ethnic groups and, if we take the case of Northern Ireland, a further distinction can be made between Protestants and Catholics. What is true of the majority ethnic group is also true of the two minority ethnic groups we earlier distinguished. They originate from different countries and, in the case of Asians, adhere to different religions. And so we could go on sub-dividing further the three ethnic groups we identified above. The crucial point is that different boundaries are drawn in different contexts. Thus, people who think of themselves as Scottish in one context may see themselves as British in another and people who define themselves as Indian in one context may identify with the wider category of British Asians in another. Whatever ethnic groups we distinguish, we must be alert to the sources of diversity within them. When we think of the group with whom we find it easiest to identify, we are aware that it is by no means homogeneous. Such a group will contain, for example, gender differences, class differences and generational differences. It is from such internal tensions, as well as external pressures, that cultural traditions may be challenged or reinforced and ethnic groups reconstructed. We shall return to the issue of ethnicity later, but in the meantime let us turn to our second set of material on 'race' and ethnicity.

——————————————— ACTIVITY 6 ———————————————

You should pay particular attention to three issues as you read the article from *The Independent* on page 81:
1   What does the article add to your understanding of the experience of people from minority ethnic groups?
2   What difference does it make to define groups as 'racial'?
3   What explanation is given for the increasing violence faced by some groups?

While the statistical data revealed that the ethnic minorities we distinguished above, namely Afro-Caribbean and Asian, were disadvantaged relative to white people in an area of central importance to people's life-chances, such data are inevitably 'cold'. The article, by contrast, gives us a much better feel for what some groups have to confront, and alerts us to the fact that vulnerability (if that is not too weak a word) pervades their lives.

You will have noted that the article utilizes the term 'racial' and does suggest that the classification of people in such terms does make a significant difference to the lives of some groups. The notion that people can be classified on the basis of biological criteria into a limited number of fixed and discrete 'races' emerged in the nineteenth century. For many scientists of that period such a classification accounted for the observed physical and cultural differences between people and the assumed superiority of the West. Such a theory is no longer accepted by biologists. Two factors in particular need to be stressed. Firstly, the essential condition for 'race' is that populations remain insulated from each other so that inter-breeding does not occur. This condition has not been met for many years, especially since the expansion of Europe from the fifteenth century. Secondly, the discovery of genetics has resulted in the realization that the visible differences between people are biologically trivial and that there is far greater genetic variation *within* than *between* groups previously defined as 'races'.

As Germans protest over racism, Heather Mills reports on increasing violence in Britain

Knock on the door brings growing fear of racial abuse and attack

JOREENA ALI's children watched helplessly as their mother — pregnant with her third child — was punched in the face and stomach in the hallway of their home. Mrs Ali had answered her door to a white woman who screamed "Paki bastard" as she made her attack. Mrs Ali was treated in hospital for eye injuries and bruising to her stomach. Four days later she miscarried.

The attack was part of a persistent campaign of racist abuse against Mrs Ali, 31, and her family, living in an area of south London which has seen three racially motivated killings in the last 18 months.

Mrs Ali has now been rehoused. She said she was finally driven out by local people who piled rubbish at her door, threw bricks at her house, put nuts and bolts in the children's rabbit cage, called her a "Paki slut" and in one incident stuck a penknife in her husband's arm.

Terror has meant she and her children now live in isolation. They feel obliged to keep their new address and telephone number a secret for fear of revenge attacks for her determination to press charges and campaign against racism.

"I cannot describe to you how I felt, I was terrified to go out of my house — but I was not even safe in it. The effect on the children has been dreadful. One has started wetting the bed and the other has had screaming fits."

Their experience is not unique. The Greenwich Action Committee against Racist Attacks has recorded more than 200 racist incidents in the past year — more than half of the 177 assaults were against women and most were against families living on the borough's council estates.

Trevor Walsh, white and married to a woman from the Seychelles, who lives on the Thamesmead Estate, described how they had to put up with years of taunts, of having excrement thrown at them and lighted cigarettes put through their letterbox and finally physical assaults.

Dev Barrah, co-ordinator of the action committee, who was set upon by a gang of skinheads last July,

puts much of the rise in racist attacks down to the arrival of the neo-Nazi British National Party in Greenwich. BNP graffiti and stickers stain the walls near the committee's offices, declaring "rights for whites" and "put British people before aliens". What is most worrying is the increase in the viciousness of the attacks.

Last July, Rohit Duggal, 16, became the third fatal victim of the heightened violence. He was stabbed to death as he and two friends went in search of a mini-cab

Trevor Walsh, whose family has suffered years of racial attacks, with a cousin of the murdered Rohit Duggal

and encountered a group of about 12 white youths. But these incidents are not confined to one area.

In August, Ruhulla Aramesh was beaten to death with an iron bar by a gang of about 15 youths who broke down his front door in Croydon, south London. In Hounslow, west London, an 11-year-old boy was stabbed by a gang who attacked the bed and breakfast premises where he and his family were staying. Increased violence is being reported from all over the country. Six Asian men have been killed this year. Of

concern to some welfare agencies is that refugees — having fled war and persecution — are faced with violence as they try to find asylum in Britain. On the Teviot housing estate in east London, one-third of the 323 racist attacks recorded in a 12 month period were directed at refugees, mostly Somalis.

The British Refugee Council believes some of the assaults on refugees may have been prompted by television reports of attacks on refugee hostels in Germany.

But attackers in the UK tend to

pounce when refugees are isolated and even more vulnerable. The council said: "Refugees would be safer if the government and media took care not to inflame racist and criminal tendencies with announcements suggesting that many asylum-seekers should not be here."

Even Home Office figures for racial attacks have shown a steady rise since the mid-1980s to nearly 8,000 a year. It accepts these are only the tip of the iceberg. A committee of European MPs last year put the figure at about 70,000.

In the 1980s, anti-racist initiatives and policies were implemented by local councils, the police and the Government in an effort to tackle the problem of racial attacks. Some housing authorities have started evicting the harassers rather than the victims — moves are apparently currently underway to evict some of Mrs Ali's tormentors.

But according to Colin Hann of the Commission for Racial Equality paper policies are all too rarely implemented in practice. There are already signs that high unemployment, poverty and the social crisis of economic recession are providing fertile recruiting grounds for extreme right-wing groups who seek to blame minorities for their own plight. Kenneth Clarke, the Home Secretary, cites fear of the kind of violence seen in Germany as one of the reasons behind his moves to restrict refugees coming to Britain.

But civil rights activists and welfare groups say this amounts to the Government bowing to racist views. They want to see new laws introduced to make racial harassment and attacks a specific offence.

Labour MPs, lawyers and campaign groups, including the CRE, will this week seek cross-party support for a revised Racial Harassment Bill. They argue current legislation has not halted racial violence.

While hundreds of thousands protested in Berlin at mounting racism at the weekend, Saturday's comparatively modest "stop racist murders" march in south London passed almost unnoticed.

Joreen Ali, who was forced from her home by racists *Photographs: Kayte Brimacombe*

Source: *The Independent*, 9 November 1992

This raises a paradox. On the one hand, we have good scientific evidence to conclude that 'there's no such thing as "race"'. On the other hand, we know, as the article disturbingly demonstrates, that classifying people in 'racial' terms has real effects. The paradox is solved once we realize that, as W.I. Thomas put it, 'If men (sic) define things as real, they are real in their consequences'. This means that physiological differences in skin colour, although in themselves as insignificant as differences in height, can become significant because of the importance attached to them by people's beliefs. Let's take a particular example. Below is a short extract from the diary of a man who describes an early experience he had travelling through the southern states of the USA in the 1960s:

> I walked up to the ticket counter. When the lady ticket-seller saw me, her otherwise attractive face turned sour, violently so. This look was so unexpected and so unprovoked I was taken aback. 'What do you want?' she snapped. Taking care to pitch my voice to politeness, I asked about the next bus to Hattiesburg. She answered rudely and glared at me with such loathing I knew I was receiving what the Negroes call 'the hate stare'. It was my first experience with it. It is far more than the look of disapproval one occasionally gets. This was so exaggeratedly hateful I would have been amused if I had not been so surprised. I framed the words in my mind: 'Pardon me, but have I done something to offend you?' But I realized I had done nothing — my colour offended her.
>
> (Griffin, 1964)

Griffin was in fact white, but had artificially darkened his skin so as to give the appearance of a 'Negro'. Because of the way he was defined, he endured a catalogue of humiliations from people who, if they had known he was white, would have treated him with courtesy. Being black was here considered to be significant and as a result was.

We must not assume that historically skin colour has been the only indicator of 'race'. Here is Charles Kingsley, author of *The Water Babies*, writing to his wife during a visit to Ireland in 1860:

> But I am haunted by the human chimpanzees I saw along that hundred miles of horrible country. I don't believe they are our fault. I believe there are not only many more of them than of old, but that they are happier, better, more comfortably fed and lodged under our rule than they ever were. But to see white chimpanzees is dreadful; if they were black, one would not feel it so much, but their skins, except where tanned by exposure, are as white as ours.
>
> (quoted in Husband, 1982)

What, then, does the article from *The Independent* add to our understanding of the experience of members of minority ethnic groups in Britain?

The article suggests that some are defined as 'racially' inferior and, as a result, face the threat of violence. They do not, as we have seen, in fact constitute 'races' (hence the use of inverted commas around the term), but they are seen as essentially different. Whether such racism is characteristic of a minority of extremists or is more pervasive is not clear, but it is clearly an issue to which we must return.

SUMMARY

- 'Race' and ethnicity involve drawing boundaries between people. 'Racial' boundaries are drawn on the basis of physical markers such as skin pigmentation, hair texture and facial features, while ethnic boundaries are drawn on the basis of cultural markers such as language, religion and shared customs. These boundaries are socially constructed and not fixed. They can, and do, change over time.

- It should be noted that although there is a conceptual distinction between 'race' and ethnicity, in practice the distinction is not so clear-cut. The statistical data we have looked at identify the majority ethnic group on the basis of skin colour and others by place of origin.

- The Afro-Caribbean and Asian communities can be seen as distinct ethnic groups but have been defined by some as 'racially' different. These ethnic minorities experience disadvantage not only in employment but also in other areas of their lives.

3   'RACIAL' DIVISIONS IN BRITAIN

Before moving on to look at explanations for the disadvantages faced by Afro-Caribbeans and Asians, we need to ask why it is that social scientists have only recently been concerned to explore social divisions *in* Britain which centre upon 'race' and ethnicity. The answer revolves around post-war immigration to Britain and the reception met by the newcomers.

3.1   POST-WAR IMMIGRATION TO BRITAIN

After the Second World War a significant number of people emigrated from Britain's old colonies to settle in Britain. There have, of course, been significant waves of immigration before. Thus in the nineteenth century, the combination of a rising population and bad harvests encouraged a major movement of the population from Ireland, and around the turn of the century virulent anti-Semitism prompted the movement of Jews from Eastern Europe. But population movements have not been one way. Millions of people have emigrated from Britain in the last two centuries to settle in new lands and indeed, except for relatively short periods, more people have emigrated from Britain than immigrated into the country during this time. Migration, therefore, is nothing new. Nor is the presence of black people in Britain, which goes back at least 400 years.

Nevertheless, the immigration of Afro-Caribbeans and Asians to Britain after the Second World War has been seen by many as magnifying ethnic diversity and the visibility of black people. People from the Caribbean were the first to migrate to Britain, with the majority coming from one island, Jamaica. Like other Caribbean islands, Jamaica had been colonized by white people from Western Europe. By the time England captured Jamaica from the Spanish in the seventeenth century, the original inhabitants, the Arawak Indians, had been wiped out, so that the population of the island comprised mainly immigrants from England, who managed the plantations, and people imported from Africa, who worked as slaves. The economy was geared to the needs of Britain: sugar was exported to Britain, and with it the profits from the trade. Starved of investment, the Jamaican economy was unable to develop. This underdevelopment still persists, in spite of the country becoming self-governing in 1944 and independent in 1962: the economy continues to be dominated by plantation agriculture and dependent on a few multinational corporations (Pryce, 1986). (You might remind yourself here of the problems faced by the sugar industry — see Unit 1, p.26.)

Despite the abolition of slavery in 1833, the majority of Jamaicans have seen little improvement in their economic situation. The paucity of adequate farmland and the lack of sufficient jobs have thus encouraged many Jamaicans — and other Afro-Caribbeans — to look to emigration either to South America, North America or Britain as a way of improving their situation (Foner, 1979).

A participant in the multi-ethnic Notting Hill Carnival, Europe's biggest street carnival, which celebrated its 25th anniversary in 1990

In India a similar process of underdevelopment occurred. After the setting up of trading posts by the East India company in the seventeenth century, the British gradually took power. With the defeat of the French in the eighteenth century and recognition by the British government of the importance of India in the nineteenth century, the stage was set for the British Raj. As in Jamaica, the economy was made to serve the needs of Britain. The local textile industry was destroyed, being seen as a competitor to the Lancashire-based one; indeed India became a key market for cotton goods from Britain. Since a large market is necessary for industrialization to take place, as the economic historian Eric Hobsbawm (1969) has argued, the possession of India and other colonies was critical for Britain's Industrial Revolution. There seems little doubt that as the nineteenth century wore on, India became 'the jewel in the Imperial diadem'

(Barratt Brown, 1970), which Britain increasingly leant on as other countries 'caught up economically'. This is not to say that Britain did not invest in India. In the course of the nineteenth century, significant investments were made, for example, in communications, but these did not prevent the Indian economy from being underdeveloped and dependent on British society. The consequence has been the inability of the economy to generate enough jobs to meet the needs of a rapidly increasing population. Again the result has been for people to look to migration as a solution. Some migrated to other parts of the British Empire under a system of indentured labour, whereby they were contracted to work for a particular employer for a number of years. In some cases, they stayed when the contract had expired and brought their families over to join them, to be followed later by other immigrants. In this way, Indian settlements developed, for example in East Africa. Migration is, therefore, not a new phenomenon for South Asians. Indeed, independence itself, which was only achieved in 1947 after a long struggle, entailed further migration. The struggle between the two major religious groups, the Hindus and Moslems, resulted in the partition of India to create Pakistan, which comprised two territories at the eastern and western extremities of Northern India, and was predominantly Moslem, and India, which was predominantly Hindu. Not surprisingly, given the intensity of the preceding struggles, many people migrated to join their co-religionists. The countries have remained relatively poor so that some have continued to look to emigration as a way of improving their economic situation. It is in this context that migration to Britain needs to be seen.

Under the British Nationality Act of 1948, citizens of the British Commonwealth were allowed to enter Britain, to seek work and settle here with their families. Some took the opportunity to do so. Afro-Caribbeans were the earliest to come, but were soon followed by Southern Asians — Indians, Pakistanis, Bangladeshis (East Pakistan became the independent state of Bangladesh in 1972) — and East African Asians, from countries such as Kenya and Uganda, who had opted on the independence of these countries for British citizenship. All in all, immigration from the New Commonwealth and Pakistan since the Second World War has brought a significant increase in the proportion of people of colour in Britain. Some notion of the range of such groups can be gleaned from Figure 4.

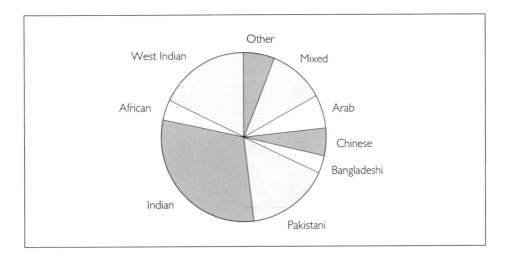

Figure 4   Estimated minority ethnic group populations as a proportion of the total ethnic group population of Great Britain, 1986–8

Source: Williams, 1992

——————————————— ACTIVITY 7 ———————————————

I would like you to answer a question asked in a national survey of 'racial' attitudes in Britain:
'How many black people or Asians do you think there are in Britain (population 55 million)?'

———————————————————————————————————————

You will find the most recent estimate below. We need, however, to get matters in perspective. People from the New Commonwealth comprise well under half the overseas-born population in Britain and none of the black minorities is as large as the Irish (Skellington, 1992). What is more, immigration from the New Commonwealth and Pakistan is to all intents and purposes at an end. It reached a peak in the early 1960s, but has been, with the odd temporary increase caused by the expulsion of East African Asians, on a downward trend since. Immigration Acts, beginning with the Commonwealth Immigrants Act 1962, have made it increasingly difficult for black people in particular to emigrate to Britain, with the result that the vast majority of citizens from the New Commonwealth and Pakistan now accepted for settlement are dependants, i.e. mainly wives and children, and even they face difficulties.

I wonder how you answered the question above? The figure for all minority ethnic groups, according to the 1991 Census, is 3 million people or 5.5 per cent of the British population (see Table 7). You may well have given a higher figure, particularly if you are white. For in a large-scale study conducted in 1991, over half the white sample thought the true figure was 5 million and a quarter thought it was 10 million (Runnymede Trust, 1991). There are a number of reasons why there is a tendency to overstate the number of people from minority ethnic groups. Can you think of any? I can think of two. You might live in an area where minority ethnic groups form a high proportion of the population (see Figure 5) or you might have been influenced by the mass media, which have tended to focus on the question of 'numbers' and present Britain as being, in the words of an ex-Prime Minister, 'swamped by people with a different culture' (Thatcher quoted in Skellington, 1992).

Table 7   Ethnic group composition of the population in 1991, from the Census County and Region Monitors (thousands of persons)

OPCS Ethnic group	Great Britain	England	Wales	Scotland
White	51,843.9	44,114.6	2,793.3	4,936.1
Black – Caribbean	499.1	496.3	2.7	0.0
Black – African	207.5	203.2	2.3	2.0
Black – Other	178.5	172.9	3.5	2.4
Indian	840.8	823.9	6.7	10.2
Pakistani	475.8	448.8	5.8	21.2
Bangladeshi	160.3	156.1	3.4	0.8
Chinese	157.5	142.4	4.9	10.2
Other – Asian	196.7	189.7	3.5	3.5
Other – Other	290.1	273.3	7.7	9.2
All minorities	3,006.5	2,906.5	40.5	59.5
Total population	54,860.2	47,026.5	2,835.1	4,998.6

Source: Owen, 1993

In the course of discussing the entry of immigrants from the New Commonwealth and Pakistan into Britain, you may have noticed that three terms have been used interchangeably to refer to them and their children — 'black people', 'people of colour' and 'minority ethnic groups'. All these terms try to pick out colour because this has been a salient feature of their immigration for many of the indigenous population and has resulted, as we shall see, in black people/

people of colour/minority ethnic groups sharing a common experience. None of the terms, however, is uncontested. In much of the literature, 'black' is used, but while Afro-Caribbeans often define themselves as black and see this as a positive source of identity, many Asians prefer to define themselves in religious and other ways (Modood, 1992). 'People of colour' has become a popular term in the United States, where there have been attempts to create an alliance between diverse ethnic groups who feel excluded because of their colour, since it more successfully includes Chinese and Hispanic groups, for example. The term has not yet caught on here and does not wholly escape the criticism previously levelled at the term 'coloured people' — aren't we all people of colour? 'Minority ethnic group' is the term used in the tables and figures we've looked at, but, in terms of our earlier discussion of ethnicity, there is no good reason why the term should necessarily exclude white minorities such as people of Italian or Polish origin. In view of the essentially contested nature of these terms, I shall refer to specific groups as much as possible. Where there is a need, however, to point to a common experience based on colour, I shall, with some hesitancy, use the term 'black'.

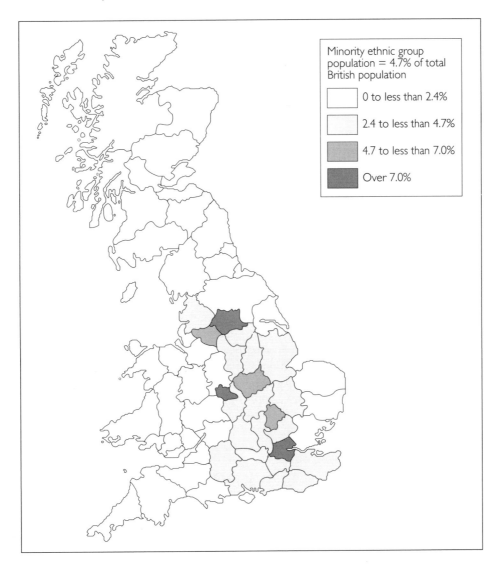

Figure 5   Estimated* minority ethnic group population as a percentage of the total population by county or region, 1986–8

*Percentages estimated from surveys carried out in 1986–88 (omitting Northern Ireland): see text and Table 7 for 1991 Census figures.

Source: Skellington, 1992, Map 1.1; data from Haskey, 1991, p. 28

What, then, caused Asians and Afro-Caribbeans to migrate to Britain after the Second World War? It is convenient to distinguish here between push factors and pull factors (Banton, 1972). Push factors refer to those which encourage people to leave their country of origin and pull factors refer to those which encourage people to come to Britain (or to other developed economies). The principal push factor has been poor opportunities in the country of origin where, for instance, the population may have grown at a pace which their underdeveloped economies could not sustain. This is not to say that there has been a mechanical association between the degree of poverty and emigration. Most of those who have emigrated have been people with some wealth from areas with a tradition of migration. Most initially expected their stay to be temporary and have maintained close contacts with their homelands, including sending back remittances (Watson, 1977). The other major push factor relates to the East African Asians, who were in most cases forced to leave Africa as a result of the adoption of an 'Africanization' policy by some governments. To point to these push factors does not, however, explain why such people have come to Britain. In order to understand this we need to turn to the pull factors. The first has been the closing of other avenues and, particularly for Afro-Caribbeans, the difficulty of gaining admission into the United States as a result of the McCarren-Walter Act of 1952. This has meant that those who wished to migrate had to go elsewhere. They chose to migrate to Britain because of two further pull factors — the connection with Britain which stems from the fact that their countries had been part of the British Empire and, most importantly, Britain's labour shortage at the time.

Although there was, immediately after the war, a substantial group of Polish immigrants and other refugees and displaced persons who came as European Volunteer Workers, the labour shortage which Britain, along with other West European countries, experienced when the economy began to expand, was met through immigration from the New Commonwealth. In a few cases, people were recruited for specific jobs. More often they came to Britain having heard that jobs were available. Although the period of migration was generally a time in which the economy was booming and there was a consequent shortage of labour, there were occasions when the demand for labour fell. Remarkably, Afro-Caribbean movement to Britain seems to have responded with extraordinary sensitivity to the demand, with net migration tending to go down as unemployment went up in the period for which appropriate figures are available (Peach, 1968 and 1978/9). The only exception seems to have been from 1960 to 1962, immediately prior to the first Commonwealth Immigrants Act, when anxiety about impending immigration control led some to 'beat the ban'. What is true of Afro-Caribbean migration has also been shown to be true, although to a lesser extent, of Asian migration (Robinson, 1980). Labour demand has been an important determinant of Asian immigration into Britain too.

3.2   NEWCOMERS OR 'BLACKS'?

The question we now turn to is how Afro-Caribbeans and Asians have been received in Britain. Two broad answers have been put forward. One emphasizes that black immigrants are immigrants; the other emphasizes that black immigrants are black. Let us outline each view in turn and then evaluate their merits.

The first position is well exemplified by Patterson (1965) but hints of it can be found in much of the early post-war writing on 'race' in Britain. Immigrants, it is argued, have to go through two processes before they can be absorbed or assimilated into the society they have entered; they have to adapt themselves to and at the same time be accepted by the host society. Neither of these two processes is likely to take place in the life-span of one generation, with the result that the reception black people meet is at least temporarily a negative one. On the one hand, some immigrants find difficulty in making what is often a move from a rural to an urban existence and in many cases a transition from one culture to another, with all that this implies in terms of language, religion and family structure. On the other hand, the host society finds difficulty in coming to terms with people who don't show an understanding of the implicit norms governing behaviour and therefore seem strangers.

Although most of the writers who have expounded the 'immigrant–host' framework recognize that there is a degree of cultural antipathy to black people in Britain which makes what they call 'absorption' more difficult, the overriding mood is one of optimism. It is assumed that the discrimination which 'dark strangers' presently confront will, with the passage of time, and a new generation, be transcended. As support for this thesis, attention might be drawn to the experiences of immigrant groups in the nineteenth and early twentieth centuries, for example, Irish and Jewish immigrants into Britain and European immigrant groups generally in the United States. Although later generations still tend to retain traces of their roots (Glazer and Moynihan, 1970), the two key processes pointed to — namely adaptation on the part of the immigrants and acceptance on the part of the host society — have been to a large extent completed and the earlier hostility and discrimination overcome.

——————————————— ACTIVITY 8 ———————————————

The immigrant–host framework derives mainly from one of the four traditions distinguished in Unit 5. Can you identify which one? (If you need to remind yourself of their main features, look at the summary in Block I, p.197.)
What assumption does the immigrant–host framework make about (a) the nature of British society and (b) assimilation?

———

It seems to me that the immigrant–host framework flows mainly from the conservative tradition. Society, in this view, is held together by common values — the shared customs and traditions of 'community' and 'nation' — so that immigration, inasmuch as it involves groups with different customs and traditions, constitutes a potential threat to social order. Assimilation or 'absorption' is therefore considered crucial. In line with this tradition, the immigrant–host framework pictures British society as culturally homogeneous prior to the advent of immigrants after the Second World War. Although these newcomers initially seemed strange, there are no significant barriers (given, it is assumed, traditional British tolerance) to prevent their assimilation, a process thought important for social stability.

Needless to say, proponents of other traditions (in particular Social Reformism and Marxism) challenge the assumptions built into the immigrant–host framework. Has Britain ever been a culturally homogeneous society? Hasn't it been characterized, for example, in the last two centuries by social classes with different customs and traditions and hasn't there been significant conflict between these social classes? Is assimilation into a uniform culture, in fact, desirable? Doesn't the co-existence of a plurality of cultures make a society more vibrant and allow its members more options? Isn't the demand that ethnic minorities assimilate 'asking for conflict and destabilization and the fragmentation of communities that are currently the sources of stability, group pride and self esteem?' (Modood, 1992). And, anyway, aren't there significant barriers to assimilation? Doesn't the evidence that 'even the relatively small-scale black settlements that took shape in the inter-war period were perceived as alien and a possible threat to the British way of life' (Solomos, 1989), suggest that the British are not so tolerant after all? While some immigrant groups have indeed been assimilated, they were white in skin colour, so that later generations are not easily distinguishable from the indigenous white population. The children of black immigrants do not share this physical similarity to the indigenous population. If skin colour is seen as an indicator of difference, aren't they liable, therefore, to experience more lasting patterns of hostility? This brings us on to the second account of how New Commonwealth immigrants have been received in this country.

This stresses the low status attached to black people in British society and is the view found in much recent writing on the subject. Attention is drawn, in this approach, to imperialism, which involved the domination of black people by white European countries. The development of the West facilitated not only exploration of the world, but also enabled it to control what were for Europeans newly discovered lands. In the 'New World', such colonialism involved the mass transfer of people from Africa to work as slaves on the plantations. Needing to reconcile their treatment of slaves as mere objects and their dimly recognized humanity, beliefs emerged which classified such people as inferior. Such beliefs spread from situations of slavery to other situations of colonialism, so that the image of the inferior slave tended to be stamped on all who were colonized. In the process, white domination of black people was justified. These beliefs, it is argued, are still endemic in British culture, so that the arrival of black people from countries which had formerly been part of the British Empire was met with a degree of hostility which would not have been triggered by the entry of white immigrants. Indeed, white Australians, South Africans, Canadians and New Zealanders, for example, have been readily absorbed into Britain.

For those who point to the prevalence of such beliefs, the passing of time and a new generation will not necessarily entail a dramatic diminution in 'racial' discrimination. As support for this more pessimistic outlook, attention might again be drawn to the United States, but this time to an early immigrant group forcibly taken there, notably black people. Unlike other immigrant groups, most of whom arrived later, black people in the USA have found that, over one hundred years after the abolition of slavery, it remains extremely difficult for them to be treated equitably.

The two accounts we have considered of the reception met by black immigrants in Britain, involve a process of intellectual abstraction. They pick out and focus on what are taken to be the really significant issues and they ignore a great deal of detail. Both accounts agree on picking out discrimination as significant in the reception met by the first generation, but they differ in their choice of what constitutes the basis for this discrimination. In the one case, their status as newcomers is highlighted and in the other case their status as black people is highlighted. Although we might have an intuitive preference for one or other of these two accounts, to assess which, if either, is better supported, we need to look at some empirical data.

The best evidence we have seen comes from the two Political and Economic Planning Studies directed by Daniel (1968) and Smith (1977) and the Policy Studies Institute project directed by Brown and Gay (1985). Together these studies provide, over a twenty-year period, the most systematic data we have on the extent of discrimination. To ascertain the level of discrimination and whether it was based on newness or colour, Daniel conducted a series of situation tests in which actors applied for jobs, housing and commercial services in a series of carefully controlled circumstances. Here, a black immigrant (Afro-

Caribbean or Asian), a white immigrant (Hungarian) and a white native, matched in terms of age and claiming equivalent occupational qualifications or housing requirements, applied (in that order) for a job, a house, or a commercial service on offer to the public. Discrimination was defined as a case in which one tester was made an offer or a better offer and the other(s) none or a worse one. What Daniel discovered was that the black immigrant met by far the most discrimination. Despite legislation since then, designed to combat 'racial' discrimination, the later studies reveal that it still remains considerable and is based predominantly on colour. While Smith detected a fall in the level of discrimination between 1967 and 1973, Brown and Gay — utilizing both actor testing and a form of situation test, pioneered by Smith, known as correspondence testing, in which matched written applications were sent in reply to advertised vacancies — found little evidence to suggest that the level of 'racial' discrimination (found in 1984–5) had decreased since 1973. At least a third of employers still discriminated against black applicants for jobs.

The extensive research available indicates that the basis for the discrimination met by immigrants and their children is 'race' and not, as some have thought, newness. What we have examined so far, however, is only one form of discrimination — direct discrimination. It remains important and does not vary between manual and non-manual jobs nor between Afro-Caribbean and Asian applicants. There is, however, a more subtle form of discrimination, sometimes labelled 'institutional racism', but which we shall call here indirect discrimination. This refers to institutional practices which, however unintentionally, have the consequence of systematically operating to the disadvantage of groups seen as 'racially' different.

—————————————— ACTIVITY 9 ——————————————

If you are white, try to identify any practices which, perhaps unintentionally, disadvantage Afro-Caribbeans and Asians in an organization with which you are familiar. If you are Afro-Caribbean or Asian or from another minority ethnic group, can you identify any from your own experience?

Here are a few examples I have identified:

(a) a school uniform policy which has the consequence of prohibiting the wearing of turbans;

(b) the practice of allocating apprenticeships in an informal way to the 'lads of the dads', a practice which clearly disadvantages people who are not part of this network;

(c) restrictions on the size of council houses, a policy which may particularly affect groups who wish to live together as an extended family;

(d) immigration rules which do not give British citizens the automatic right to be joined by their wives/husbands and children;

(e) using behavioural as well as academic criteria to allocate pupils to streams, a practice which (if, for instance, teachers stereotype Afro-Caribbean pupils as less well-behaved) disadvantages a group seen as 'racially' different;

(f) a 'colour-blind' approach to the selection of juries, which can result in black defendants being judged by all-white juries;

(g) recruitment to an all-white workforce by word of mouth.

These are only a few examples from my reading of the research literature, but they do indicate that indirect discrimination is very extensive (Braham *et al.*,

1992). No doubt you have come up with further examples. Inevitably, however, when we look at specific cases, problems arise. We find that practices may also disadvantage other groups. And we find that the distinction between direct and indirect discrimination is less clear-cut in practice. Many of these practices, it is now known, are indirectly discriminating and yet persist. What's more, some of them may, on examination, turn out to have been motivated by 'racial' considerations. Nonetheless, the distinction between direct and indirect discrimination is a useful one and the evidence does indicate that 'racial' discrimination is extremely pervasive.

SUMMARY

- Social scientists have only been concerned with social divisions centred upon 'race' and ethnicity in Britain relatively recently. The concern arose from the post-war wave of immigration from the New Commonwealth and Pakistan and the reception met by the newcomers and their children.

- Post-war immigration to Britain was occasioned, as it was throughout much of Western Europe, by a labour shortage. It has made Britain a more ethnically diverse society and increased the visibility of black people.

- Both Afro-Caribbeans and Asians have been subject to discrimination because they have been defined as 'racially' different. 'Racial' divisions have, therefore, become more evident in Britain since the Second World War, with the result that social scientists now recognize that Britain, like other capitalist societies in Western Europe and North America, is characterized both by class and 'racial' divisions.

---

4   EXPLAINING 'RACIAL' DIVISIONS

There is a danger involved in pointing to the extensive disadvantage faced by Afro-Caribbeans and Asians and I'm not sure that this has been wholly avoided so far. The danger is to present black people solely as victims. In turning to explanations of 'racial' divisions, therefore, we shall seek to combat this danger by pointing to the ways in which the explanations account not only for disadvantage, but also for resistance.

There are a wide range of explanations. We shall, however, concentrate on three sociological ones. The first two flow from the work of Marx and Weber and thus return us to a central concern of the first half of this unit, while the third seeks to move beyond these analyses. All three seek to account for 'racial' divisions but each, it should be noted, addresses the issue in a different way.

At first sight, it seems odd to return to Marx and Weber. For although aware of the significance of 'racial' and ethnic inequality as a source of identity and a generator of conflict in particular societies, their emphasis on those features which are characteristic of all capitalist or industrial societies led them to discount 'race' and ethnicity as of central importance. Indeed, both 'social theorists tended to regard ethnicity as a spent force' (Parkin, 1979). While Marx pointed to capitalism as the key factor behind the erosion of 'racial' and

Bill Morris, Britain's first black leader of a large trade union, the Transport and General Workers' Union

ethnic identity and conflict, Weber regarded features of industrial society, especially bureaucratization, as central to the declining significance of 'race' and ethnicity.

Our concern, therefore, is not strictly speaking with the work of Marx and Weber, who were mistaken in this particular case, but rather with the work of writers who have sought to apply their analyses to what is now recognized to be a salient social division.

4.1 MARXISM: CAPITALISM, CLASS AND MIGRANT LABOUR

─────────────── ACTIVITY 10 ───────────────

Before reading this section, you should remind yourself of the central features of Marx's analysis of modern society by re-reading Section 3.1 in Part I of this unit. How do you think a marxist could account for 'racial' divisions?

Although there are a variety of marxist approaches (Solomos, 1986), there is general agreement that a marxist analysis 'begins with the concepts of capitalism and class' (Phizacklea and Miles, 1980). An analysis which starts there 'and then proceeds by introducing the concept of migrant labour' has been developed to account for the entry and reception of black people in Britain since the Second World War.

The expansionist nature of capitalism, it is argued, led it to seek out new sources of profit throughout the world. One form such a search took was that of colonialism, which entailed the conquest of non-capitalist countries. The exploitation of the colonies fostered Britain's economic development but at the same time distorted their development. You have already come across an example of the way colonialism affected non-capitalist societies in Chapter 2 of the Reader. In this situation, sections of the population turned to migration to improve their economic position. While a negative image of black people predated this period of colonialism, such an image was reinforced by ideas suggesting the inherent inferiority of black people and was used to justify further colonialism, so that by the end of the nineteenth century 'racism ... had a circulation throughout the class structure of Britain' (Miles, 1982). When, therefore, migrants from what were now ex-colonies responded to the demand for labour after the Second World War, and chose Britain as their destination, they were confronted by racism. This framework of ideas and attitudes was taken up by sections of the working class who sought a simple explanation for the material decline of their own areas. This meant that, despite the fact that there was little competition for jobs, because the migrants were taking up jobs being vacated by white people, a further source of division within the working class had opened up. Such a division from the point of view of the dominant class had two advantages. Firstly, it ensured the availability of a visible 're-serve army of labour' and, secondly, it helped to inhibit class solidarity among the workforce.

Although such an analysis does recognize that people who have been categorized as belonging to a particular 'race' are seriously disadvantaged, we are urged to move beyond 'the way in which the social world appears immediately to the observer' to 'the essential relations which, in turn, can be used to explain why the social world appears as it does' (Miles, 1982). On a marxist view, these relations are, of course, the social relations of production. While it is recognized that black people are subject to racism, stress is placed on the context within which this occurs — namely, capitalist social relations. The availability of black migrant labour is traced back to the devastation wreaked on the colonies as a result of a previous stage of capitalist development. What is more, the position of black migrant labour in the social relations of modern capitalism is seen as deriving from the need of capital for a cheap, reserve labour force available to be employed in a boom and to be unemployed in a recession. Black migrants are working-class, but, because they were recruited for a particular role and because they are subject to racism, they constitute a subordinate 'fraction' of the working class. The implication of such an analysis seems to be that 'racial' disadvantage can only be successfully resisted through united action by white and black workers.

─────────────── ACTIVITY 11 ───────────────

We shall be looking at ways in which we can assess theories in Unit 9, but at this stage I would like you to begin a preliminary assessment. What are the strengths of this marxist explanation? What are the weaknesses?

───

An attractive feature of this explanation to me is its comprehensiveness. Not only is a form of inequality which is seemingly inimical to a marxist analysis accounted for, but so are a wide range of apparently unrelated facts (colonialism, migration, racism etc.). What's more, the focus on 'migrant labour' reminds us that the solution Britain adopted in response to its labour shortage was by no means unique. Western European countries generally responded to their labour shortage by importing 'migrant labour'. The marxist stress on capitalism can account for these similarities among Western societies.

In view of the fact that black people are predominantly working-class, it is anticipated that their response to disadvantage will (at least eventually) take a similar form to that of their white comrades. And there do indeed seem to be signs of such similarities. The evidence indicates that black workers are just as likely as white workers, in fact more so, to vote Labour (Saggar, 1992) and to join a trade union (Brown, 1984). Electoral support for Labour and trade union membership do not, of course, necessarily indicate class consciousness. The former partly results from a preference for a party which is rather more reform-ist than its main rival on 'race' relations, while the latter partly reflects the fact that black workers are disproportionately found in manufacturing. Neverthe-less, evidence of a willingness on the part of black workers to participate in industrial action, such as strikes, alongside white workers, does point to a degree of class unity. Despite the fact that industrial disputes have often brought black and white workers together in opposition to management, there has been a tendency on the part of some writers to think that disputes which primarily involve black people are complicated by a 'racial' element. We must be wary of making such an assumption. Take for example, the dispute which arose at Burnsall Ltd., a small metal finishing company in Smethwick in 1992. Here, the basic demand of the strikers was to gain union recognition from an employer who had refused to accept one. The fact that the strikers were pri-marily Asian women does not make this an atypical dispute (Hill, 1993).

To point to positive features in a marxist explanation is not to say that it is without its critics. Wasn't colonialism in the nineteenth century primarily motivated by political rather than economic considerations? Isn't there greater variation in the economic position of different ethnic minorities and within them than is implied? And, above all, isn't this particular marxist analysis — in seeing 'racial' divisions as deriving from, and being sustained by, the needs

Asian women on the picket line outside Burnsall's in Smethwick, Birmingham, October 1992

of capitalism — underplaying the significance of 'race' and virtually ignoring ethnicity, that is cultural differences between groups? Let us turn, then, to an alternative account.

4.2   WEBERIAN THEORY: STATUS AND GROUP CLOSURE

——————————————— ACTIVITY 12 ———————————————

Before reading this section you should remind yourself of the central features of Weber's analysis of modern society by re-reading Section 3.2 in Part I of this unit. Note in particular Weber's distinction between class, status and party. How do you think a Weberian theorist would account for 'racial' divisions?

Weberian theory does not have to wrestle as hard as does marxist theory with this phenomenon because it is not tied to the assumption that in some sense the economy is of primary importance and that class conflict is central in capitalist societies. In terms of Weber's three dimensions of stratification, 'racial' inequality comprises an example of *status inequality* and as such may be as significant as class inequality.

Status for Weber arises out of the tendency of human beings to evaluate each other, to express respect for some human attributes and contempt for others. The result is the existence of prevalent beliefs and values concerning the criteria for social worth or esteem. What human attributes are evaluated, and how they are evaluated, varies from society to society, but the consequence of such evaluations is that some groups will be able to benefit from, and actively exploit, such beliefs and values.

One analysis which uses the Weberian concept of social closure to show how groups exploit such beliefs has been put forward by Parkin (1979). Social closure refers to the process by which groups seek to maximize their rewards by restricting access to resources and opportunities to a limited circle. Two strategies are identified. The first is known as *exclusion* and involves the operation of power in a downward direction. Here, more privileged groups seek to exclude other groups from sharing their advantages by defining them as inferior or ineligible. An example of this strategy was evident during the disputes in the 1970s at Mansfield Hosiery Ltd and Imperial Typewriters, when the white-dominated unions were more anxious to restrict access to promotion opportunities to white people rather than represent the interests of Asian workers. The second strategy is known as *usurpation* and involves the operation of power in an upward direction. Here, less privileged groups seek to gain access to advantages from which they have been excluded. An example of this strategy was again evident during the disputes mentioned above. The Asians were 'forced to organize as an Asian workforce, relying on the resources of the Asian community rather than their unions' (Moore, 1982). In other words, they turned to 'ethnic organizations'. These two strategies are not, of course, mutually exclusive; some groups, such as trade unions, use both exclusion and usurpation.

In the course of competing for scarce resources, dominant groups take advantage of prevailing beliefs and values to define competitors as inferior and ineligible. Which attributes are used as criteria for exclusion varies from society to society, being dependent not only on the beliefs which are prevalent, but also on the policies of the state. One such attribute is 'race'. Its use as an exclusionary device means that 'race' can be as significant, if not more so, than class. Let us look at two examples.

Under the system of apartheid in South Africa, the population was rigidly classified by 'race', as black, white, Asian or coloured, with each category having different entitlements. Such a system entailed the exploitation of black people by white people and meant that the dominant social division was a 'racial' one.

In Britain the population was not classified in this way and the boundaries between groups were much more fluid. Nonetheless, some Weberian theorists argue that the status division between 'whites' and 'blacks', with its concomitant belief in the superiority of white people, which developed under colonialism, still persists. It is reinforced when social groups (including the white working class) attempt to maximize their rewards by restricting the access of other groups, who are defined as 'racially different', to resources and opportunities. If racial discrimination results in black people being restricted to those occupations which are characterized by low pay, poor job security and few promotion prospects, status disadvantages are being translated into class disadvantages and we can talk of a black underclass. Just such an outcome was detected by Rex and Tomlinson. On the basis of a study of Handsworth in Birmingham they argued that there were clear differences in life-chances between Afro-Caribbeans and Asians on the one hand, and the white British on the other hand, such that the former had 'a different kind of position in the labour market, a different housing situation and a different form of schooling' (Rex and Tomlinson, 1979). Subject to racism and distinctly disadvantaged in these three sectors, the ethnic minorities constituted, in their view, an underclass in British society, increasingly conscious of their subordinate position, below the white working class, and of the need to pursue their interests in a distinct and militant fashion.

Although it is recognized that 'race' can be a marker of difference, it is stressed by Weberian theory that it is only one of a range of markers which can enable 'us' to distinguish ourselves from 'them'. Which markers are used depends on what suits our interests in a particular context. This means that groups which may be in competition at one time may be in alliance at another time. Wallman (1986) gives two examples from her fieldwork in London of the way in which different markers are used in different contexts. In one ethnically mixed residential area, where the local authority had placed homes in a 'housing action area', the boundaries between the ethnic groups were less significant than between 'us' — the locality — and 'them' — the local bureaucracy. In another area she discovered among the Asians a variety of boundaries in operation between Indians, Pakistanis, Bangladeshis and Kashmiris, between Hindus, Sikhs and Muslims and between Punjabi, Gujerati and Urdu speakers. However, faced by a common form of discrimination in which they were all treated as Asians, the separate groups developed a common identity as Asians ('us') as against the majority white ethnic group ('them').

—————————————— ACTIVITY 13 ——————————————

How does the Weberian explanation differ from the marxist one which we looked at earlier?

An attractive feature of Weberian theory is its sensitivity to the variety of groups which form as people struggle to maximize their own rewards and minimize those of others. While the marxist account recognizes that class solidarity may be inhibited by 'racism' so that class unity is not always forth-coming, Weberian theory takes much greater cognizance of the way in which groups organize around ethnicity. It is, therefore, able to appreciate how ethnic minorities have not only created a plethora of neighbourhood-based organiza-tions to enable their community life to function, but have also used these organizations to further their interests in the wider society.

Alongside such an appreciation of complexity, however, goes a certain hesi-tancy in a Weberian perspective towards providing a general explanation of 'racial' inequality which links the range of factors addressed by marxism. While Weberian theory certainly does not underplay the significance of 'race' and does point to the salience of ethnicity, it emphasizes that the importance of these phenomena can only be gauged through empirical investigation and that their importance is likely to vary enormously. Some Weberian theorists, as we have seen, argue on the basis of their research that 'race' is so central to an understanding of British society that a new social division is opening up between a black underclass and the white majority. This thesis (of which this is only one version) will be explored further in the second part of Unit 8. You might begin a preliminary assessment of this thesis by re-examining Tables 5 and 6. Do the data challenge the thesis in any way?

4.3   GLOBALIZATION AND CULTURAL IDENTITY

────────────────────── ACTIVITY 14 ──────────────────────

Before we move on to examine a third explanation of 'racial' disadvantage, I would like you to read a short extract from a speech made by a British MP, and come to a judgement as to whether this comprises an example of racism:

> The fact that the Hong Kong Chinese are very hard-working and hold British passports does not make them British. If millions of Chinese come to the UK, they would not integrate and become yellow Englishmen. They would create another China, another Hong Kong in England, just as former immigrants have created another Pakistan in Bradford.
>
> This possibility should make us consider what has already happened to this green and pleasant land — first as a result of waves of coloured immigrants and then by the pernicious doctrine of multi-culturalism … Every year that goes by the English are battered into submission in their own country and more strident are the demands of ethnic nationalism. The British people were never consulted as to whether they would change from being a homogeneous society to a multi-racial society. If they had been, I am sure that a resounding majority would have voted to keep Britain an English-speaking white country.
>
> (Townsend, quoted in Miles, 1990)

Racism is a term of very recent origin. It emerged in response to two phenom-ena: firstly, a growing body of scientific evidence which challenged the nine-teenth-century doctrine that people belong to a limited number of discrete 'races', some of which are inherently superior to others; and, secondly, the realization that Nazism had used this doctrine to define Jews as an alien and inferior 'race' and thus justify genocide (Miles, 1989). The term still carries a strong moral charge so that people are generally reluctant to admit that what they say amounts to racism. I suspect that Townsend is no exception. Whether you consider this extract 'racist' or not will depend primarily on how you define the term. If you define racism as a set of beliefs which not only purport to identify a number of distinct 'races' but also allege that some are superior to others, it follows that the speech is not an expression of racism. For Townsend does not claim that people from Hong Kong or Pakistan are biologically inferior. If you define racism, however, as a set of beliefs which involve distinguishing groups on the basis of physical markers, seeing these groups as permanently and essentially different and asserting that their interaction produces undesirable consequences, it follows that the speech is an expression of racism. For Townsend distinguishes three distinct groups (English/British, Chinese, Pakistanis) on the basis of skin colour, sees the first group as permanently and essentially different from the other two and asserts that the presence of these two groups in Britain is undesirable.

For proponents of the third explanation of 'racial' divisions — which we shall now turn to — this extract does indeed constitute racism and as such illustrates a central feature of British national culture. While it is recognized that references to the alleged 'racial' inferiority of particular groups are now relatively rare outside the confines of neo-fascist parties, it is argued that references to supposed essential differences between minority ethnic cultures and the national culture are commonplace. As one writer puts it:

> A form of cultural racism which has taken a necessary distance from crude ideas of biological inferiority now seeks to present an imaginary definition of the nation as a unified cultural community. It constructs and defends an image of national culture, homogeneous in its whiteness, yet precarious and perpetually vulnerable to attack from enemies within and without.
>
> (Gilroy, 1987)

Here Gilroy is following another writer, Anderson, in visualizing the nation as an 'imagined community' — 'imagined because the members of even the smallest nation will never know most of their fellow members, meet them, or even hear of them, yet in the minds of each lives the image of their communion' (Anderson, 1983). When we actually examine the nation-states of the West, we discover that they have never in fact been culturally homogeneous nor comprised unified cultural communities but 'are without exception ethnically hybrid — the product of conquests, absorptions of one people by another' (Hall, 1992a). The British people, for example, are the product of a series of such conquests — Celtic, Roman, Saxon, Viking and Norman. What national cultures seek to do is 'to represent what is in fact the ethnic hotch-potch of modern nationality as the primordial unity of "one people"' (Hall, 1992a) and to create amidst the social divisions which characterize a nation an 'imagined community'. (How this is achieved will be discussed by Gregor McLennan in relation to Scotland in Unit 17 and explored further in TV 10.)

It is conceivable that British national culture will one day embrace black people, but at the moment this seems a forlorn hope. Afro-Caribbeans are frequently presented as belonging to a pathological culture and thus prone to criminality, while Asians are often presented as a threat to the British way of life by virtue of the strength and cohesiveness of their cultures: 'For different reasons, both groups are judged to be incompatible with authentic forms of Englishness ... The process of national decline is presented as coinciding with the dilution of once homogeneous and continuous national stock by other strains' (Gilroy, 1987).

The 'three wise men' in a school Nativity play. From the left: a Sikh child, a Muslim child and a Christian child (Claremont Primary School, Nottingham)

====================================== READER ======================================

If you have time, I would like you read Chapter 5 by Solomos in the Course Reader. Does his analysis of recent political discourses support Gilroy's contention that British national culture excludes ethnic minority groups? In a tutorial you might look at the way the mass media present news which deals with 'race' and ethnicity. Does your analysis support Gilroy's contention, or not? (You will find a discussion of two newspaper articles which concern the 1985 Tottenham 'riot' in Britain in Unit 17.)

==

A central feature of the explanation, which we are examining, is its insistence that our identities (including our national identities) are socially constructed, that is to say informed by our culture and thus changeable. (This argument will be developed in detail by Margaret Wetherell in Unit 20.) It is further argued that this process can only be fully understood in a global context. European contact with populations elsewhere involved a process of representation and, with European expansion, a construction of the West's sense of itself through its sense of difference from others. The consequence was the emergence of a discourse which represented 'the world as divided according to a simple dichotomy — "the West/the Rest"' (Hall, 1992b).

In the course of exploring representations generated within the Western world about populations elsewhere, Miles provides two examples of this division. The first is based upon colour: 'in the act of defining Africans as "black" and "savages", and thereby excluding them from their world, Europeans in the eighteenth and nineteenth century were representing themselves as "white" and "civilized".' The second is based upon culture: 'European representations of the Islamic world extensively utilized images of barbarism and sexuality in the context of a Christian/heathen dichotomy' (Miles, 1989). Miles emphasizes that representations of the Other (and by implication oneself) only utilized the concept of 'race' from the late eighteenth century. 'Races' themselves do not exist; rather at a particular period populations began to be represented as 'races'. Representing the Other in 'racial' terms was significant, however, both because it represented differences as fixed by biology and therefore unalterable and because it provided scientific legitimacy for excluding the Other. As such, this representation has had, and continues to have, real effects — justifying, for example, the domination of non-white, non-European peoples by white Europeans.

While globalization, in the sense of the interconnectedness of societies, has been a feature of modern societies since the sixteenth century, a number of social scientists have suggested that in the last two decades we have entered a qualitatively new phase of globalization. One of its main features has been described as 'time-space compression' (Harvey, 1989) in recognition of the fact that our lives are increasingly and remarkably quickly influenced by distant events. An example of this was the British government's sudden exit in 1992 from the ERM (European Exchange Rate Mechanism) as a result of worldwide speculation on the pound. As this example demonstrates, globalization proves unsettling to seemingly established national cultures. In the case of Britain, a period of economic and political decline has coincided with threats from above and below. From above, increasing integration into the European Community is felt by some members of the dominant ethnic group to threaten sovereignty; and from below, the formation of ethnic minority 'enclaves' within the nation-state is felt by some members of the dominant ethnic group to be a threat to the British way of life. The response has been, as we illustrated earlier, 'a particularly defensive, closed and exclusive definition of "Englishness" being advanced as a way of warding off or refusing to live with difference' (Hall, 1992a).

Such a definition of Englishness/Britishness (the terms are significantly not distinguished) has underpinned state policy especially in the last decade. This representation in short has had real effects. Two examples will suffice. Immigration and nationality legislation has been discriminatory, its 'real purpose' from 1962, as a former government minister has pointed out, being 'to restrict the influx of *coloured* immigrants' (Deedes quoted in Solomos, 1988). And the Education Reform Act of 1988 has been ethnocentric in, for example, reasserting the primacy of Christianity and attempting (not wholly successfully) to transmit a particular version of the nation's past within school history (Whitty, 1992).

How, then, have Afro-Caribbeans and Asians responded to globalization? This account stresses the diversity of responses. Some, faced by cultural racism and exclusion have retreated 'to the familiar certainties of the past' where 'the meaning of life is deemed to be permanently and incorrigibly revealed in a sacred text, body of rituals, or a pool of inherited and inviolable traditions' (Parekh, 1989). This response has been particularly evident among some Muslims who, for instance, have felt insulted by the attacks upon their religion, symbolized by the publication of Salman Rushdie's *The Satanic Verses*. Others have attempted to draw upon cultures developed by black populations elsewhere in the world to 'redefine what it means to be black, adapting it to distinctively British experiences and meanings' (Gilroy, 1987). This response has been found among some Afro-Caribbeans who have drawn on Rastafarianism to recognize blackness as a central aspect of their identity, take pride in their colour and feel opposition towards a society which they realize can meaningfully be described as Babylon. And yet others have sought to produce new identities. A good example is 'those new identities which have emerged in the 1970s, grouped around the signifier 'black', which in the British context provides a new focus of identification for *both* Afro-Caribbean and Asian communities' (Hall, 1992c). While these communities are culturally different, some Afro-Caribbeans and Asians — recognizing that they are similarly subject to cultural racism and exclusion — have sought to represent their common situation by taking on a 'black' identity.

Although a variety of responses to globalization can be detected among both the majority ethnic group and the minority ethnic groups, they tend towards one of two kinds. The first kind of response seeks to retreat to the familiar certainties of the past — cultural racism and what has become labelled as 'fundamentalism' comprise examples. The second kind of response rejects both these and seeks to draw on different cultures to construct new identities.

ACTIVITY 15

How, if at all, does the third explanation of 'racial' divisions — which centres on globalization and cultural identity — move beyond the marxist and Weberian explanations, which we examined earlier?

It seems to me that the third explanation accepts both the marxist premise that an essential context for understanding cultural racism and exclusion is 'the international crisis of the capitalist world economy and the deep-seated crisis of the British social formation' (Centre for Contemporary Cultural Studies, 1982) and the Weberian premise that primacy should not necessarily be given to economic factors when accounting for 'racial' divisions. Where I think the third explanation moves beyond the others is in linking the 'global' and the 'local'. The marxist account, which we examined, stressed the 'global' and in the process was able to account for the pattern of post-war migration experienced by many Western societies. The Weberian account, on the other hand, focused on the 'local' and was able in the process to point to the variety of groups which form as people compete for scarce resources. What the third explanation does is to link the two — the 'global' and the 'local'.

Danny Chovanji, presenter of BBC Radio 5's and BBC Radio WM's *Eastern Beat* for Britain's Asian youth

To point to positive features of this explanation does not mean that queries can't be raised. I will raise two here. The first revolves around the question of how pervasive cultural racism is. The examples frequently given come from speeches and writings of some modern liberals, often referred to as the 'New Right' (we looked at one earlier during Activity 14) which, with the advent of the Conservative government in 1979, did gain more currency. There are, however, competing notions of Britishness around. Here is the vision of society put forward by the Swann Report's inquiry into the education of children from minority ethnic groups: one which 'enables, expects and encourages members of all ethnic groups, both minority and majority, to participate fully in shaping the society as a whole within a framework of commonly accepted values, practices and procedures, whilst also allowing, and where necessary, assisting the ethnic minority communities in maintaining their distinct ethnic identities within this common framework' (DES, 1985).

While I recognize that multiculturalism may, in practice, not be wholly exempt from the charge that it presents minority ethnic cultures as the Other, it does seem to me that multiculturalism presents a very different conception of Britishness than cultural racism. My second query concerns the question of how racist state policy has been. It seems to me to have been contradictory, involving alongside discriminatory immigration and nationality legislation, attempts (however ineffective) to combat 'racial' inequality through anti-discrimination legislation. Perekh put it well:

> The immigration policy rested on the assumption that black immigrants were less desirable than white, and were to be allowed in only when Britain could not dispense with their services. The anti-discrimination legislation rested on the opposite assumption. Furthermore, the immigration policy assumed that Britain was a homogeneous *nation* that could not integrate people of different 'stocks' and 'races', whom it must keep out if it was to preserve its national 'identity'. By contrast, the anti-discrimination legislation assumed that the UK was a *state*, an inherently open institution based on little more than collective subscription to a common authority and capable of accommodating people of all races and cultures.
>
> (Parekh, 1991)

SUMMARY

Marxism: capitalism, class and migrant labour

- 'Racial' divisions can only be understood in the context of the development of capitalism. Historically, it created 'racial' divisions and currently it sustains them.

- Both the availability of black migrant labour in the post-war period and the representation of the Other in 'racial' terms need to be understood against the backdrop of colonialism, which itself was a product of the expansionist nature of capitalism.

- Black migrants were recruited to play a particular role as a cheap reserve labour force within the capitalist relations of production. Racism ensures that the migrants and their children constitute a subordinate 'fraction' of the working class.

- Resistance takes a number of forms, including a class form.

Weberian theory: status and group closure

- 'Racial' divisions can only be understood in the context of the competition of groups for scarce resources.

- Groups draw on a range of markers to exclude others, one of which may be 'race'.

- The use of 'race' as a marker is consequent upon beliefs generated during the colonial era.

- Since the significance of 'race' depends on prevailing beliefs it is a form of status inequality and is conceptually distinct from class inequality.

- The use of 'race' as an exclusionary device can result in status inequality being translated into class inequality, i.e. an underclass.

- Resistance takes a number of forms, including an ethnic form.

Globalization and cultural identity

- 'Racial' divisions can only be understood in the context of globalization. Historically globalization involved the construction of the Other in 'racial' terms (racism) and currently a common response to globalization has been a new form of racism, cultural racism.

- Racist discourses influence social practices, justifying for example the domination of non-white peoples.

- The current phase of globalization proves unsettling to established identities. Two kinds of response can be distinguished: the first seeks to recover old certainties; the second seeks to live with difference and construct new identities.

- Cultural racism, which is an example of the first kind, is extremely pervasive among the majority ethnic group and results in the exclusion of minority ethnic groups.

- Resistance takes a number of forms, including an ethnic form.

5   CONCLUSION

What I have sought to do in this half-unit is to introduce you to a second major social division in British society.

In the second section, I defined 'race' and ethnicity, emphasizing that the boundaries between social groups are socially constructed. In the process we addressed one of the course themes — *representation and reality* — and saw how the process of representation can have significant effects.

In the third section, I pointed to some evidence which indicated that 'racial' divisions are significant in British society. Not only is there evidence that the Afro-Caribbean and Asian communities are disadvantaged relative to the majority ethnic group, but also that this stems from 'racial' discrimination of both a direct and indirect kind.

In the fourth section, I outlined three different explanations of 'racial' divisions. Although we have not had time to provide a thorough assessment of them, it does seem to me that they are not necessarily competing explanations and that each one illuminates some aspect of 'racial' divisions. In the process of exploring these explanations, we addressed a second course theme — *the local and the global* — and saw how one of the explanations sought to link them in a fruitful way.

REFERENCES

Anderson, B. (1983) *Imagined Communities*, London, Verso.

Banton, M. (1972) *Racial Minorities,* London, Fontana Collins.

Barratt Brown, M. (1970) *After Imperialism*, London, Heinemann.

Braham, P., Rattansi, A. and Skellington, R. (1992) *Racism and Antiracism: Inequalities, Opportunities and Policies*, London, Sage/The Open University.

Brown, C. (1984) *Black and White Britain: The Third PSI Study*, Aldershot, Gower.

Brown, C. and Gay, P. (1985) *Racial Discrimination: Seventeen Years after the Act*, London, Policy Studies Institute.

Centre for Contemporary Cultural Studies (1982) *The Empire Strikes Back: Race and Racism in '70s Britain*, London, Hutchinson.

Daniel, W.W. (1968) *Racial Discrimination in England*, Harmondsworth, Penguin Books.

DES (1985) *Education For All*, The Report of the Committee of Inquiry into the Education of Children from Ethnic Minority Groups, Department of Education and Science, London, HMSO.

Foner, N. (1979) *Jamaica Farewell*, London, Routledge.

Gilroy, P. (1987) *'There Ain't No Black in the Union Jack': The Cultural Politics of Race and Nation*, London, Hutchinson.

Glazer, N and Moynihan, D. (1970) *Beyond the Melting Pot*, Cambridge, Mass., MIT Press.

Griffin, J.H. (1964) *Black Like Me*, Panther Books.

Hall, S. (1992a) 'Our mongrel selves', *New Statesman and Society*, 19 June.

Hall, S. (1992b) 'The West and the rest: discourse and power' in S. Hall and B. Gieben (eds) *Formations of Modernity*, Cambridge, Polity Press/The Open University.

Hall, S. (1992c) 'The question of cultural identity' in S. Hall, D. Held and T. McGrew (eds), *Modernity and its Futures*, Cambridge, Polity Press/The Open University.

Harvey, D. (1989) *The Condition of Post Modernity*, London, Oxford University Press.

Haskey, J. (1991) 'The ethnic minority populations resident in private households: estimates by county and metropolitan district of England and Wales', *Population Trends 63*, OPCS, London, HMSO.

Hill, D. (1993) 'Smethwick crucible', *The Guardian*, 2 January.

Hobsbawm, E. (1969) *Industry and Empire*, Harmondsworth, Penguin.

Husband, C. (ed.) (1982) *'Race' in Britain*, London, Hutchinson.

Miles, R. (1982) *Racism and Migrant Labour*, London, Routledge.

Miles, R. (1989) *Racism*, London, Routledge.

Miles, R. (1990) 'Racism, ideology and disadvantage', *Social Studies Review*, vol.5(4).

Modood, T. (1992) *Not Easy Being British*, London, Runnymede Trust and Trentham Books.

Moore, R. (1982) 'Immigration and racism' in R. Burgess (ed.) *Exploring Society*, British Sociological Association.

Owen, D. (1993) 'Local census data for ethnic groups in Great Britain', *New Community*, vol.19(2).

Parekh, B. (1989) 'Between holy text and moral void', *New Statesman and Society*, 23 March.

Parekh, B. (1991) 'Law torn', *New Statesman and Society*, 14 June.

Parkin, F. (1979) *Marxism and Class Theory*, London, Tavistock.

Patterson, S. (1965) *Dark Strangers*, Harmondsworth, Penguin Books.

Peach, C. (1968) *West Indian Migration to Britain: A Social Geography*, London, Oxford University Press.

Peach, C. (1978/9) 'British unemployment cycles and West Indian immigrants 1955–1974', *New Community*, vol. VII (1).

Phizacklea, A. and Miles, R. (1980) *Labour and Racism*, London, Routledge.

Pryce, K. (1986) *Endless Pressure*, Bristol, Classical Press.

Rattansi, A. and Donald, J. (eds) (1992) *The Question of Racism*, London, Sage/The Open University.

Rex, J. and Mason, D. (eds) (1986) *Theories of Race and Ethnic Relations*, Cambridge, Cambridge University Press.

Rex, J. and Tomlinson, S. (1979) *Colonial Immigrants in a British City*, London, Routledge.

Robinson, V. (1980) 'Correlates of Asian immigration, 1959–1974', *New Community*, vol. VIII (1 and 2).

Runnymede Trust (1991) *Race and Immigration*, Bulletin 247, London, Runnymede Trust.

Saggar, S. (1992) *Race and Politics in Britain*, Hemel Hempstead, Harvester Wheatsheaf.

Skellington, R. (1992) *'Race' in Britain Today*, London, Sage/The Open University.

Smith, D. (1977) *Racial Disadvantage in Britain*, Harmondsworth, Penguin Books.

Solomos, J. (1986) 'Varieties of Marxist conceptions of "race", class and the state' in Rex, J. and Mason, D. (eds).

Solomos, J. (1988) *Black Youth, Racism and the State*, Cambridge, Cambridge University Press.

Solomos, J. (1989) *Race and Racism in Contemporary Britain*, London, Macmillan.

Wallman, S. (1986) 'Ethnicity and the boundary process in context' in J. Rex and D. Mason (eds).

Watson, J. (ed.) (1977) *Between Two Cultures*, Oxford, Basil Blackwell.

Whitty, G. (1992) 'Education, economy and national culture' in R. Bocock and K. Thompson (eds) *Social and Cultural Forms of Modernity*, Cambridge, Polity Press/The Open University.

Williams, J. (1992) '"Race" in Britain', *Sociology Review*, vol. 2(2).

FURTHER READING

A relevant and useful book in this area, if you are interested in reading further is:

Skellington, R. with Morris, P. (1992) *'Race' in Britain Today* (with an introductory essay by Paul Gordon), London, Sage/The Open University.

ACKNOWLEDGEMENTS

Grateful acknowledgement is made to the following sources for permission to reproduce material in this unit:

Text

Johnson, F. (1989), *The Sunday Telegraph*, 23 April 1989, © The Daily Telegraph plc; Walden, B. (1989), *The Sunday Times*, 23 April 1989, © Brian Walden; Kettle, M. (1989), *The Guardian*, 20 April 1989, © The Guardian; Mills, H. (1992), 'Knock on the door brings growing fear of racial abuse and attack', *The Independent*, 9 November 1992.

Figure

Figure 1: Wright, E.O. (1985), *Classes*, Verso; *Figure 2*: Central Statistical Office (1989), *Social Trends 19*, © Crown Copyright, reproduced with the permission of the Controller of Her Majesty's Stationery Office; *Figure 3*: Heath, A. (1987), 'A class in the classroom', in Cosin, B., Flude, M. and Hales, M. (eds), *School, Work and Equality*, Hodder and Stoughton; *Figure 4*: Williams, J. (1992), 'Race in Britain', *Sociological Review*, vol. 2, no. 2, Routledge; *Figure 5*: Haskey, J. (1991), *Population Trends*, 63, © Crown Copyright, reproduced with the permission of the Controller of Her Majesty's Stationery Office.

Tables

Table 1: Goldthorpe, J.H. and Payne, C. (1986), 'Trends in intergenerational class mobility in England and Wales, 1972-1983', *Sociology*, vol. 20, 1986, copyright © John H. Goldthorpe and C. Payne/BSA Publications Ltd; *Tables 3 and 4*: Central Statistical Office (1993), *Social Trends*, *23*, © Crown Copyright, reproduced with the permission of the Controller of Her Majesty's Stationery Office; *Table 5*: Brown, C. (1984), *Black and White Britain*, Gower; *Table 6*: Department of Employment (1991), 'Ethnic origins and the labour market', *Employment Gazette*, vol. 99, no. 2, © Crown Copyright, reproduced with the permission of the Controller of Her Majesty's Stationery Office; *Table 7*: Owen, D. (1993), 'Local census data for ethnic groups in Great Britain', *New Community*, vol. 19, no. 2, Commission for Racial Equality.

Photographs/Illustrations

p.49: Courtesy of Liverpool Football Club; *p.74*: Leonard Freed/Magnum; *p.82*: The Independent/Richard Ratner; *p.84*: The Independent/Kayte Brimacombe; *p.87*: Ulrike Preuss/Format; *p.95*: T&G Publications/Roy Peters; *p.98*: The Guardian/John Robertson; *p.102*: The Independent/Richard Ratner; *p.105*: BBC Pebble Mill/Danny Choranji.

UNIT 8 GENDER DIVISIONS AND THE INTERACTING DYNAMICS OF CLASS, 'RACE'/ETHNICITY AND GENDER

Prepared for the Course Team by Norma Sherratt (Part I) and Andrew Pilkington and Norma Sherratt (Part II)

CONTENTS

PART I: GENDER DIVISIONS

1 INTRODUCTION

In Unit 7 you explored two major divisions in British society — divisions of class and divisions of 'race' or ethnicity. You were given the opportunity to think about the ways in which people from different classes or ethnic groups have different life-chances and life experiences and you were introduced to different explanations for the prevalence and continuation of these divisions. In the first half of this unit we shall be looking at a third major line of division in Britain, that of gender, and asking the same kinds of questions:

1 How do the life-chances and life experiences of women in Britain today differ from those of men?

2 How can we explain these differences?

Gender is not an easy area to study. Almost certainly every one of you reading this half-unit will have some ideas already, possibly very strong ones, about the differences between men and women. They are part of your own lived experience and you may well have discussed them with family, friends or colleagues — discussed them, too, with great intensity! Some of you, in addition, may well be more closely involved with exploration of the differences, on a professional or personal level, and in challenging existing divisions. In writing this half-unit I have tried to recognize the many different starting-points you will be coming from.

Gender is not only a difficult subject to study. It is also a very wide-ranging subject. During the past twenty years there has been an upsurge of research and writing, exploring gender divisions in many different fields — science, technology and the arts as well as the social sciences. Within the social sciences there is increasing awareness of the relevance of gender divisions in every topic or discipline studied. Certainly, in D103, an awareness of the way in which men and women experience our society differently is not limited to this half-unit.

This is, however, the only opportunity you will be given in D103 to explore gender divisions in some depth and in particular to work on the different theoretical frameworks which have been developed to address gender divisions. Getting to understand, compare and assess different theories is not easy, as you have probably already realized. So in order to make your task (and mine) easier, I am going to focus in on just one aspect of gender divisions for most of this half-unit. We are going to be looking in particular at the differences between men's and women's lives at home and at 'work'. Although British material is the main source of examples, many of the same issues arise in other Western societies. In Section 1 we shall be concerned with describing the situation in the early 1990s; in Section 2 we shall be looking back to put this picture into a 'historical context'; and in Section 3 we shall be looking at a range of explanations for the divisions we have been describing. This work on theories will then be picked up again, both in Part II of this unit, where one of our concerns will be to put together all the theoretical frameworks you have been looking at in this block, and in Unit 9 where we shall carry further the question of how to assess these different frameworks.

2   WOMEN'S WORK AND MEN'S WORK

- Women work in paid employment in the *public* sphere, outside the home; they also work inside the home in the *private* sphere.

- Women are a crucial part of the workforce of Britain in the 1990s (and their wages are essential to the well-being of most families); but at the same time they are largely responsible for the domestic and caring work which is carried out in the home.

- It is men who are often still thought of as family 'breadwinners' and yet in 1990 only 8 per cent of men in employment were sole breadwinners for a totally dependent wife and children.

It is this 'dual role' of women which we will be exploring in this section — the kinds of work that women do both outside and inside the home, and the way in which our ideas of what is the 'normal' division of labour between men and women continues to have consequences for all of us.

You may not be familiar with the use of 'work' in this way to refer to both paid employment in the public sphere and activities in the *private* sphere of the home. 'Work' is often defined more narrowly as what happens in the public sphere. However, this is a usage which is increasingly being explored by social scientists. You will have more opportunity to look at the distinction, and the reasons for the distinction, when you come to Unit 10.

2.1   WORK IN THE PUBLIC SPHERE

When I was a small child in the 1950s the mothers of most of my friends did not go out to work. Indeed, certainly in the part of the north-west where I lived, the few children whose mothers did go out to work were seen as 'different', they did not have a 'normal' family life. In the 1990s the situation would seem to be very different as you can see from the newspaper report below.

Most mothers reject home role to go back to work

Most mothers – including nearly half with children under five – have turned their backs on the role of home-maker to go back to work, according to official figures released yesterday.

As a result seven out of 10 of all parents of babies and toddlers rely on childcare, acording to the Office of Population, Censuses and Surveys.

Preliminary findings of its 1991 General Household Survey – based on interviews with almost 10,000 households and 20,000 adults –

also show 47 per cent of others with children under five are in work or seeking work – a leap of 20 per cent on 1973 and a 2 per cent rise on 1990. And more mothers with children over five are also working.

Part-time jobs have the greatest appeal among mothers with very young children. Numbers working full-time have risen from 7 per cent in 1973 to 13 per cent; while part-timers have increased from 18 per cent to 29 per cent over the same period.

Source: *The Independent,* 23 September 1992

In the 1990s the majority of women are in paid employment outside the home or seeking paid employment, even those with very small children. Department of Employment figures show that in December 1992 there were 10,682,000 men in employment and 10,142,000 women. The gap which has existed for many years between men and women seems to be closing. I will return to this trend and the question of the 'feminization' of the labour force later in this section. But let's first look more closely at these figures.

What exactly do women do when they 'go out to work'. Are women's employment patterns the same as those of men?

———————————————————— ACTIVITY I ————————————————————

Use Figure 1 and the photograph below to describe the kinds of work that women do.

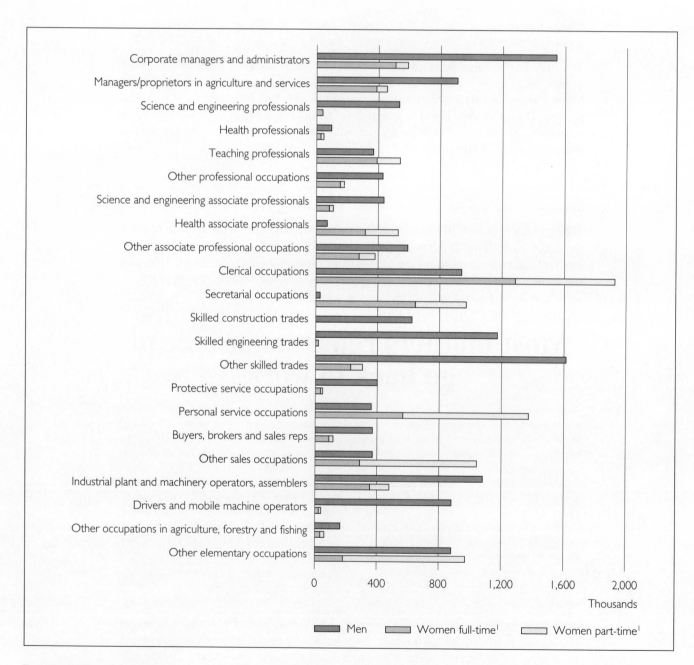

Figure I   Numbers of women and men of working age in employment by Standard Occupational Classification, Great Britain, Spring 1991
I Based on respondents' self-assessment

Source: data from 1991 Labour Force Survey estimates; table from *Employment Gazette*, September 1992

Marlow Day Hospital celebrates its first birthday: secretary Sylvia Rowe, ocupational therapy helper Beverley Hamer, Sister Veronica Checksfield, occupational therapist Ann McIntyre, consultant Dr Adrian Wilson, clinical assistant Dr Evelyn Taylor, physiotherapy helper Louisa Vendelis and physiotherapist Linda Howle

Figure 1 shows that although similar proportions of men and women are 'economically active', they are actually in very different types of work. As you can see, women are concentrated in certain types and certain areas of work. The highest percentage of women is in clerical work, followed by 'personal service' occupations (this means hairdressing, waiting at table, receptionist-type work), sales occupations (other than buyers, brokers and reps), secretarial occupations and 'other elementary occupations'. In each of these a large percentage of the women are part-time workers. Correspondingly the percentage of men who are employed in these areas is relatively small. Men are concentrated in quite different areas of work (as corporate managers and administrators, and in the skilled trades especially) in which there are very few women.

According to Figure 1 there *are* a few areas of employment in which the numbers of men and women are roughly equal — health professionals, for example, and teaching professionals. In fact, though, what these statistics do not show (but which the photograph illustrates well) is that, within these areas, there is a further division. The occupations in which women are more likely to be found are those which do not have attached to them the same pay, status and power as the occupations in which men are more likely to be found. Even in those areas of work in which women form the greatest number of employees — teaching, social work, nursing — the higher the level of work, the greater will be the percentage of men occupying posts. Furthermore, when we move to the very highest levels, particularly those positions which confer quite substantial amounts of power over other people's lives, then the percentage of women is very small indeed. In 1992, for example, women constituted fewer than 7 per cent of MPs, 4 per cent of judges and 7 per cent of civil servants at the level of Under Secretary or above.

The picture is, however, much more complex than this. One reason is that we have to be careful about making overall generalizations about women's employment patterns.

——————————— ACTIVITY 2 ———————————

How does Table 1 below add to our knowledge of women's employment patterns?

Table 1   Economic activity rates[1] by ethnic origin and sex, average, Spring 1987–89, Great Britain (percentages)

	All	Males	Females
All origins[2]	79	88	70
White	80	89	70
Ethnic minority groups	68	80	56
West Indian/Guyanese	80	85	76
Indian	71	84	58
Pakistani/Bangladeshi	51	77	21
All other origins[3]	67	74	59

[1] Persons of working age (16–59/64). [2] Includes those who did not state origin. [3] Includes those of mixed origin.

Source: *Employment Gazette*, February 1991

As Table 1 shows, the extent to which women are economically active varies according to ethnic group. During 1987–89, 76 per cent of West Indian/Guyanese women were economically active compared with 70 per cent of white women, 58 per cent of Indian women and only 21 per cent of Pakistani/Bangladeshi women. In addition, of course, what is not shown in this table is that there are further variations according to whether the work is full-time or part-time. (A far lower proportion of white women are in full-time employment than West Indian women or Asian women.) Finally, there are variations according to ethnic group in the *kinds* of work women do. Whilst the clothing and textiles trade accounts for a large percentage of the Asian women in employment (many as home-workers or in Asian-run businesses), West Indian women are more likely to be found in the health industry or engineering, while a high percentage of white women are employed in clerical work.

To these ethnic variations we also need to add a further division, one linked closely to status and to education. There is a vast difference between the lives of the large army of women working for low wages, often part-time, in unskilled work (as cleaners, shop assistants, waitresses) and those from more privileged backgrounds, usually with higher educational qualifications (and this number includes a high percentage of Asian women). Indeed if we add office work as a third grouping, then any suggestion that we can talk easily about women's experience of employment in general begins to seem more and more unrealistic.

Whatever the class or ethnic background of women, however, the picture is still one of women being concentrated primarily in *non-manual* work and in *service* industries. As you can see from Table 2 opposite, whereas men are spread almost equally over manual and non-manual work, far more women are employed in non-manual work, whatever the industry. In terms of industry, a far higher percentage of women (82 per cent) than men (54 per cent) are employed in the service industries.

Table 2   Employment by occupation and industry, Spring 1991, persons of working age in employment, Great Britain (thousands and percentages)

	Women	Men
All occupations[1,2]	10,711	14,129
Non-manual occupations	69	48
Manual occupations	30	51
All industries[2,3]	10,711	14,129
Agriculture, forestry etc.	1	3
Energy and water supply	1	3
Manufacturing	14	28
Construction	2	12
Services	82	54

[1] Numbers shown include those not stating occupation but percentages are based on totals which exclude this group. [2] Thousands = 100 per cent.
[3] Numbers shown include those for whom industry was not specified or whose workplace was outside Great Britain but percentages are based on totals which exclude this group.
Source: *Employment Gazette*, September 1992

This is what brings us back to the question of the 'feminization' of the labour force which was mentioned at the start of this section. In the early 1990s the proportion of women in the workforce was increasing, and the proportion of men decreasing. The gap between them was closing. This was mainly because it was the areas of employment in which women are most likely to be found which were the expanding ones. There has been a shift from manual to non-manual work; a shift from manufacturing to the service sector; and a move overall to patterns of 'flexible' working whereby an increasing number of jobs will be part-time and temporary (McDowell, 1992). The newspaper article below describes clearly some of these processes. (Although it can certainly be argued that it presents an overoptimistic picture of the future, as you will see when you read Section 4.)

Small rise in jobs after recession 'to favour women'

By Barrie Clement, Labour Editor

Few extra jobs will be created after the recession and nearly all will be taken by women as "brain replaces brawn" at the workplace.

In the period up to 2000, about 1.9 million new jobs will appear in "skills-intensive, knowledge-based" occupations, but more than 1.2 million blue-collar jobs will disappear, according to forecasts published today.

The net increase of 700,000 jobs is only 2.5 per cent more than now and unemployment is likely to remain above 5 per cent.

In a report prepared for the Institute of Careers Guidance and the Centre for Research in Employment and Technology in Europe, Amin Rajan predicts that there will be a 1 million decrease in employment in manufacturing in general with 250,000 job losses in engineering alone.

The report says that primary industry and the utilities, covering agriculture, oil, gas, electricity and water supply, will lose about 200,000 jobs. On the plus side the hotel and catering sector will create 243,000 jobs, more than offsetting 148,000 redun-dancies in other distribution industries such as retailing, wholesaling and transport.

Employment will increase by 416,000 in business services, such as banking and insurance; 650,000 in miscellaneous services, including recreation and "non-market" services such as health and eduction. Mr Rajan says that the shift towards white-collar jobs will particularly favour women. "Indeed, forecasts suggest that they will takenearly all of the additional jobs thereby shifting the gender composition of the workforce."

The author argues that the "occupational segregation" of women will weaken, partly because demography will ensure that they form a larger part of the workforce and partly because of equality initiatives like Opportunity 2000. In general, the number of full-time jobs will decline and self-employment among both sexes will rise "modestly".

Six occupational groups are predicted to grow. These are professional such as scientists, lawyers and marketing specialists; associate pro-fessional and technical posts in science, engineering, law and accountancy; managers and administrators; personal andprotective services covering travel attendants, catering and police, fire and security services; sales jobs; clerical and secretarial.

Among the factors influencing the changes will be greater concern for the environment, unemployment, more individuality in products and services and demographic changes, which will mean an ageing population. There will be a move towards alliances and networks in business rather than mergers and acquisitions.

1990s: Where will the New Jobs Be?, Institute of Careers Guidance, 27a Lower High Street, Stourbridge, West Midlands DY8 1TA; and Centre for Research in Employment and Technology in Europe, 2 Holly Hill, Vauxhall Lane, Southborough, Tunbridge Wells, Kent TN4 0XD.

Source: *The Independent*, 12 November 1992

2.2   WORK INSIDE THE HOME

We have just been looking at work outside the home, in the public sphere. The picture which was emerging was one of the majority of women working outside the home for most of their working lives. However, another kind of work in our society takes place in the private sphere, inside the home — looking after children or other dependants, and generally doing 'domestic' work.

—————————— ACTIVITY 3 ——————————

Look at the two pieces of information below and then answer the following questions:

1   Using Table 3, how would you describe the sexual division of labour in the home?

2   From the information available in Figure 2 would you agree with the statement that 'women fit work around their family?'

Table 3   Who does the chores? (percentages)

	Done mainly by man	Done mainly by woman	Shared equally
Shopping	8	45	47
Evening meal	9	70	20
Evening dishes	28	33	37
Cleaning	4	68	27
Washing and ironing	3	84	12
Repairing equipment	82	6	10
Money and bills	31	40	28

Source: *The Guardian*, 11 February 1992; data from British Social Attitudes Survey

1   As Table 3 shows, there is a sexual division of labour in the home in the private domestic sphere as well as in the public sphere of paid employment (and note that we have not yet included childcare in our discussion). It is women, not men, who are primarily responsible for the day-to-day running of the home — the cooking, washing and cleaning (shopping is the only chore shared almost equally; you can relate this back to your study of Unit 3). Men are involved in work in the home but for the most part (and, of course, there are exceptions) the work they do does not demand the same regular and continuous commitment that the work of a woman does.

2   Extending our analysis of the sexual division of labour now to *include* childcare, what Figure 2 shows is that the economic status of women varies according to whether or not they have dependent children and the age of those dependent children. The likelihood of a woman being in full-time employment increases as the responsibility for dependent children decreases. This would seem to support the statement that women seem to fit work around their families. For the majority of women it is their domestic responsibilities which take precedence over their lives outside the home (and increasingly now in the early 1990s these domestic responsibilities extend to the care of old people, as I show below).

Here again, however, as in the case of paid employment outside the home, there are very significant variations in terms of class and ethnic group. The division of labour and the expectations in some families are far more 'traditional' than in others. In many Asian families, for example, there is very marked role segregation, whilst West Indian women are more likely than most other

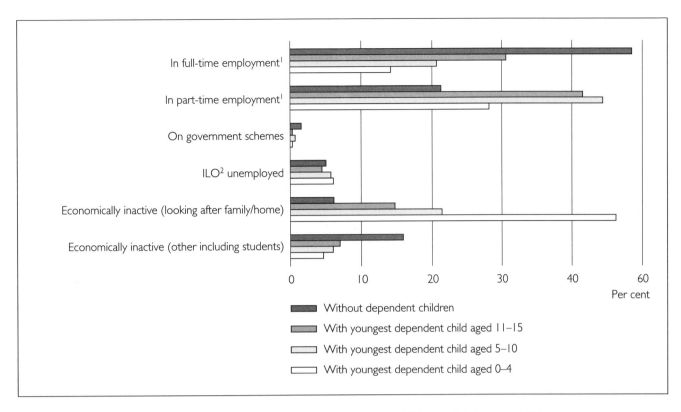

Figure 2   Economic status of working age (16–59), by age of youngest dependent child, Great Britain, Spring 1991

[1] Based on respondents' self-assessment

[2]International Labour Organisation's definition of unemployed

Source: Employment Gazette, September 1992

women to be the main breadwinner in a family. Similarly there are some middle-class women who have been able to resist traditional pressures and reduce their domestic responsibilities by buying the services of other women to provide childcare and other help in the home.

Buying the care of other women, or relying on family or friends, is, however, the only significant way women can obtain help. Most importantly, in Britain there is very little help from the state. State support for childcare has always been minimal. Britain has one of the lowest levels of state childcare in Europe (only 2 per cent of the 0–2 age group are in state-run nurseries). Furthermore, changing state policies of recent years in relation to old or disabled people (specifically the replacement of institutional care by community care) has meant increased responsibilities for women. Community care, in times of scarce resources, has come to mean family care (Finch and Groves, 1985). Just as it is considered 'normal' for women to be primarily responsible for the care of dependent children, so it is considered 'normal' for it to be the women in the family who will take on further caring work when it is needed. (According to the 1988 General Household Survey 6 million adults are involved in community care, the vast majority of these being women.) Central to all state welfare policy and legislation is an association between women and caring; the conviction that it is women's 'natural' role to be in the home; and a conviction that strong, healthy families are dependent on women fulfilling this role.

Moreover, recent changes in the way we actually live as families have not resulted in any signficant shift in these ideas. As you can see from Figure 3 overleaf, the number of lone-parent families has increased since 1971, the majority of them headed by women. But how far this marks a real change in the 'normal' division of labour is open to question.

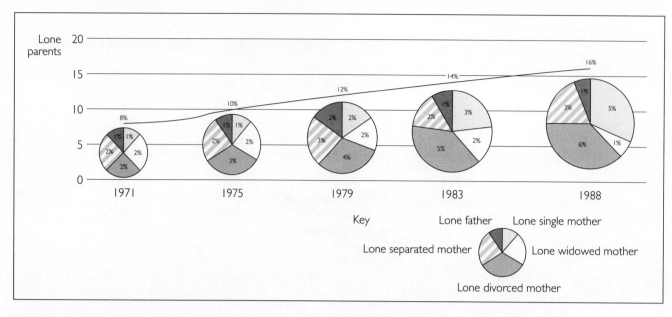

Figure 3   Lone-parent families with dependent children, by marital status, 1971–88

Source: Kiernan and Wicks, 1990; data from Office of Population Censuses and Surveys, 1990

The way in which people live is changing. But most accounts of life as lone parents, by men and women, show very little change has occurred in expectations of what are normal family roles; nor has there been any change in the way these expectations are reflected in and reinforced by state policies. All lone parents face problems because the 'norm' in British society is that of a two-parent family. They also face problems because the way they are living challenges the normal division of labour. Men who are lone parents may be carers; women who are lone parents may be trying to support the family as the sole breadwinner. But for both men and women the difficulties they experience reflect the continued strength of traditional expectations.

We have a picture, therefore, of women continuing to bear quite substantial domestic responsibilities. The division of labour is one in which the well-being of the family is seen to be dependent on the wife and mother carrying out to the full her domestic responsibilities. Even though a woman may work outside the home, and even work full-time; even though it is increasingly recognized that women are a crucial part of the workforce of the country and that their wage is essential to the economic well-being of the family; still her main role is perceived as being in the home, just as her husband's main role is perceived as being outside the home as the breadwinner.

2.3   CONCLUSIONS

At the start of this half-unit I said that one of our aims was to look at the differences in life-chances and life experiences between men and women. In many ways, as I have shown, it is difficult to generalize about women's experiences and similar problems emerge in relation to men. However, I think we can nonetheless point to a number of very significant differences:

1   Men's and women's experiences of paid employment are different. There are differences of status, of power, of opportunities for promotion and of pay. The low pay of women is reflected in poverty statistics (you could remind yourself of these by turning back to Section 3 of Unit 3 Part I).

2   Men and women experience the private world of the home differently. Whilst both are involved in the home, women do more domestic and

caring work. Home is seen as another workplace for women rather than a place of relaxation. Most women have to attempt to combine two work-roles in a way which most men do not.

3 Both men and women are constrained by the division of labour we have been describing. Just as it is difficult for a woman to advance in her career in a way she might wish, so it is difficult for a man to participate fully in family life. Each is constrained by the need to conform to their respective gender expectations and there are financial as well as social penalties for those who do not conform.

The picture is not, however, a static one. Even within the very brief period we have been looking at there have been changes and some of them raise quite significant questions about the division of labour. In Section 4 we shall be turning to some explanations for this division of labour and for the changes we have identified. But first we shall make a slight detour to help you to put the picture we've been looking at into historical perspective.

3 GENDER ROLES IN HISTORICAL PERSPECTIVE

This detour takes the form of a quiz. In Section 2 we were trying to build up a picture of the working lives of women and men in one particular historical period, loosely defined as the 1980s and early 1990s. The aim of this section is to sketch in a little of the background to this picture. But it *is* only a little; and furthermore it is *my* selection of what I think are useful questions and answers. So do be prepared to question what I have decided is relevant — and what I have omitted. If this is the first time you have studied this particular subject you may feel a little unsure of the answers. Have a guess at them. The aim of the quiz is not to test your knowledge of British history, but to enable you to build up a picture for yourselves of how women's lives have changed; and to show you how seemingly simple questions can have very complex — and different — answers. In fact, in most cases there is no *one* 'right' answer. Make notes for yourself on why you decided on your answer.

QUIZ

RING THE 'CORRECT' RESPONSE.

1 Britain has been an industrialized country for the past ...

100 years   200 years   400 years

2 The emergence of industrial capitalism in Britain was accompanied by radical and long-lasting changes in the lives of all women.

True or false?

3 The percentage of married women in the workforce in 1911 was:

5%   11%   30%

4 The two World Wars did very little to change women's position.

True or false?

5 'In any measure of social policy in which regard is had to facts, the great majority of married women must be regarded as occupied on work which is vital though unpaid, without which their husbands could not do their paid work, and without which the nation could not continue.'

This statement was made in:

1900   1945   1990

6 Black women who came to Britain in the 1950s, '60s and '70s did so because they were recruited by British employers to do skilled work in Britain.

True or false?

7 The Sex Discrimination Act 1976 had a great impact on women's lives.

True or false?

8 As we move into the twenty-first century we can expect most inequalities between men and women to disappear.

True or false?

1   Britain has been an industrialized country for the past ...

I hope this didn't sound too much like a return to school history books. Social scientists are very aware of the difficulties involved in setting dates to important social processes — certainly we could at this point enter into a long discussion around the meaning of industrialization. I decided to start with this question, however, because we all need to be reminded that this kind of society — an industrialized, urbanized society — is only of recent origin. Britain during the seventeenth century and early eighteenth century was certainly changing in many ways. It is the period between 1780 and 1830, however, which is often identified as the period which marks the emergence of industrial capitalism in Britain. This was the crucial period in the beginning of a gradual changeover from a society where most people worked in agriculture or agriculture-related industries and lived in small villages and towns to a society in which most people worked in industry, primarily as wage labourers, and lived in urban areas.

2   The emergence of industrial capitalism in Britain was accompanied by radical and long-lasting changes in the lives of all women.

This question needs quite a lot of unpacking. Certainly the changes taking place in the economy during the eighteenth century and early nineteenth century had consequences for the lives of everyone. However, the focus here is on one particular change — the increased separation between the private world of the home and the public world of work. During the nineteenth century, work came to be something done outside the home, for a wage, as far as the majority of the population was concerned; and eventually it came to be defined as what *men* did outside the home. The lives of most women consequently became more restricted to the home; the activities they were involved in were domestic activities. They became defined as full-time housewives.

(You will have more opportunities to explore the significance of this when you come to study Block III of this course. But it is important to note how different this situation was from all previous ones. Before the development of industrial capitalism, work was probably best defined as activities of any type which contributed to the survival of the household. Men, women and children were all likely to be involved and although some of this work might have been wage labour it was not necessarily the most significant for a household's well-being, nor necessarily performed by men.)

It is important, however, to be wary of making sweeping generalizations about these changes. The *speed* at which they happened, and the *extent* to which they happened varied across classes.

It was with the middle classes that the separation of home and work, the development of separate spheres for men and women, first took shape. The lives of middle-class women at the beginning of the nineteenth century were becoming increasingly separated from the lives of their husbands. Instead of sharing in the running of the family business, they were retreating into a home-based life where their primary function was to raise children and oversee the running of the house.

As the century progressed, working-class women too began to withdraw from the public sphere. But this took much longer for them. In the early years of the century many women (and children) were working alongside men; and they continued to do so right throughout the first half of the century. The cotton factories, which were being established in the 1830s, were originally staffed mainly by women and children. The most important Factory Acts limiting the working day and occupations of women and children were not until the 1840s. Moreover the idea that a 'woman's place is in the home' simply did not extend to many married women, who *had* to work (Phillips, 1989).

Gradually, however, even if somewhat unevenly, the workforce came to be composed largely of men. Men were defined as the breadwinner, supporting dependent wife and children on a 'family wage'. Consequently, women during the nineteenth century became more dependent and economically vulnerable. (These inequalities extended, of course, beyond women's working lives. Even in the late nineteenth century women did not have the vote, they had few civil or legal rights, and they suffered from restricted educational opportunities.)

3   The percentage of married women in the workforce in 1911 was:

The percentage of married women officially in the workforce in 1911 was 11 per cent. Only married women who had to work outside the home to survive — those with husbands who were unemployed or earning very low wages — were left in the workforce by the end of the nineteenth century. The only exceptions to this pattern were those areas of the country where women have always been an important part of the workforce as in the cotton factories of Lancashire.

However, it is important to note that we are only talking here about married women. Single, working-class women had always worked outside the home. Right through the nineteenth century large numbers of them, mainly young, worked in domestic service: in 1911, 35 per cent of 14–18 year old girls were in domestic service. Single women were also beginning to work in the new types of office work that were emerging towards the end of the century. In addition, by the beginning of the twentieth century middle-class, single women had begun to gain entry into the professions, following very determined action in the second half of the nineteenth century to open up a range of educational opportunities for them.

4   The two World Wars did very little to change women's position.

This question is best answered in two parts. On the one hand there is no doubt that *during* both wars there were quite dramatic changes in that women were encouraged out of the home and into production. This happened both in 1914 and in 1939. Women in 1914 moved into male civilian jobs (shop assistants, bus drivers, bank clerks and jobs in industry). In 1939 women were again encouraged into production with the corresponding provision of crèche facilities.

In some ways the working lives of women were different *after* each war too. Certainly new employment opportunities were opening up for women in the 1920s, with the growth of office and shop work. Similarly, there were new opportunities for employment in the period after the Second World War with the expansion of part-time work. Part-time work had been virtually unknown before the war and many of the part-time jobs created by the state in the service sector (in teaching, nursing and clerical work) were taken up by married women.

On the other hand, however, it seems that very little changed in the years after each war. The 1920s and '30s were marked by a closing off of some employment opportunities for women. For example the 'marriage bar' (which debarred women upon marriage) was introduced into the civil service and teaching in the 1920s and it was revived in domestic service after the war. During the 1930s it continued to be the norm for women to stop work when they married. A non-working wife was a mark of family status.

Similarly the late 1940s and '50s, after the Second World War, were marked by a renewed emphasis on men's and women's 'traditional' roles. Family life was expected to return to normal — women to their 'natural' roles. This was the period when the term 'maternal deprivation' became used to denote ways in which, it was claimed, both individual and social well-being might be adversely affected if early bonding between a child and its mother did not take place. (The name most closely associated with this approach is John Bowlby, a psychoanalyst whose work on the effects of maternal deprivation on child development became the focus of study and discussion after the late 1940s.)

So in 1955, out of a workforce of 21.5 million, only 7.5 million were women, and fewer than half of these were married: i.e. in 1955 a high proportion of married women were still full-time housewives.

5 **'In any measure of social policy in which regard is had to facts, the great majority of married women must be regarded as occupied on work which is vital though unpaid, without which their husbands could not do their paid work, and without which the nation could not continue.'**

This is William Beveridge, often seen as the person most responsible for developing the rationale for the 'welfare state' in the UK, in 1942; and it is one of the statements underpinning the welfare legislation of the late war and immediate post-war years. The intention of the Labour government 1945–51 was to improve the position of the family, and to do this through securing the position of women in the family. The institutions and legislation of the post-war welfare state (for example, the system of tax and social security) were built on the assumption that men were the family breadwinners and that wives and children were their economic dependants. Motherhood was defined as a labour of love, private and unpaid.

6 **Black women who came to Britain in the 1950s, '60s and '70s did so because they were recruited by British employers to do skilled work in Britain.**

This is partly true. Many of the Afro-Caribbean women who came to Britain in the 1950s came as a result of recruitment campaigns by, for example, London

Transport and the National Health Service. There was intensive advertising in the West Indies during this period for skilled workers who were in short supply in Britain. There was, however, a more general labour shortage as well. So the black women who came to Britain in the 1950s fell into two large work categories — those who had been specially recruited for their professional skills, such as nurses, and those who entered low-skilled, low-paid manual work for which there was no competition from any men (whatever their ethnic origin) or from white women.

However, as you saw in Unit 7, Asian women (from India, Pakistan and Bangladesh) who came to Britain in the 1960s and '70s, were for the most part coming as the dependants of Asian men who had arrived earlier (in the 1950s); they were not coming in response to any kind of recruitment drive. Nor were the East African Asian women who arrived with their families in the 1970s, but were fleeing from the political situation in East Africa.

7   The Sex Discrimination Act 1976 had a great impact on women's lives.

It is certainly the case that many more opportunities did seem to be opening up for women in the 1970s. For a start, more women were working outside the home. In 1976, 25 per cent of all children under 5, and 40 per cent under 11, had mothers in employment, but mostly part-time. There was by now a general acceptance that married women would be employed until the birth of the first child and that they would return to work part-time when not occupied full-time with childcare.

Other changes were taking place too during the 1960s and '70s. To name just a few:

- More girls were entering higher education, particularly after the Robbins Report (1965) had identified girls as one of the 'untapped pools of ability'.

- Although the changes in family life were not as pronounced as those commentators who heralded the arrival of the 'egalitarian' family would have liked to believe, there were certainly signs of change in family life, changes which did mean a lessening of inequalities.

- Along with other disadvantaged or marginalized groups, women seemed to be becoming more powerful and gaining a voice. This was the time of the re-emergence of feminism, as well as of gay rights and black power.

However, to explain *why* these changes were taking place in the 1960s and '70s is difficult. The fact that in some ways women's position started to improve *before* the equal opportunities legislation of the 1970s, and the fact that in some ways there was a retreat during the Thatcher years of the 1980s, suggests that legislation is not the whole answer.

8   As we move into the twenty-first century we can expect most inequalities between men and women to disappear.

This question is almost impossible to answer. There is certainly no right answer and the reason for this is very important, not only in terms of your understanding of gender divisions, but also in terms of your own development as social scientists.

The task of the social scientist is to describe and explain; to understand more thoroughly what is happening (and has happened) in society; to answer the 'why' questions that we all ask — but in a more rigorous way; and possibly to use the answers to these 'why' questions as a starting-point for thinking about what is going to happen in the future.

So far, all we have done is to *describe* the divisions of labour in society, not to attempt to explain it. We have shown that:

1   There is a division of labour in Britain today which results in men and women having different life-chances and life experiences (Section 1).

2   This division of labour has certainly been in existence for the past two hundred years although the extent of the difference between men and women's activities has varied from one period to another and also from one group to another (Section 2).

We have not yet, however, asked any 'why' questions. For example: *Why* did women increasingly withdraw from the public sphere in the nineteenth century? *Why* did employment opportunities for women improve in the 1960s? *Why* does the state emphasize so strongly women's 'natural' role as carers? So, on the basis of the work we have done so far, we cannot think clearly about whether or not inequalities will lessen in the future.

In the next section, however, we do go on to address these 'why' questions. We shall be moving away from the *description* of gender divisions which has formed the subject matter so far, to attempts to *explain* them. I am not promising that by the end of this section you will be able to predict what women's lives will be like in the twenty-first century. But you will be more aware of the possible answers and of the complexity of the question.

4   EXPLANATIONS

Why do we have a division of labour between men and women? Why does it take the form it does? How long has it been in existence? And why is it still in existence?

We are going to look in this section at a range of theories which each offer explanations for the gender divisions that so far we have simply been describing. Of course, as you know already from the work you have done in Block I, facts and theories cannot really be distinguished as simply as this. A particular theory will direct your attention to some 'facts' and not to others. Furthermore theories themselves are dependent on the facts we have at our disposal. However, for the moment it will help you to think of this section as a kind of jump in the work you are doing. You are moving from the less obviously disputable areas of facts to the much more disputable area of explanations. In addition, an important part of your work here will be to assess the strengths and weaknesses of each framework as a way of explaining the divisions we have been looking at so far.

One important point should be made at this juncture. As this is a social science course, it is not my intention here to explore in detail the enormous range of work that looks at the biological differences between men and women. The extent to which there exist genetic, physiological, hormonal and psychological differences is a huge area of study in itself. Moreover whilst some differences are undisputed, the evidence by and large seems to be contradictory and certainly far too complex for us to examine here.

What is important, however, for us as social scientists to recognize, is the complexity of the link between the biological and the social. Even if differences between men and women can be proved to exist in certain areas, it is still not the case that these biological differences *in themselves* can account for differences of behaviour, or of life experiences, in any given society. At the end of the day what matters is the whole social context within which these differences are situated. If, for example, there were to be increasing evidence that men are more 'aggressive' than women (and this is one of the differences that is increasingly interesting those involved in this area of research, and is a matter of substantial controversy), it still would not be possible to use this evidence *on its own* to explain why there are very few women boxers, why domestic violence more often involves aggression by the man rather than the woman, why it is males who generally make up the fighting forces of a society, why more women than men are involved in the teaching and nursing professions. For a full explanation we would need to look at the society itself — its institutions, values, and in particular the sets of interpretations, meanings and definitions that guide people's behaviour. We cannot simply jump from basic biological differences to the complex differences displayed in the social world.

We need to start, then, with the differences between 'sex' and 'gender'. 'Sex' refers to being biologically male or female — to having male or female genitals and to the ways in which we develop anatomically in certain predictable ways. Sex can be distinguished at birth or even earlier. 'Gender' refers to the social characteristics of masculinity and femininity — what it means in a particular society to be a man or a woman. It is based on cultural expectations and is adaptable. Women in different societies may perform very different roles and behave differently; and, as we saw in Section 3, there have been changes in women's roles and behaviour over a period of time even within Britain. These historical and cultural variations demonstrate the extent to which differences are *socially* constructed.

We shall, then, be looking at explanations which emphasize that the differences between men's and women's lives need to be understood as *socially* constructed. (This is taking you right back to the arguments that Stuart Hall presented in Unit 6 and you might find it useful at this point to re-read quickly Section 1 of Unit 6, 'Making sense of "the social"'.) We shall be looking in this section at three theories, each of which provides an explanation of gender divisions. These theories are all *feminist* theories in the sense that they have developed out of the body of thought and social movement known as 'feminism', rather than directly out of one of the four traditions you have been working with so far in D103. (It might thus be useful here to consider the definition of feminism. In the D103 *Glossary* feminism is defined as: 'Feminism: a body of thought and a social movement which rests on the acceptance of the underlying equality of the sexes. It incorporates a historical analysis of the oppression of women and the restriction of women's roles in society. There are different viewpoints within feminism (e.g. Marxist, liberal, radical) (*see also* gender, patriarchy).')

However, two of the theories do draw closely on one or more of the traditions you have met in D103: liberal feminist explanations draw on social reformism and liberalism; marxist feminist explanations draw on marxism. There are also links between those explanations which focus on biological differences between men and women and the conservative tradition with its emphasis on 'women's place is in the home'. So you should try to relate as much as possible your study of these feminist theories to your work on the traditions.

I will give you the main outlines of each theory and then ask you to note its strengths and weaknesses. We shall be doing more of this 'assessing' work in Unit 9 so all I want you to do at this stage is to ask yourself how much the theory explains and how much it cannot explain. Can it explain some of the patterns we have been looking at in Section 2 of this half-unit? Can it explain some of the changes we identified in Section 3? Can it account for those aspects of gender divisions which *you* are most aware of in your own life? Is it an explanation which is applicable to *all* women in *all* societies? I will give you my own assessment after each Activity but you will find it helps if you jot down your own ideas *before* going on to read what I have to say.

4.1 LIBERAL FEMINIST EXPLANATIONS

As you saw in Unit 5, central to liberalism in general are ideas of the autonomy of the individual, equality of opportunity, open competition, and personal freedom and choice — for men and women. These ideas have informed the analysis of many of those working in the past, and present, to improve women's position in society. For early 'feminist' writers (Mary Wollstonecraft is one example) inequalities existed because men were educated and economically independent and because women, restricted to a domestic sphere, lacked very basic legal, political and educational rights. In the 1990s we can see the same kinds of explanations at work. Attempts to increase the percentage of women in parliament, to encourage more girls and women to study science subjects and to persuade ecclesiastical hierarchies to ordain women are all working within a similar explanatory framework. According to this argument, gender divisions exist because we do not have equal opportunities. They exist because of individual prejudice and discrimination. They exist because we have not yet tried hard enough to get rid of them. They are a result, it is assumed, of being unenlightened and not yet extending to women the chances open to men.

From this perspective what is needed to remove the inequalities, then, is more 'positive action', including legislation, so that women can enjoy the same freedom of choice as men. These are the ideas which have underlain, and still do underlie, many of the efforts made by women to improve their position in

Minister attacks slow progress for women

WOMEN face "glass walls" as well as glass ceilings to hinder their progress up career ladders, Gillian Shephard, the Employment Secretary, said yesterday on the first anniversary of the Opportunity 2000 campaign.

Mrs Shephard welcomed the fact that companies covering more than a quarter of the workforce have signed up with Opportunity 2000, which was set up by the Business in the Community charity last year to encourage employers to meet measurable targets for increasing opportunities for women. But corporate Britain was slow at tackling outdated and unfair treatment of women at work.

"Progress is being made, but almost everywhere you look an all too familiar picture still emerges," Mrs Shephard said. "The simple fact is that in many professions and at many levels women are not taking a fair share of the opportunities available. There are no-go areas, occupations which are automatically assumed to be the province of men, and there are areas where women make up the majority of the workforce but are segregated at the bottom."

She complained that only 3 per cent of university and polytechnic lecturers, 15 per cent of medical consultants, 2 per cent of chartered engineers, 10 per cent of accountants and 4 per cent of senior business managers were women. Mrs Shephard said it was "startling that men are 50 per cent more likely to have had job-related training than women" and she announced a plan for regional "opportunity shops" in the new year to provide information and training for women.

The Opportunity 2000 campaign, chaired by Lady Howe and launched with much razzmatazz by the Prime Minister in the run-up to the general election, has increased its group of 61 founding employers to 141, covering both the public and private sectors and including banks, government departments, industrial conglomerates and universities.

Its first year report shows that member companies — many of which already had relatively good equal opportunities records — have adopted measures to improve employment practices, such as flexible work arrangements, positive action on recruitment, common terms and conditions, better childcare, action to reduce sexual harassment and encouragement to return to work.

But the report reveals that in many cases a formal commitment to equal opportunities at the top has failed to translate into change lower down the organisation. "More work needs to be done to encourage line managers' commitment to equal opportunities," the report says. "There is clearly still a lot of communication work left to do both inside organisations and out . . . many organisations recognise that the Opportunity 2000 message has not filtered down." The report argues that changes in corporate culture and "family-friendly practices" are vital to improving employment practices.

Marjorie Mowlam, Labour's spokeswoman for women's issues, said the Opposition welcomed Opportunity 2000. "But . . . the central limitation is that it wholly ignores the issue of women's pay. A few higher paid women in an organisation will not solve the problem of women's pay inequality. Trickle down equality policies are simply not enough."

Source: *The Guardian*, 18 November 1992

society. They underlay the struggles of the nineteenth-century activists for women's rights to university education and to enter the professions. They are the ideas, too, which underlie much current equal opportunities legislation and other kinds of action.

One example of a contemporary initiative is Opportunity 2000 which is explained and commented on in the article on the previous page.

—————————————— ACTIVITY 4 ——————————————

1   What are the strengths of liberal feminist explanations?

2   What are the weaknesses?

There is little doubt that in many ways these seem to provide an adequate explanation for gender divisions. Looked at in one way the story of the past one hundred years is very much one of women gaining increasing equality as entrenched attitudes and discriminatory laws are challenged. Opportunity 2000 is just one example of the way in which patterns of inequality may be changed by this kind of positive action.

Looking at the article through a different pair of spectacles, however, we can identify strong elements of disquiet. There is also a suggestion that not much has changed or is really going to change (and this can be paralleled in other spheres — in relation to attempts to increase the percentage of women MPs, for example).

This brings us to what some see as a major weakness of liberal theory. At the heart of any assessment of liberal explanations must be a critique of liberalism itself — the way in which it starts with the individual and makes the assumption that change can be brought about with enough time and commitment and individual effort; that prejudice is a matter of attitudes, and change comes through simply changing these attitudes. Liberalism ignores the much wider and deeper question to do, not just with the existence of unequal opportunities, but with why these differences exist in the first place and why they persist and are maintained.

To answer these questions we need to look at the structure of society, and the unequal distribution of power which is inherent in this structure. (You might find it useful to turn back at this point to Section 4 of Unit 6 where Stuart Hall identifies the three key dimensions of a society's structure.) We need to look beyond the attitudes, actions and initiatives of groups or individuals in which we are aware, to the processes and relationships that lie beneath the surface.

The key concept in relation to gender divisions is *patriarchy*. We shall explore the nature and significance of patriarchy more fully below, but you should note here that 'patriarchy' refers to the *systematic* nature of men's power over women; the way in which this power is embedded in, and reinforced by, all the institutions and organizations of society, and the way it operates regardless of the wishes or actions of any one group or individual.

We are now going to examine explanations which look at the nature and origins of patriarchy. However, although bound by a common concern, they differ in approach and particularly in terms of where they locate the roots of patriarchy. Very broadly marxist feminist explanations see patriarchy as having its roots in capitalism, whilst radical feminists see patriarchy as existing far more 'in its own right'. It is these two approaches, and the differences between them, which form the core of the work you need to do in this section. We shall start with the way in which feminists have been able to apply marxist analysis to understanding the form taken by the sexual division of labour, and move on to those explanations which work from the premise that patriarchy has a far more substantial life of its own than marxist feminism would suggest. However, you do need to be aware that the theories do not lend themselves easily to hard-and-fast divisions; furthermore they are continually developing and changing, as I shall show later.

4.2   MARXIST FEMINIST EXPLANATIONS

As we saw in Unit 7, marxist explanations in general are those which start from the fact that we live in a capitalist society and that central to the workings of capitalism is the need to maintain and indeed increase (accumulate) profits from production. It is this which is central to both the organization of production and the way in which labour is used. Explanations of any division in society, then, have capitalism and the needs, or interests of, capital as their starting-point. Class is the main division in society and all other divisions can be explained in terms of the way they relate to class divisions.

Within this basic set of ideas, marxist analysis is always changing, and being reworked as society itself changes. Furthermore, of those who work within the marxist tradition, not all have applied marxist ideas to the analysis of gender divisions. (Indeed, it was precisely the reluctance of many marxists in the 1960s and '70s to take account of gender that resulted in the development of alternative explanatory frameworks, as you will see below.) However, what marxist feminists have shown is that answers to questions about women's inequality *can* come from within the marxist tradition.

One of the earliest and most significant marxist feminists was Sheila Rowbotham. The extract below, taken from *Woman's Consciousness, Man's World*, introduces the key concepts which continue to direct the work of marxist feminists:

> ... the sexual division of labour means that men and women are at different points in the structure of social relationships. Men as a group have a different relation from women as a group to the means of production. Women enter commodity production, and, like men, produce goods which circulate as commodities; they thus share the exploitation and experience of alienation of male workers in capitalism. But, because within the social division of labour in capitalism the task of maintaining and reproducing commodity producers is largely given to women, the expenditure of female labour power in procreation and in the nourishing of men and children at home determines how much female labour can be expended in the production of commodities.
>
> (Rowbotham, 1973, pp.58–9)

As you can see, the concern of marxist feminists is with women in relation to the means of production, and specifically to the form this relationship takes under commodity production. (If you remember, the development of capitalism as a system of commodity production was one of the main stories of Unit 1.) So what are these relationships? How are women involved in production?

The development of industrial capitalism involved — as I showed in Section 3 — the separation of home and work, the creation of distinctions between the private world of the home and the public world of production. It involved, according to marxist feminists, the development of a sexual division of labour whereby, as Rowbotham says, 'men as a group have a different relation from women as a group to the means of production'. It was men who came primarily to be most involved in production outside the home. Women came to have the primary responsibility for what happened *inside* the home (even though, of course, as we have seen, this responsibility has often been combined with a role as wage-earner).

Describing the sexual division of labour in this way immediately gives rise to two questions. First of all, why is woman's role in the home so important within a capitalist society? Secondly, how can marxist analysis, which tends to concentrate on production in the public sphere, claim to address the experience of women when much of that experience is outside the realms of production? The answers to both these questions are contained within the Rowbotham extract.

One reason why women's role in the home is so important to capitalism relates to the need of capital for a workforce which is cheap and flexible. Women workers do share the 'exploitation and experience of alienation' of male workers, but there is also a long history of women working for lower pay than men because they have not traditionally been seen as the main breadwinners of a family. The notion that women only work for 'pin money' has taken a long time to die and it has clearly been a notion that it has not been in the interest of employers to challenge. In addition, women provide a *flexible* workforce. Women workers are available as a 'reserve army of labour' which is readily available to be pulled into the labour force during times of economic expansion (or, for instance, in times of war), yet can be pushed out with very little bother if, during periods of recession, their labour is not needed (Breugel, 1979). Women are easily 'disposable'. They can be easily re-absorbed into the home when necessary, possibly without even adding to unemployment figures, certainly with no great upsurge of national disquiet. All that is needed is a re-affirmation of women's 'true' role as 'homemaker'.

However, women are important to capitalism, not only as workers directly involved in production but also because of their role in the home 'maintaining and reproducing commodity producers'. Women are responsible for making sure that the labour force is maintained in size and quality. This means not only giving birth plus all the associated acitivities of child-rearing, instilling values and safeguarding the health of the *future* workforce, but also means being actively involved in maintaining the *present* workforce. Women 'service', at very low cost to capital, the men who form the bulk of the wage labour. If women were not available in the home, capital itself would have to bear these subsistence costs. Women's unpaid domestic labour thus contributes indirectly to capitalist accumulation.

So far we have stayed very firmly within the analysis offered by Rowbotham in the extract above. It is important, however, at this juncture to point out one way in which marxist feminist analysis has moved on or developed since she wrote *Woman's Consciousness, Man's World*. The key concept here is 'reproduction'. 'Reproduction' usually refers to the processes of procreation. In recent years, however, marxist feminists have widened the usage of the term to refer to *all* the activities carried out by women in the home to maintain the future and existing workforce — cooking, cleaning, serving the sexual and emotional needs of men, as well as childbirth and child-rearing. Furthermore, with the increasing recognition of the importance of this 'reproductive labour' to the whole productive process, strong arguments are now advanced for extending the idea of production to include reproduction. The unpaid reproductive labour which mostly women do in the private sphere of the home, it is argued, is as much part of the productive processes of a society as what men or women do as paid work in factories or offices in the public sphere ('productive labour'). ('Reproductive' and 'productive' labour are, however, closely related. Attempts to understand the nature of the divide between the two have been at the forefront of much marxist feminist analyses of recent years. You will have the opportunity to explore this divide further in Unit 10 of Block III.)

I hope that you have been able to pull out from this analysis answers to the two questions I set out near the start of this section. Women's role in the home is important for capital because it ensures a cheap, flexible, healthy and well-disciplined workforce. Marxist feminists address women's experiences in the home, as well as their experiences as members of the labour force, precisely because of this. What they do in the home — their 'reproductive labour' – makes a direct contribution to the economy.

Women are, then, according to marxist feminists, doubly exploited both as producers *and* reproducers primarily in the interests of capital. Any questions about how to bring about changes in this situation would need to address primarily the way we organize production in our society and women's role in those productive processes.

ACTIVITY 5

What are the strengths of marxist feminist explanations?
What are the weaknesses?

There are aspects of the division of labour which do seem to be explained in a very adequate way by this kind of framework. In particular, it provides a very reasonable explanation for the existence of what all frameworks recognize to be crucial in understanding women's experiences — the division between production and reproduction, the *public* and the *private*. These divisions are seen to be an integral part of the development of industrial capitalism whereby *waged* labour, work engaged in outside the home for employers, became the main source of income for most families.

Also, by focusing on the needs of capital, it can explain the diversity of women's experiences which we identified in Section 2. Women of different classes, different ethnic groups (and different parts of the UK too, as you will see when you study Block VI) do not have the same life experiences and life-chances. This can be understood in terms of the different roles they play in the labour process and in terms of how capital uses groups of women in different ways according to the needs of the economy.

Finally, marxist feminist analysis can offer explanations for changes in women's work roles. For example, the vast increase in the numbers of women at work in the 1960s can be understood in terms of the needs of an expanding economy for more workers. The feminization and potential feminization of the workforce that we referred to in Section 2 can be understood in terms of the present 'restructuring' of the labour market towards more flexible, temporary workers as economic conditions change. (You will be able to go into this more fully in Block III.)

Marxist analysis does, however, have a number of weaknesses. The first major problem is that a very simplistic marxist explanation implies that gender divisions are a direct product of the way production is organized, along capitalistic lines. It is in fact clear, however, that gender divisions predate capitalism and, as the articles on the opposite page show, are a feature of other societies which are not capitalist.

The second major problem is that there are limits to the range of women's experiences which can be explained by this framework. Women experience oppression in many different ways, and an analysis which starts from class and capitalism may not be able to take account of all of these. It is not clear, for example, how a marxist feminist analysis can *fully* explain the significance of

Impoverished queens of the mountain kingdom

AN AID project was delighted with a new bean it had introduced to Lesotho. It grew well, it had high nutritional value and the farmers were delighted. Then a woman pointed out that it took too long to cook and they didn't have any fuel.

The anecdote is recounted by Idriss Jazairy, the Algerian diplomat who heads the UN's International Fund for Agriculture and Development (Ifad). The moral of the tale is simple: no one cuts through theory more quickly than a woman; and no agricultural project will work in Lesotho unless women are involved. Ifad, with an annual budget of $3.1 billion, aims to help the rural poor. But a review in 1985 of its 160 projects found that only 38 per cent of them were benefiting women.

A big shift in emphasis followed, and women are now seen as Africa's best hope. The development agencies have discovered women are a good bet: they repay credit, they're good at business and, importantly, they invest extra income in the family — unlike men. Throughout sub-Saharan Africa women are producing 90 per cent of the food, they work twice as hard as men and the number of women-headed households is rising.

Nowhere are these facts better illustrated than in the tiny, mountainous kingdom of Lesotho, landlocked by South Africa. Rakoloi is a small cluster of mud-baked round huts in an expanse of drought-dried fields where the maize stalks of a failed harvest still rustle. Nine widows and one man gather, with blankets pinned around their shoulders in the cool winter breeze, to tell how their trials with Ifad's new method of ploughing — designed to save water and stop soil erosion — has been ruined by the drought.

The season before last Rakoloi had the best maize crop in the country. This season, encouraged by early rains, villagers raided their savings to plant all the seed they could. But they haven't enough maize until the next harvest, nor do they know where the seed will come from for the next planting. It's not panic on their worn faces, but a slow, dull resignation to the cruel blows Lesotho's unpredictable climate deals them.

Asked why there are not more men in the group, they laugh. Mathabiso Mphasa, mother of six and caring for six grandchildren, said: "They're slow to understand new things, they like to argue and waste time. They don't like hard work."

Seventy-two per cent of Lesotho households are headed by women, partly because 95,000 men work in the South African mines. But even those that don't work in the mines have little inclination for "women's work" — the painstaking cultivation of the scattered strips of land.

Lesotho does not produce enough to feed its 1.3 million population and the shortfall is growing. Women of Mathabiso's age remember how they could often store 42 kg of grain after each harvest. Crop yields have dropped dramatically as millions of tons of soil are washed away every year. She doesn't know what to do. Fertiliser may help, but it is so expensive.

Fertiliser cannot combat Lesotho's climate, a catastrophic cocktail of drought, torrential rain storms and strong winds. Drought kills the plant life that

could protect the soil and the rains carve 12-foot gullies into the slopes, cutting fields into ribbons. Nearly 30,000 gullies in the Lesotho lowlands have destroyed acres of productive land.

In the mountains — about 90 per cent of Lesotho is above 1,800 metres — the soil has been washed away to expose patches of bare rock. Cattle, kept as a traditional form of investment, have overgrazed communal pastures.

The expansion of South Africa forced the Basotho into the highlands. This austerely beautiful but fragile environment is snow-covered in winter and crops are frequently hit by early frosts. The land simply cannot sustain the human and animal population, and one aid project after another has failed as the country lurches from crisis to crisis. South Africa benefits, exporting the food Lesotho needs. The Pretoria government provides 97 per cent of Lesotho's imports and 100 per cent of its energy.

"I feel a fraud," Letla Mosenene, the agro-forestry officer, said on hearing Mathabiso's story. "Every year we don't reach the harvest we expect. There's always an excuse: frost, drought. But that's Lesotho and I'm paid to come up with solutions."

Ifad's Special Programme for Africa aims to devise simple and effective means of increasing agricultural yields, conserving water and stopping erosion. But Lesotho has no money for expensive, imported technologies. "If people are reluctant to take part in a project, then it is not making commercial sense to them and we have to go back to the drawing board," Bahman Mansuri, Ifad's Africa director, says.

But Mathabiso's "ripping" has proved so effective her neighbours are copying her. A ripping plough cuts below the normal water penetration level, breaking up the soil and helping water seep through. Ifad loans the ripper plough and provides seed and fertiliser, while Mathabiso must save manure for the fields instead of using it as fuel. Ifad's

efforts to prevent soil erosion on communal grazing lands have been less successful.

Animals from Ha Mosa used to graze on the hillside above the village but the soil has been so badly eroded there's little grass left. Malankisi Moleleki and a group of women enlisted Ifad's help to plant grasses and trees. It was going well until a neighbouring village disputed their right to the land and sent its cattle to graze on the new plants. The project has been halted while the dispute goes to court.

Farming is a precarious livelihood but there is little industry and few indigenous crafts to supplement family incomes. In the southern province of Quthing Ifad is helping women to find alternative ways of earning money. It has loaned money for sewing machines, wool and shoe leather. But it is a struggle finding customers, says Emily Machachamise, who runs a sewing group. Mass-produced clothing from South Africa, which is sold in the markets, always undercuts locally produced goods.

The Basotho now have a taste for patent leather, heels and fancy buckles, which leaves Mabohlokoa Sekotlo with few customers for her soft, hand-made moccasins. But there are some successes: Makhethisa Mokhosi has learnt to knit beautiful jumpers, which are exported to the Netherlands and Germany. One woman has earnt enough from her sewing to send a child to college and two children to secondary school.

This kind of grass-roots micro-development is laborious work. The success stories hearten the aid workers but are dwarfed by the thousands still trapped in a set of historical, environmental and political circumstances which consign them to a grinding poverty.

Source: *The Guardian*, 5 November 1992

Third-class citizens

WOMEN stand on the frontline in the struggle against environmental degradation. As deserts spread through overgrazing, as soil is eroded because of intensive farming and poor conservation methods, and as forests are felled for commercial sales, cash cropping or construction projects, so women spend more time foraging for food and fuel and fetching water.

Women in the developing world perform these tasks day after day, year after year. According to Ifad, the crisis for rural women has reached alarming proportions: 565 million women are living in poverty. Poverty for rural men has risen by 3 per cent over the past 20 years; for women the increase has been 48 per cent.

Yet in rural areas of the developing world, women are often denied ownership of the land they work. In Islamic law women's rights to land are clearly defined, but the threat of divorce and other sanctions force women to pass control of the land to men. Even when women have rights to certain fields their responsibilities will include helping in their husbands' field — as well as looking after the family.

In Africa, the trend is going against women, as they work harder and their status

as secondary to men shows little sign of changing. Women rarely own or inherit land. In 10 African countries women and children constitute 77 per cent of the population. But they have a legal right to own property in only 16 per cent of the households in those 10 countries.

The fragility of our world becomes more apparent daily. It is the poor who live in the areas under greatest threat — where it rains least and where survival is hardest. And yet, over the years, the people's need to make a living from the land has been ignored by those who thought they knew better.

The truth is that population control and its environmental implications depends on the reduction of child death rates. This will only come when parents feel confident about health, education and survival for themselves and their family.

Whatever we say about birth control and however much is spent on propaganda, women and men cannot see any personal advantage in having smaller families. On the contrary, when children are the only future means of support, control of family size is seen as a source of poverty not wealth.

Glenys Kinnock is chairwoman of One World Action.

Source: *The Guardian*, 5 November 1992

A woman's work is never done … the matriarchs of Rakoloi, a Lesotho village of mud-baked huts, must cope with sexual apartheid as well as southern Africa's worst drought for 50 years

pornography or other forms of violence against women; or the extent to which women are marginalized in other spheres of life — the religious, for example, or the arts — which have little to do with production.

4.3   RADICAL FEMINIST EXPLANATIONS

At the same time as many feminists were attempting to extend marxist analysis, the 'second wave' of feminism was giving rise to a set of explanatory concepts which had a different starting-point and focus from the marxist emphasis on class and capitalism. The starting-point for radical feminism was precisely the way in which marxist thought of the early 1970s was dominated by men and male concerns.

Whilst agreeing with marxist feminists that gender divisions are about struggles, power and oppression, radical feminists argue that gender divisions cannot be understood simply as a form of the class divisions of capitalism. They need to be explored and explained in their own right, as separate lines of division. The key concept in this kind of explanation is *patriarchy*, rather than capitalism. Nearly all known societies, according to this perspective, have been patriarchal and this should therefore be the starting-point for explaining the differential experiences of men and women. From this perspective the gender divisions and specifically the sexual division of labour can be understood in terms of the way it serves, not primarily the needs and interests of a capitalist system, but the needs and interests of men.

What, then, is meant by 'patriarchy' and 'patriarchical'?

Below is an extract from *Sexual Politics* by Kate Millett, a figure as significant for the emergence and development of radical feminism as is Sheila Rowbotham for marxist feminism:

> What goes largely unexamined, often even unacknowledged (yet is institutionalized nonetheless) in our social order, is the birthright priority whereby males rule females. Through this system a most ingenious form of 'interior colonization' has been achieved. It is one which tends moreover to be sturdier than any form of segregation, and more rigorous than class stratification, more uniform, certainly more enduring. However muted its present appearance may be, sexual dominion obtains nevertheless as perhaps the most pervasive ideology of our culture and provides its most fundamental concept of power.
>
> This is so because our society, like all other historical civilizations, is a patriarchy. The fact is evident at once if one recalls that the military, industry, technology, universities, science, political office and finance — in short, every avenue of power within the society, including the coercive force of the police, is entirely in male hands.
>
> (Millett, 1970, pp.24–5)

As you can see, Millett is stating very clearly here the case for studying gender divisions in their own right. The relations whereby men dominate women are, she argues, 'sturdier', 'more rigorous', 'more enduring' than any other system of relationships. Furthermore, they exist not just in people's lived experience but also inside their heads; they have been thoroughly internalized (this is what she means by 'interior colonization') and this gives them even more strength.

Patriarchies are societies in which men have power over women. They are characterized by patterns of male dominance and decision-making, by the systematic exclusion or closing off against women by those who exercise power. According to Millett patriarchy is universal. It characterizes every known society (although the form it takes will vary in its expression) and it characterizes every aspect of life in all societies. She reminds us that 'every avenue of power in a society ... is essentially within male hands'. Thus the power structures of law courts, schools, parliament, state, financial empires, armed forces, belief systems are patriarchal. Furthermore, patriarchy — according to radical feminists — is also embedded in scholarship, in arts, literature and social science. It is even embedded in language (Spender, 1980).

Millett makes it clear that what we are talking about here — patriarchy — is a *systematic* set of social relationships through which men maintain power over women. This means that we are not talking about individual people's achievements or inclinations. So, for example, having a few women in decision-making posts makes very little difference. The women who occupy such posts accept and reinforce patriarchy through their decision-making because the whole system is patriarchal. Similarly, although this is not an argument developed strongly by Millett, the fact that some men do not want power over women need not serve to weaken the radical feminist argument. Men, too, can be victims of patriarchy: 'Men (especially white ones) do have more than their fair share of power at the expense of women. Yet there are some men who do not want power, who do not know how to get rid of it, and who do not know what to do about it' (Murphy, 1989, p.360).

How, then, have men acquired this power? How have they managed to maintain it? How might radical feminists be expected to work to change patriarchal systems?

One way, they argue, of understanding how and why patriarchy developed might be to look at the way in which women's reproductive function has made them dependent on men. The fact that until recently in all societies women spent a large part of their lives in child-bearing has enabled men to gain control over them. Moreover, even today in the UK, although women's lives are not dominated to such a large extent by childbirth and child-rearing, the technology which has 'freed' them as well as the decision-making power over that technology are still in men's hands. For example, scientific research into contraception is for the most part controlled by men; more men than women occupy the most powerful positions in all medical hierarchies including obstetrics.

An extension of this explanation is one of cultural control — that men have gained control of women through laws, custom, myths and ideologies which result in women behaving in ways that suit men's interests. Primarily this means women serving men's needs within the family — an example of this cultural control from Western society would be the idea of 'romantic love' which some would argue leads women to want, and then to accept, a way of life which

The cabinet of the UK Conservative government, April 1991: there was protest at the absence of any women in John Major's first Cabinet. By September 1993 there were two.

does very little to serve their own interests but which rather fulfils men's needs. But it may also refer to what happens in the workplace. Paid work, too, is a site of patriarchy with the same processes of cultural control at work. At work, women are largely defined as different from, and subordinate to, men. These definitions create and maintain power divisions. They serve to further men's interests in the workplace. For example, there has always been, in most industries, a distinction between men's jobs and women's jobs, with the work that men do being defined as 'skilled'. The nature of these jobs and the differences between men's and women's jobs may change with technological progress. But divisions will be maintained and with them the definitions which justify men's higher pay, higher status etc.

Alongside this focus on cultural control there has developed, not unexpectedly, a concern on the part of radical feminists with the re-evaluation of what is distinctively feminine. The emphasis in recent years has not been on what prevents women from being equal to men but on understanding where women's strengths lie. This entails re-evaluating the many spheres of women's experience which have been defined away, or put into second place, by men and in exploring ways in which women can become autonomous, powerful beings in their own right (Rich, 1979, 1980). These are the theoretical concerns and ideas which have helped, for example, to make male violence a public issue and which, for instance, play a part in the increasing recognition of women's creativity.

So the way forward for radical feminists is not necessarily the same as for marxist feminists. If the key to understanding women's experiences is the power relations by which men dominate women, then it is these relations, and all the different ways in which they are supported, which need to be challenged.

─────────────── ACTIVITY 6 ───────────────

What are the strengths of radical feminist explanations?
What are their weaknesses?

───

Like marxist feminist analysis these explanations do provide answers to the question of why, despite all the recent changes, and efforts at change in society, major differences remain. This analysis, too, attempts to explore what it is about society which means gender differences are so deeply embedded, not only in our institutions and practices, but in the very way we think about what is 'normal'.

However, perhaps it can go further. When discussing the weaknesses of marxist feminism we noted its inability to explain violence against women fully and adequately; and many women would argue that sexual violence, or at least the threat of sexual violence, experienced as child abuse, sexual harassment at work, domestic violence, sexual assault or rape, is one of the major features of women's lives. This *can* be explained by radical feminist theories — as a form of male control over women. Similarly, once we work from a perspective which draws attention to the way being male is seen as the norm, and how women are 'the Other' to be understood, interpreted and defined through men's eyes, then we can begin to understand the marginalization of women in all spheres of life — something which marxist analysis has difficulty addressing. Finally, radical feminist theories take account of one of the major weaknesses of marxist theory — the limitation of gender divisions to capitalist societies. According to this perspective, patriarchy is a characteristic of all societies.

On the other hand, looking at this explanation in its simplest form, we could argue that there is a major weakness in that it seems to assume that all women

A poster from the 'Zero Tolerance' campaign organized by Edinburgh District Council Women's Committee; it links all forms of violence against women, identifying them as male abuses of power

have, and have had, the same experiences. It does not take account of the way in which the inequalities may vary between historical periods. Nor does it take account of different kinds and degree of inequality *between* women. *All* women seem to be controlled by *all* men.

4.4 MOVING ON ...

In summary, marxist feminists focus on the way in which patriarchy is rooted in capitalism, whilst radical feminists focus solely on patriarchy and the way it manifests itself in all spheres of life.

However, as feminists have attempted to develop their understanding of the relationship between capitalism and patriarchy, and in particular to debate the question of which concept is the main explanatory one, so the clarity of these distinctions diminishes. There is not space here to outline, even in a minimal way, the range of work of this kind, developing out of both marxist feminism and radical feminism. However, the ideas of Heidi Hartmann, a North American economist whose work on 'dual systems theory' lies in the marxist feminist tradition, will serve as just one example.

Hartmann (1981) defines patriarchy as 'a set of social relationships between men which have a material base and which, though hierarchical, establish or create interdependence and solidarity among men that enables them to dominate women'. Central to her analysis is men's control of women's labour power both in the home (women's domestic labour) and in the workplace (their wage labour). This is 'the material base on which patriarchy rests' (p.15). Looking specifically at women's place in the labour market, she has argued that during the twentieth century what has emerged is a *partnership* of capitalism and patriarchy. Women's secondary place in the labour market is a consequence of patriarchal gender relations operating in the workplace as in every other sphere of life. They exist and need to be studied in their own right and not simply as a by-product of capitalism. At the same time, however, capital can exploit women's weaker labour market situation to its own advantage by using women as cheap labour. That is, patriarchal definitions and relations can be used by employers to further *their* own interests. What Hartmann has been able to show, then, is how capitalist and patriarchal interests may coincide and interlock. So that to understand the position of any one group of women we would need to look at the way both the relations of capitalism *and* patriarchal relations interact in particular historical and social contexts and circumstances.

We are going to leave the analysis of feminist theories at this point, although this is certainly not the end of the story. Recent years, in particular, have seen the emergence of theories which question the value of using such overarching concepts as capitalism and patriarchy. The emphasis in these more recent ideas is on the diversity of women's experiences — the way gender identity, ethnic identity and class identity cross-cut each other, and combine with other sources of identity such as religion, age and sexual orientation to produce a fragmented social structure.

We shall be returning to some of these issues in Part II of this unit. For the moment I want you to finish this part by reflecting on what you have done.

SUMMARY

1 In this section we have moved from describing women's lives, and the way women's lives differ from those of men, to explaining these differences.

2 The three explanations we looked at in detail were similar in that they all recognized the differences as socially constructed.

3 However, there are also important differences between them:

(a) in terms of whether they start from individual or group attitudes, initiatives etc. or from the structure of society:

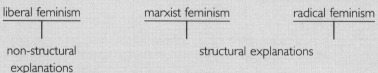

(b) in terms of what is seen as the most important characteristic in terms of a society's structure:

4 It is not enough as social scientists simply to present these different theories. You also need to be able to assess them.

5 Feminism as a complex body of thought is developing all the time. However, the framework you have here is a sound basis for any further work you do in this area.

REFERENCES

Bowlby, J. (1965) *Childcare and the Growth of Love*, abridged and edited by M. Fry, 2nd edn (based on World Health Organization Report, *Maternal Care and Mental Health*), Harmondsworth, Penguin Books.

Bruegel, I. (1979) 'Women as a reserve army of labour', *Feminist Review*, no.3.

Bruegel, I. (1989) 'Sex and race in the labour market', *Feminist Review*, no.32.

Finch, I and Groves, D. (1985) 'Community Care and the family: a case for equal opportunities?' in C. Ungerson (ed.) *Women and Social Policy: A Reader*, London and Basingstoke, Macmillan.

Hartman, H. (1981) 'The unhappy marriage of Marxism and feminism: towards a more progressive union' in L. Sargent (ed.) *Women in Revolution*, London, Pluto Press.

McDowell, L. (1992) 'Gender divisions in a post-Fordist era: new contradictions or the same old story?' in L. McDowell and R. Pringle (eds).

McDowell, L. and Pringle, R. (eds) (1992) *Defining Women: Social Institutions and Gender Divisions*, Cambridge, Polity Press/The Open University.

Millett, K. (1970) *Sexual Politics*, New York, Doubleday.

Murphy, P. (1989) 'Towards a feminist masculinity', *Feminist Studies*, no.15, Summer.

Phillips, A. (1987) 'Classing the women and gendering the class' in *Divided Loyalties: Dilemmas of Sex and Class*, London, Virago (edited version reprinted in L. McDowell and R. Pringle (eds) (1992)).

Rich, A. (1979) *Of Woman Born: Motherhood as Experience and Institution*, London, Virago.

Rich, A. (1980) 'Compulsory heterosexuality and the Lesbian existence', *Signs*, vol.5(4).

Rowbotham, S. (1973) *Woman's Consciousness, Man's World*, Harmondsworth, Penguin Books.

Spender, D. (1980) *Man Made Language*, London, Routledge.

Wollstonecraft, M. (1975) *A Vindication of the Rights of Women*, New York, Norton.

PART II: THE INTERACTING DYNAMICS OF CLASS, 'RACE'/ETHNICITY AND GENDER

1 INTRODUCTION

We are now moving towards the end of this block on divisions in society and, in this half-unit, we are going to ask you to do some work which is rather differ-ent. So far, your work on divisions has followed a clear pattern. In Unit 6 you explored the meaning of 'the social', the basis for all the work to follow; then in Unit 7 and Part I of Unit 8 you were presented with accounts of the form taken by, respectively, class divisions, divisions based on 'race' or ethnicity, and gen-der divisions. We also set out for you different explanations for each set of divisions. In Unit 9 we shall do some more work on these explanations, particu-larly looking at the ways in which we can assess them. Here, however, we shall approach the whole question of divisions from a slightly different angle.

You may well have been saying, as you worked through the material so far, that somehow all this seems too neat and tidy and 'packaged'. You now have a reasonably clear understanding of the different theories, but how far do these really take us in understanding lived experience — why people have the lives they do, why they see themselves the way they do? In this half-unit we aim to complicate the analysis so far, by opening up a range of questions to do with divisions in society. By looking at five key questions, we are going to pull together the issues raised so far in the block:

1   Is one of the divisions we have been looking at more important than the others in 'determining' people's life-chances and life experiences? Is it, for example, your class, gender or ethnic origin which is *most* likely to influence the kind of education you get, your experiences of employment, your chance of being the victim of violence, your health patterns, the likelihood of being discriminated against? Is there one particular line of division which we, as social scientists, should see as the most significant, as the starting-point for any attempts to explain the life-chances and experiences of any one group in our society?

2   And what of the 'subjective' rather than the 'objective' importance of these divisions? Is there any one line of division which is more important in terms of people's identity — in terms of who they think they are, how they see themselves, how they think other people see them?

3   Maybe, in relation to both these first two questions, we ought also to be looking at other lines of division. So the next question is whether there are other important lines of division in addition to gender or class or 'race'/ethnicity. Perhaps in some cases it is where you live, or your age, or your sexual orientation, or whether or not you are able-bodied, which are the most important influences on both your 'objective' life-chances and experiences and on your identity.

4   These questions in themselves may have limited usefulness. It can be argued that contemporary society is a *fragmented* society in which lines of division cross and re-cross each other. Rather than attempting to work out which is the most significant social division, should we rather be focusing upon the way in which the relationship between different kinds of division varies according to the situation — the way divisions may intertwine, in different ways at different periods and in different places?

5   Not only may divisions relate to each other in different ways, but account also needs to be taken of the ways in which 'oppressed groups'

seek to resist the effects of such divisions. Should we, then, be moving away from the notion of 'determination' to recognizing rather that people may negotiate their way through a series of pressures, expectations and constraints, sometimes with quite unexpected outcomes?

There is no 'right' answer to these questions. However, the activities which make up the rest of this half-unit will give you the opportunity to think about them much more closely and begin to recognize their complexity and their importance.

2   CASE STUDY I: EXPLAINING THE RIOTS

To begin with Question 1 above, while social scientists concur in seeing Western societies as characterized by class, 'racial'/ethnic and gender divisions, they often differ over what they consider to be the central social division. Article 1 'privileges' one social division.

──────────────── ACTIVITY I ────────────────

As you read the article by Young, write down which social division he sees as central to an understanding of the 'riots' in the 1980s and early 1990s.
Underline the points at which you find him prioritizing this division.
Before you read on, think for a couple of minutes about how those who wish to prioritize other divisions might respond to Young's analysis. Write down some of these criticisms.

For Young, the social division which is central to an understanding of the riots is that of social class. As he puts it, 'It is class, not "race", which unites rioters today'. The presence of black youths at the forefront of the riots in the early 1980s misled many commentators into thinking that 'race' or racism was the most fundamental factor. In fact, 'whenever a part of the community is economically marginalised and feels politically impotent, riots occur'. Black youths 'were the first to face the cutting edge of the recession', but they have since been joined by white youths.

A central concept in Young's analysis is that of 'underclass'. It is not altogether clear, however, what he understands by the term. At one stage he seems to have in mind 'young people who face a lifetime on the dole', while at another stage he seems to be referring to the wider category of 'have-nots'. His position seems to be as follows.

Economic changes since the mid-1970s have entailed polarization. This development has been particularly evident since 1979 with the election into government of the Conservative party, whose economic restructuring involved significant unemployment and whose New Right ideology advocated welfare cuts. While for most of the population economic restructuring and growing inequality have been accompanied by an increase in standards of living, a growing stratum has become relatively deprived (Halsey, 1989). This stratum was referred to as 'the poor' in Block I and grew significantly during the 1980s, with one study indicating that the number of people who could not afford three or more necessities, as defined by most people, had risen from seven and a half million in 1983 to eleven million in 1990 (LWT, 1991). The poor fall into a

number of groups — the unemployed, lone parents, pensioners, families where someone is infirm or disabled, and low-paid workers. Some of these groups, it is

Riotous rage of the have-nots

Jock Young on how the politics of despair spread from blacks to disaffected whites

Two youths stole a police BMW motorbike in Hartcliffe, Bristol, on Thursday night; in the subsequent police chase they crashed, and were killed. Trouble ensued: crowds of young people, white and black, set fire to the local library and community centre, and looted shops. The following night, there were more riots. It is a familiar pattern, repeating what has occurred in depressed estates from Teesside to Salford.

After the riots of 1981 and 1985, the immediate response, from all parts of the political spectrum, revolved around race. For the right, an unassimilated black minority was simply displaying its inablility to act in an orderly British fashion. For the left, the problem was racism: a minority barred from jobs because of prejudice and treated unfairly by police, had been driven beyond their tether. Both interpretations conveniently forgot that many of the rioters, in Brixton and elsewhere, were white.

We can now see the secondary nature of the race factor. In the 1980s it would have been possible to pinpoint the sites of rioting by marking on the map where there were concentrations of blacks or Asians. Brixton, Tottenham, Handsworth and Toxteth all fit this pattern Now the dots on the map are more widespread: in cities or districts with no black concentrations: Meadow Well on Tyneside, Coventry, Oxford and Ordsall in Salford. As the recession has spread, the white population of the depressed areas has joined the ranks of the violently disaffected.

Riots are the politics of despair, the collective bargaining of the dispossessed. Whether in Brixton or Los Angeles, whenever a part of the community is economically marginalised and feels politically impotent, riots ocur.

But history never repeats itself, and the causes of riots today are specific to the modern recessions. First, there is a notion of consumer citizenship. With political and social rights, the affluent societies of the West have fostered new expectations. Advertising and the rules of an economy based on mass consumption teach us that if we are truly to belong to our society we must possess its glittering prizes. Hunger no longer propels the riot: in its place is the video-recorder, the BMW and the mountain bike. Kids may be robbed, not for their pocket money, but for their trainer shoes or designer clothes.

Second, although black youths were certainly to the forefront in the riots in Britain of the early 1980s, this was simply because they were the first to face the cutting edge of the recession. It is class, not race, which unites rioters today. The distinction was clear in Los Angeles, where the targets were not only whites and Asian business people, but also better-off blacks.

Much play has been made of the word "underclass", which, in the work of the neo-conservative Charles Murray, has the resonance of a groupd which has lost all motivation and, shored up by welfare, is unwilling to help itself. But there is another definition of underclass, which does not contrive to blame the poor for their own misfortunes: those yong people who face a lifetime on the dole, whose welfare benefits are being cut, who regard the police as persecutors, who are impotent to make any change in their livs and who, perhaps most pressingly, are chronically and endlessly bored.

The police recognise that their task is made more difficult by the recession. As the Avon and Somerset constabulary put it in the Operational Police Review: "Is it a coincidence that, at the depths of the 1980–81 recession, when unemployment began to rise sharply from its 1970 base, the first urban riots of the modern era occurred in St Paul's, Bristol, and Brixton? Is it again a coincidence that, as unemployment approached its peak, a series of disorders occurred in 1985 in Brixton, Tottenham and Handsworth?"

However correct their diagnosis, much is lacking in police practice. Survey after survey on poor housing estates reveals widespread experience of gratuitous police violence, assault and the improvisation of evidence. It is not just in the headline cases that such lapses ocur; there is a vast undertow of malpractice. And the antagonism between police and youths becomes a game. A status-symbol motorbike is stolen; the police chase which ensues is an entertainment feature on the estate; two young men die. The riot which occurs in protest is irrational in its targets. The library, the community centre and the lcoal shops: the infrastructure of the community – *their* community – is attacked.

Riots and distubances will not go away, and the people affected are not just an underclass on some far distant estate. Beneath the overt riot is the vast slow riot of crime which affects us all. Last year more than five million offences were known to the police; in 1980 it was 2.5 million; in 1950 half a million. Crime is no longer a chance misfortune but an ever-present threat, yet ministers still blithely blame lack of parental discipline and the decline of religion: anything to avoid the economic explanation.

It is riots and crime which confront the "haves" with the despair and hopelessness of the "have nots". No society can permanently exclude so many people from the rewards and prospects which the majority takes for granted, without bearing these consequences.

Professor Jock Young, of the Centre for Criminology, Middlesex University, is co-author of 'What's to be Done about Law and Order?'

Article I   Source: *Independent on Sunday*, 19 July 1992

argued, are effectively excluded from citizenship rights enjoyed by the bulk of the population and thus constitute an underclass. For one writer, this class comprises the long-term unemployed, lone-parent families and elderly pensioners (Field, 1989). Young's concern in the article is with the first of these groups.

Unemployment, Young is at pains to point out, does not necessarily lead to rioting. For poverty can just as easily, as he indicates in an earlier article, 'be associated with quiescent fatalism and the acceptance of adversity. The root causes of rebellion invariably develop when a group of people feel they are doing badly compared with another significant group' (Lea and Young, 1982). Young people now comprise the age group most prone to unemployment and it is among this group that such a sense of relative deprivation is keenly felt. This is less true of Asian youth because of 'the distance between Asian culture and indigenous British culture'. Afro-Caribbean and white youth, however, 'have assimilated the expectations of the majority culture only to be denied them in reality' (Lea and Young, 1982), and thus feel acutely deprived. One response, found among both black and white youth, is the creation of deviant subcultures in which criminality is taken for granted.

The latter sets the 'scene', as Lea and Young point out, 'for the development of a vicious circle whereby relations between police and community deteriorate in such a way that each step in deterioration creates pressure for further deterioration'. For there to be 'consensus policing', a community must act as a source of information to the police so that the latter can 'catch and/or deter individual law breakers'. As unemployment generates more crime, however, the police begin to adopt a more aggressive policing policy and turn to operations which involve the 'random stopping of "suspicious" youth'. This inevitably results in large numbers of innocent people being stopped and searched. Once this happens, the community 'begins to become alienated from the police'. It 'comes to see any attempt at an arrest by officers as a symbolic attack on the community', and ceases to provide the police with any information which can help to identify individual offenders. Faced with this situation, the police adopt an even more aggressive policing policy and so the vicious circle continues. In this context, any perceived instance of police malpractice can trigger off a riot. If riots are to be avoided, the authors argue that the conditions which generate crime need to be attacked and that the police need to be made more accountable to the community (Lea and Young, 1982).

We have spent some time spelling out a necessarily condensed newspaper article to bring out the subtle way Young seeks to relate a number of factors in his analysis. To point to positive features of this account does not, however, mean that it is without its critics (for example, see Hughes, 1991). You might have noted, for instance, that there is no discussion of gender. What role do women play in the riots? Are men primarily involved because they feel frustrated that they can't perform their traditional role as 'breadwinners'? Are the participants operating with a particular conception of 'masculinity'? You might have wondered whether the riots of the 1980s and early 1990s really were the same phenomena. One review of the riots in the 1980s (Benyon, 1987) lists five characteristics common to the areas where rioting occurred, namely:

1   Racial disadvantage and discrimination.
2   High unemployment, particularly affecting youth.
3   Widespread deprivation.
4   Political exclusion and powerlessness.
5   Widespread resistance of, and hostility to, the police among certain sections, particularly the young.

The first factor may be less evident in the early 1990s' riots, but didn't its presence in the earlier riots make a significant difference?

Our central concern in Case Study 1 has been with the first question we identified earlier. Social scientists often try to weigh up the relative importance of different social divisions and in the process seek to prioritize one division. Such attempts, however, are open to challenge from other social scientists.

The fact that we have chosen to include a newspaper article by a social scientist, Jock Young, is indicative of the fact that social science does not operate in a vacuum. Concepts developed by social scientists to illuminate social reality can be, and often are, taken up by politicians and journalists and thus gain a wider currency. Our second case study focuses on one such concept.

3   CASE STUDY 2: THE UNDERCLASS THESIS

The term 'underclass', has been extensively employed in the last decade to point to what many consider a major new social division between what Galbraith (1992) calls the 'contented majority' and the rest. The concept, however, is highly contested.

Firstly, the term itself is rather nebulous. It is used in a variety of ways but tends to carry with it particular connotations, representing the underclass as pathological. One writer describes its use as an example of the language of disease and contamination, which encourages a view of the underclass as 'the Other' rather than one which links their plight to a denial of the full rights of citizenship (Lister, 1990). Secondly, the groups which are deemed to constitute the underclass vary enormously — the poor or a subgroup of the poor; minority ethnic groups or a particular minority ethnic group, and (occasionally) women or a 'fraction' of women (Gallie, 1990). In short, the concept has been used to prioritize each of the social divisions highlighted in this block. Thirdly, the explanations proffered for the emergence of this new division are radically divergent. Those writing from a conservative or liberal tradition emphasize cultural factors and see the emergence of an underclass as stemming from the adoption by individuals of deviant values and corresponding deviant patterns of behaviour. Those writing from a marxist or social reformist tradition stress structural factors and see the emergence of an underclass as stemming from the structure of society, whether this is seen as primarily capitalist, racist or patriarchal.

———————————————— ACTIVITY 2 ————————————————

Article 2 presents one version of the underclass thesis. When you have read it, write some brief notes in answer to the following questions:
Which group or groups are seen as comprising an underclass?
How is the underclass characterized?
What explanation is given for the emergence of an underclass?
Does this version of the underclass thesis flow from any particular tradition of social thought?

Racism is not the reason

The riots that turned much of Los Angeles into Beirut on a bad day were an American urban nightmare waiting to happen. No society can tolerate such a large, dispossessed, alienated, armed and violent underclass and expect social tranquility. If the injustice meted out to Rodney King had not been the spark, some other incident at some other time and some other place would have ignited the American tinderbox. It says much for white fear of black violent crime that the jury was prepared to fall over backwards to give the police the benefit of the doubt, despite the frenzy of thuggery the police had used to subdue Mr King. The murder and mayhem, the shooting and looting that followed say even more about the degradation of the black underclass.

Most whites, and America's many affluent non-white minorities, have preferred to ignore the transformation of huge chunks of their cities into urban hell-holes. They usually live a long way from them, and nobody has any convincing answers about what to do with them. Best just let them fester, and try to stop their crime, violence and drugs from infecting the rest of society. The scale of the Los Angeles riots, and the fact that they brought death and destruction to the richer districts as well as the ghettos, means that America can no longer afford to ignore its most pressing problem: the tragic condition of much of its black population.

The scale of the problem is daunting and it is by no means certain that it can be tackled, much less solved. Before policies can be devised it is necessary to have a proper understanding of the black experience in America, particularly why American blacks have more problems than most in securing their share of the American dream. That understanding, however, does not begin by recycling all the old cries about racism and discrimination from the 1960s, though much of America's political establishment, as if stuck in a time-warp seems determined to do just that. Of course, racism is still rife in the United States (it is on the increase in Europe too) but that alone cannot explain why blacks remain stuck at the bottom [...]

In his seminal work, Ethnic America, Thomas Sowell, a black professor, explained a decade ago how the black American family had been crushed by slavery; delivered another body blow by the huge black migration, beginning in the 1920s from the south to the northern cities (a migration in which males were often forced by economic circumstances to leave their wives and children behind); and finally destroyed by welfare, which produced a culture of dependency among single-parent mothers, encouraged them to have children they could not cope with and allowed fathers to escape their obligations. His conclusion was that the cycle of welfare dependency, with single-parent mothers on welfare rearing children who grow up to produce their own single-parent families on welfare, was the final nail in the coffin of the black family.

The problem of the policy-makers is to devise a means of breaking into this self-perpetuating cycle of despair and deprivation. Most black leaders, however, continue to speak the language of the civil rights era, believing that racism remains the cause of the black condition and calling for more affirmative action (to give blacks favoured treatment in securing jobs) and more federal funds (to finance bigger welfare programmes). But America's whites no longer feel responsible for the plight of the blacks. They see other non-white, disadvantaged groups pulling themselves up and conclude it is time the black community sorted out its own problems. That is impossible as long as black leaders sing the old songs. A new, more realistic breed is needed.

In some places, such as New Jersey, it is already emerging. Welfare reform is at the top of the agenda, with benefits being restructured so that teenage mothers are not encouraged to remain unmarried and have more children. Instead the aim is to foster small, nuclear families. It is a long, painful road and America has barely taken the first steps down it. Much more needs to be done, for example, to give the poorest blacks a choice in the schools they send their children to, so that those who care can avoid those which are ridden with violence and drugs; and the grim public housing of the ghettos needs to be handed over to the people to own and run themselves. The task is enormous. But if the public policy is directed towards rebuilding the black family, at least it will be moving in the right direction.

Article 2

Source: *The Sunday Times*, 3 May 1992

While Afro-Americans en bloc are not seen as comprising an underclass in the United States, those left behind in the ghettos are. They are characterized as suffering from a series of pathologies, which include 'crime, violence and drugs' and family breakdown. It is acknowledged that their deprivation originally stemmed from structural factors. The persistence of deprivation, however, is seen here as self-perpetuating — living as they do in a pathological culture, aided and abetted by misguided welfare expenditure. This analysis seems to stem from the liberal tradition, which sees state intervention as causing social problems — in this case, a culture of dependency which saps people's initiative.

The choice of the United States to illustrate the underclass thesis was deliberate. The term was first used to account for the persistent disadvantage of Afro-Americans and, despite its varied usage, still tends to conjure up an image of a group — predominantly black — whose members live in poor inner-city ghettos and in a culture where criminality, dependency and family breakdown are said to be the norm. The widespread adoption of the term in Britain is due, at least in part, to an American liberal theorist, Charles Murray (mentioned in Article 1), who detected an 'emerging British underclass'. 'If,' Murray argues, 'illegitimate births are the leading indicator of an underclass and violent crime a proxy measure of its development, the definitive proof that an underclass has arrived is that large numbers of young, healthy, low income males choose not to take jobs' (Murray, 1990). While, in Murray's view, the British underclass is not predominantly black, the transposition of the concept from the United States means that it is most readily applied to black people. In this context it is not surprising that in an earlier *Sunday Times* editorial we are warned that 'there are alarming signs that Britain is well on the road to creating a new black underclass' (*Sunday Times*, 15 September 1985).

Despite the fact that modern liberals have sought to popularize a cultural version of the underclass thesis, social scientists in Britain remain somewhat sceptical. Two lines of criticism have been forthcoming. The first relates to the fact that the notion of a self-perpetuating, subordinate — and dangerous — stratum at the bottom of the economic order has, as Murray recognizes, a long ancestry. But as one critic observes,

> ... while each generation has seen a sub-stratum within the working class, each period has also witnessed the rehabilitation of that stratum. The Victorian residuum appears to have evaporated in the heat of the First World War. Likewise, the class of unemployables of the inter-war period failed to survive the Second World War. Why, we must ask, have these disappeared if the values of the underclass are transmitted across generations?
>
> (Mann, 1992)

The second criticism is based on the earlier research which challenged the notion of a 'culture of poverty'. In a conservative precursor to the cultural version of the underclass thesis, Lewis (1968) had sought to explain the persistence of poverty by pointing to the existence of what he called a 'culture of poverty'. Individuals, he argued, socialized within this distinct culture, were psychologically incapable of taking up opportunities open to them and thus free themselves from poverty. Lewis's contention — which was taken up in Britain by Sir Keith Joseph and popularized as 'the cycle of deprivation' — was severely criticized. It seemed to blame the poor for their deprivation; it failed to account for the fact that people move in and out of deprivation and was unable to show that it was to any significant extent transmitted intergenerationally; it ignored the structural roots of deprivation; and it did not demonstrate that the cultural values which may develop in response to deprivation cannot be altered through structural changes.

While social scientists have tended to be sceptical of a cultural version of the underclass thesis, they have been more enthusiastic about explanations which emphasize social structure. Indeed, Article 1 draws upon such a thesis. While it is not altogether clear whether for Young the underclass refers to the young unemployed or a wider category of 'have-nots', he sees the underclass as emerging from economic factors. Despite the fact that social reformists like Young are trying to capture recent significant changes such as increasing social inequality, the rise in relative poverty, the growth of long-term unemployment and so on, through the employment of the concept of underclass, this version of the underclass thesis also has its critics (Pilkington, 1992). Perhaps the main criticism relates to the social composition of the underclass. For the underclass to constitute a group with a distinctive set of attitudes, there must be a degree of stability in its social composition. The only group this seems to apply to is the long-term unemployed which is indeed an expanding category. Although some attitudes such as fatalism may become accentuated with long-term unemployment, it should be remembered that these are by no means unique to this group (being found also among the unemployed generally and sections of the working class who are most at risk of unemployment) and that the long-term unemployed share most of the same aspirations as the rest of society (Walker, 1990).

SUMMARY

Our central concern so far in Case Study 2 has been with Question 1 which we identified earlier. We've seen that:

- despite the term 'under*class*', it's not clear which social division (class, 'race'/ethnicity or gender) should be prioritized in discussing any notion of an 'underclass'
- the 'underclass' thesis takes radically different forms
- both the cultural and structural version of the thesis can be challenged.

We have yet to examine, however, the most common structural version of the thesis. While Young, along with other structural theorists, does not restrict the application of the term to minority ethnic groups, nevertheless its most typical usage is one which does refer to minority ethnic groups, whether in Britain, the United States or Western Europe (Galbraith, 1992). We came across an example of this in Unit 7 Part II. Rex, writing from a Weberian perspective, argued that racism in Britain was creating a black underclass. We also saw earlier a not dissimilar thesis put forward by Miles (1982) who, writing from a marxist perspective, argued that minority ethnic groups in Britain constituted a subordinate 'fraction' of the working class. (You might need to remind yourself of these theses by re-reading Sections 4.1 and 4.2 of Unit 7 Part II.)

While the Weberian thesis that minority ethnic groups in Britain constitute an underclass may seem very different from the marxist thesis that they comprise a subordinate fraction of the working class, what is more noteworthy is the similarity of their analyses. On four key issues, they are in accord. Firstly, they agree that the 'economic and social requirements of British society create disadvantaged positions in the class structure and it is the racism of British society that ensures that black people continue to fill them' (Abercrombie and Warde, 1988). Secondly, they concur in recognizing that racism is extremely pervasive, affecting the position of the minorities not only in the labour market but also in other areas such as housing and education. To comprehend fully the class situation of minorities entails, therefore, an acknowledgement of the wider impact of racism. Thirdly, there is agreement that in locating ethnic minorities in the class structure, particular attention needs to be placed on the field of employment. What is apparent here — it is argued — is that they still constitute a 'replacement population', employed (if at all) in non-skilled manual work which white people are not willing to undertake. Fourthly, there is a shared recognition that the distinctive position of ethnic minorities means that their interests are not always congruent with the white working class. The result is that the minorities develop distinct forms of consciousness and action.

To discover similarities between the Weberian and marxist theses on the 'underclass' does not necessarily mean, however, that their conclusions are well-founded.

===== READER =====

Now read Chapter 6 in the Course Reader by Modood, 'The Indian economic success: a challenge to some race relations assumptions'. How does Modood challenge the thesis that racism creates a black underclass? How convincing do you find his rebuttal?

While Modood is fully aware of the existence of racism, he queries whether this leads ineluctably to the formation of a 'racial' underclass. Minority ethnic groups, he says, utilize whatever resources they have to *resist* racism. His particular concern is with one minority ethnic group in Britain — Indians — whom he argues have, as a group, been relatively successful. The data he primarily draws upon come from the annual Labour Force Survey. This source does, however, have deficiencies. Firstly, 'the Labour Force Survey has been shown to under-record the number of black-and-female-headed households in the population and is most likely to miss the poorer black households' (Bruegel, 1989). Secondly, the socio-economic categories used tend, as Modood partially recognizes, to camouflage differences in the employment position of different ethnic groups. Nonetheless the Labour Force Surveys do provide us with the most reliable data we have on the current socio-economic position of minority ethnic groups and they do indeed challenge the notion that ethnic minorities en bloc constitute a 'racial' underclass.

Modood focuses mainly on Indians. To gauge how other minority ethnic groups are faring, let us look at some of the most recent Labour Force survey data in Tables 3 and 4.

Table 3   Unemployment rates by sex and ethnic origin: average, Spring 1989 to Spring 1991

	White	West Indian/ Guyanese	Indian	Pakistani/ Bangladeshi
Men[1]	7	15	10	21
Women[1]	7	12	10	24

[1] All aged 16 and over
Source: Amin, 1992

Table 3 indicates that while all ethnic minority groups have a higher risk of unemployment than the majority ethnic group, the West Indian/Guyanese and especially the Pakistani/Bangladeshi groups have a significantly higher risk of unemployment.

Table 4 also confirms Modood's contention that Indians are more 'successful' than other ethnic groups. While Indian men are over-represented in managerial and professional occupations both West Indian/Guyanese men and Pakistani/Bangladeshi men are under-represented in such occupations.

Table 4   Employment by broad occupation, ethnic origin and sex; average, Spring 1989 to 1991: persons in employment aged 16 and over Great Britain (percentages)

	White	West Indian/ Guyanese	Indian	Pakistani/ Bangladeshi
Men				
All non-manual occupations	48	32	59	40
Managerial and professional	36	20	43	28
Clerical and related	5	*	9	*
Other non-manual	6	*	6	*
All manual occupations	52	68	41	59
Crafts and similar	25	28	16	17
General labourers	1	*	*	*
Other manual	26	39	24	41
Women				
All non-manual occupations	68	63	62	64
Managerial and professional	29	33	28	*
Clerical and related	30	26	27	*
Other non-manual	10	*	*	*
All manual occupations	31	37	38	36
Crafts and similar	4	*	11	*
General labourers	0	*	*	*
Other manual	28	33	27	*

* Sample too small.

Source: Amin, 1992

Tables 3 and 4 give us a picture of the current socio-economic position of ethnic minorities. How has it changed over time? An analysis of social mobility since 1971 'makes it clear that Britain's major black groups have seen an improvement in their aggregate social class profiles. This improvement is dramatic in the case of Indians and West Indian women, but is less so for Pakistanis and West Indian men' (Robinson, 1990).

The evidence we've been looking at indicates that there are significant differences between minority ethnic groups, so that it is scarcely surprising that cultural differences between the minorities have not been overridden by a shared colour consciousness and the need for unified black action as anticipated by some versions of the underclass thesis. Attention also needs to be given, however, to differences within minority ethnic groups. Class and gender divisions are both evident. A process of class polarization seems to be occurring within all ethnic groups, with some individuals 'experiencing improved mobility into white-collar work at the same time as ... others are experiencing downward mobility into unemployment' (Robinson, 1990). One response to unemployment is to start up a labour-intensive small business in which minority ethnic women constitute the bulk of the labour force. This option has been taken up by some Asian entrepreneurs who have used 'patriarchal attitudes and practices to discipline and control such a workforce often combined with an assertion of "ethnic" loyalty and honour' (Phizacklea, 1992). In the process such entrepreneurs have used gender divisions within their communities as a resource to improve their socio-economic position.

What conclusions can we come to? There is no doubt that Britain has become a more polarized society since the mid-1970s. Whether this has resulted in the growth of a distinct underclass, cut off economically from the working class and characterized by distinct attitudes and behaviour is debateable, however. An analysis of the way in which the term has been used indicates that it has been used to prioritize different social divisions and an examination of that section of the community most associated with the notion of the 'underclass' points to too much economic diversity, both between and within minority ethnic groups, to enable us to speak, unproblematically, of a black underclass. What we have uncovered instead is evidence of what we earlier called 'fragmentation'. Members of minority ethnic groups do not have identical life-chances and do not share the same cultural identity; rather these vary by ethnic group, class and gender.

4   CASE STUDY 3: A BIOGRAPHY

The study of social divisions need not involve only the study of those who are in 'inferior' positions in society — those who have less money, status or power than others. There is always a danger in this kind of work of forgetting that the study of social divisions is about *everyone* in a society. So we are now going to introduce an analysis of a different kind: a biographical case study about someone who is very definitely one of the more privileged people in our society.

_____ ACTIVITY 3 _____

Read Article 3, reproduced on the following two pages, and then try to write a description of Ruth Deech using not more than 25 words. Then return to the text below.

This was not just a question to give you practice in writing very brief summaries! What we hope emerged for you was the difficulty of deciding which characteristic of Ruth Deech to start with — what was the most salient characteristic to build your summary around? A middle-aged woman? A Jewish woman? A powerful academic? A campaigner on women's issues? It's not easy.

Ruth Deech is certainly now a powerful academic controlling, through her position as the head of an Oxford college, large resources and having decision-making power over the lives of many people. She has some power, status and wealth. She is also a member of a minority ethnic group and she is a woman. Our concern here is to explore the interrelationship of these divisions — both how they can explain how she has achieved her present position and also how, as presented in the article, they can help us to understand her life now.

She was born to Jewish refugee parents and we can suppose her ethnicity played an important part in at least her early academic success. Some Jewish people have tended to use both the educational system and opportunities in business to achieve upward mobility. In Ruth Deech's case it is her academic ability (and her determination to succeed academically), no doubt nurtured by the fact that her father was an academic historian, which seems to be the key to her early life, even to the extent of overcoming any constraints she may have experienced because she is a woman. In fact, questions of gender seem to feature only slightly in the biographical details we have been given. (Though we *are* told that her career has taken precedence over that of her husband's, thus certainly advantaging her over many women.) The article does, however, focus on her achievements on behalf of women at Oxford.

_____ ACTIVITY 4 _____

To what extent do you think the experience and concerns of Ruth Deech are similar to those of other women?

In a class of her own

Judy Goodkin

St Anne's College, Oxford is — to borrow Churchill's phrase — a pudding without a theme, its unremarkable terrace of Victorian houses overshadowed by the dreaming spires of Christ Church and All Souls. The same cannot be said of its principal. Ruth Deech is a woman of purpose. An hour in her company is a lightning tour of the inadequacies of British life as we live it. All the salient facts are at her fingertips, laced with insights as acute as they are broad-ranging, as she penetrates the murkier areas of British family law: fathers' rights, parental responsibility, cohabitation and divorce.

Deech is one of the most powerful women in Oxford University politics and, even in this most traditional of institutions, she gets things done. A central University nursery was debated back and forth by senior policy-makers for 21 years before Deech joined the Hebdomadal Council; now it is being built. Deech argued in favour of an Equal Opportunities Committee, now there is an office dedicated to raising awareness among those who select. In Deech, Oxford's women have a formidable ambassador.

Deech was born Ruth Fraenkel in 1943 in Clapham — "The wrong side of the river" — to Jewish refugee parents who fled to Britain from Europe in September 1939. "My parents' lives were, if not shattered by the war, then very much disrupted by it. My mother had lost all her family in the concentration camps and arrived here with no money, no possessions, no nationality — nothing. It was a very modest background, my parents always felt like refugees, rather unhappy and grieving over the past, right till the end." Ruth was their only child.

Deech grew up in a bookish house; her father was the Jewish historian Josef Fraenkel and his intellectual example was an early influence. "I began to read the papers at the age of five and somehow I gathered from my home in south London that Oxford was the best. So my little brain said to itself, 'That's what I want'."

Deech won a scholarship to Christ's Hospital school where she channelled all her endeavours to her ultimate goal. At 18, however, in what she describes as a "scarring experience", Oxford rejected her. "I couldn't accept that."

After an unhappy year at the LSE, she reapplied. In an impressive showdown, she informed her interviewer, "You saw me last year and if you don't take me this time, you'll be seeing me again next year." She got into St. Anne's (then still women-only) and took a First in Jurisprudence. "I do persist."

In 1967, she married the physicist John Deech. After they had spent ten years travelling the world as a dual-career couple in search of two good jobs, her husband sacrificed his career and requalified as a lawyer so that Ruth could remain in Oxford. "He's not a New Man but he did change careers for me and that's more than most men would do."

The fruits of his gesture are plain to see. In 1991, after over 20 years as a law tutor, Deech was elected Head of St. Anne's, making her the only female Head of a mixed Oxford college. Uniquely placed to comment on the disadvantages of the female academic, Deech's collected observations are illuminating.

Women don't shine in exams. Their steady application and diligence are repeatedly overtaken by quick flashes of brilliance from their male counterparts. "I have seen countless girls who have worked tremendously hard and put in excellent work over three years and never lagged behind, never slouched, suddenly come down at the last minute, simply because they are frightened of succeeding. And then I look at some rather, well, mediocre young man, who has done very little work for three years, who's been drunk, playing football and taking it all in his stride. He puts his head down in the last six weeks and gets a better degree than the girl."

Nurseries are pivotal to women's advancement. Deech's phone rings constantly with calls from women whose academic careers are

threatened by the conflicting demands of work and family life. They turn to her because, like most people in Oxford, they know Deech as a woman of legendary guts and determination. Senior Oxford Microbiologist professor Raymond Dwek speaks for many when he targets Deech's forthright personality and drive as her strengths: "Ruth is a super committee person who has proved her worth in the university community over and over again. No one has succeed in making us sit up and think as impressively as she did when she led the nursery appeal."

Oxford's oldest crèche is at St. Anne's — "A pioneer, as usual" — set up by a former principal 27 years ago when all the fellows happened to be pregnant at the same time. The centralized nursery, however, is Deech's project. She is proud of it, but also downcast: government legislation for the regulation of nurseries has raised the running costs to the point at which they are becoming an inhibiting influence. "This is the great hypocrisy," she says. "It's almost like asking an employer to build a private school. Oxford has raised a quarter of a million pounds in private money — what small employer could do that? If I were an MP, my first priority would be to create nurseries and make the path smoother for women. Gillian Shephard, please note!"

Women academics, she goes on to say, hunger for time. "I have watched what goes on in libraries. The man will sit there from two o'clock, having finished his teaching commitments, and stay all afternoon. Maybe at seven, he'll rush off to college for a quick meal, then carry on till late. The woman will down tools at four, or whenever school closes, dash home, cook, wash up. By then she's too tired to do much."

Without a publication record, there is no promotion. Without time, there can be no publication. "Older women, who have got their domestic problems out of the way, then begin to publish. It is usually too late."

While Deech battles for the infrastructure to help Oxford's

women, she knows that there is another, more invidious fight still to be won: the way we perceive ourselves. It irks her to reflect on the female student's failure to support women's institutions. In what she sees as "the unpalatable truth", men's colleges have stripped them of their most promising candidates.

"Until the seventies, there were only five colleges for women and we had to kill to get in at a time when men could just about walk in to Oxford. The men's colleges saw a pool of talent and clearly wanted to get some of it, so they announced that they wished to make room for more women at Oxford — a nice altruistic reason. There were polite grumblings from the women's colleges who could see what was going to happen." Once the outwardly attractive places like Wadham, Jesus and New College went mixed, all the girls from the best schools went there. Women's colleges now produce the fewest Firsts. However, despite her wish to woo the clever girls back to places like St. Anne's, Deech scrupulously resists the all-female college myth that obscures the real issues. In the fight to keep Somerville a college for women, she claims, it was in danger of becoming a fantasy.

"All sorts of people were writing letters and making speeches about how wonderful it was that there should be a college for women, where girls and ethnic minorities were welcomed, where women were running the show. They liked to think that out there in North Oxford — a part of Oxford where they never bother to go — there is a utopia for women.

"The truth is they don't send their daughters there, they won't give it any money and they probably wouldn't want a job there," says Deech, whose own daughter attended St. Anne's. "I have a very keen nose for hypocrisy and cant; I smelled it all over the place when

Somerville tried to go mixed." Deech holds that balanced co-education is the way forward, so that neither side need feel put upon.

There are privileges for a woman who holds one of the most senior academic posts in Britain. Her recent 25th wedding anniversary party was attended by 19 QCs and nine professors. But Deech is neither puffed up by prestige nor seduced by advantage. Inequality is her *bête noire* and it is extremely rare for her to allow a sighting to go

unchecked. Most recently, she was appalled to discover, on her election to full membership of the Oxford and Cambridge Club (whose constitution admits women to the secondary status of associate members only), that as a woman she is still barred from entering the club library. "What do they think that I am going to do in the library? Or what do they have in the library that they are frightened that I should see?" Ruth Deech is angry; Oxford and Cambridge Club, beware.

Article 3

Source: *The Guardian*, 22 July 1992

There are two ways of approaching this question. On the one hand, we can focus on areas of common experience. We can identify from the article some ways in which Ruth Deech's life has been similar to that of many other, if not all, women. She is, for example, married and has at least one child, and we can assume some experience of discrimination, given her emphasis on the barriers women face. She has very clear comments to make, for example, about the way in which women's domestic responsibilities limit what they can achieve and about the importance of nursery provision.

On the other hand, it does seem that what we have here is a very good example of what is referred to as the *fragmentation* of gender. The life Ruth Deech lives, and has lived, as an extremely able and increasingly powerful academic may mean that her experiences and concerns are very different from those of most other women. Women have different experiences and interests according to their class or occupation, and maybe also according to other factors such as the ethnic group to which they belong, their age, their sexual orientation etc. It is the fact that the lives of all women are *not* the same which underlies longstanding criticism of the feminist movement as one which expresses the concerns of only one group of women, namely those who are white and middle-class. Furthermore, as the extract below makes clear, once we move from a local to a global perspective, the situation becomes even more complex:

> When we talk about the need of white feminists in Britain to recognize their own ethnicity, we are relating to questions as basic as what we actually mean when we talk about 'feminist issues'. Can we automatically assume, as has been done by western feminist movements, that issues like abortion, the depiction of the family as the site of female oppression, the fight for legal equality with men and against sex discrimination and so on are *the* feminist issues?
>
> ... Feminist goals cannot be the same in different historical contexts. For instance, the family may *not* be the major site for women's oppression when families are kept apart by occupying or colonizing forces (as in Lebanon or South Africa), abortion may *not* be the major issue when forced sterilizations are carried out, nor is legal equality for women the first priority in polygamic societies where there is no independent autonomous mode of existence open to women whose husbands marry other younger and more fertile women ... Once we stop perceiving western white feminism as providing the ultimate criteria for defining the contents of feminism, we are faced with the problem of how to evaluate politically various women's struggles.
>
> (Anthias and Yuval-Davis, 1992, p.115)

The question of 'fragmentation', however, extends beyond gender divisions. Just as we can identify a debate about whether or not all women share the same experiences, so there is a similar debate in relation to 'race'/ethnicity. Is it the case that the experience of racism means that, fundamentally, all black people share a common experience; or is it the case that increasingly the black community is becoming fragmented as some of its members, as we have seen, climb the social ladder and begin to live 'middle-class' lives? Indeed this may be seen as a further line of division in that the experiences of black women have always been different from those of black men.

The discussion so far has focused on people's objective experiences. However, what about how people see themselves, how they locate themselves in society? To what extent do the social categories we belong to become a part of our identities?

─────────────────────── ACTIVITY 5 ───────────────────────

Ruth Deech belongs to a number of social categories (as, of course, we all do). Which of these categories do you think is the most important to her? Which one is most central to her identity?

We cannot say from this article whether Ruth Deech identifies herself primarily as a woman or an Oxford academic or a Jew. Or whether indeed the question is a meaningless one in that the answer would be different in different contexts. (You will be doing more work on identity and the different ways of looking at it in Block V.) But what we can do is recognize the complexity of the issue.

It may well be, for example, that her gender is an important part of Ruth Deech's identity. However, this might not be the case for women in very different situations from her for whom class or 'racial' identity may be more important. Is it, then, class identity or 'racial' identity which is most important for many of us? This is not easy to answer. According to many commentators it is class membership which more than any other has lost its importance as a source of identity in recent years with the break-up of traditional working-class communities, the decline of employment in manufacturing industries and the opportunities offered by successive governments for house ownership, share ownership etc. And in relation to racial or ethnic identity we have to grapple with questions of whether it is being black or white which is crucial, or whether other ethnic identities (Indian? Scottish? Jewish?) are equally significant.

Perhaps it is the fact that Ruth Deech is Jewish which can help us to pull together some of the strands of this discussion. From the way this article has been written, her membership of a minority ethnic group does not seem to have been of particular significance. But imagine how different the article would have been if written about a Jewish woman in the late 1930s in Nazi Germany. The significance of the division between Jews and non-Jews in both 'objective' and 'subjective' terms is less today than it was then. But it could change again. As we are writing this (in early 1993) there is increasing concern throughout Europe about the re-emergence of nationalist sentiments, the re-emergence,

Employers prepare to ditch equal opportunities at work

By Barrie Clement and Donald Macintyre

A confidential report by senior CBI officials suggests that the employers' organisation is preparing to abandon suppport for equal opportunities for women and the ethnic minorities. Other disadvantaged groups – the disabled, long-term unemployed, the over-50s and ex-offenders – would also be sacrificed.

The paper argues that rising unemployment has reduced the need for employers to concern themselves with getting previously under-represented groups into the labour force and improving their levels of skill. Unemployment is unlikely to fall below 2.5 million during the 1990s, it says.

"Clearly some of the business arguments for accessing and advancing previously excluded groups and for increasing training become less relevant," says the paper, which has been distributed to members of the CBI's employment policy committee.

The CBI's present policy is based on a report drawn up in 1989. It said that intense competition for labour would force employers
to pay more attention to the under-used potential in disadvantaged groups. Now, the confidential document, "Economic Growth and the Prospects for Employment" concludes that the "demographic timebomb" which was expected tlead to a shortage of young people in the labour market has been "defused". The labour market will probably be much slacker than expected.

It warns that the "social and political pressures on government can be expected to grow if the prospect of 2.5m unemployed (many of them long term) through the rest of the century is accompanied by evidenc of the continued exclusion from full participation in the labour market of many citizens".

Article 4

Source: *The Independent on Sunday,* 14 February 1993

not only in Germany (where admittedly the neo-Nazi movement has attracted most media attention) but throughout the rest of Europe, of a new wave of anti-Semitism. Jewishness as a social category can always be reactivated, with consequences for the life-chances and opportunities open to Jews and also for how large a part being Jewish plays in the construction of their identities.

The same applies to any other social category. The relative importance of different kinds of division will not always be the same. How they manifest themselves will depend on what is happening economically and politically in a particular society (or indeed what is happening globally) at a certain time; and how these circumstances are being defined and responded to. Indeed, as Article 4 shows, we can even extend this analysis to a debate about the commitment with which equal opportunities are pursued.

5　CONCLUSION

We started this part of the unit with five questions. These questions were about:

- The relative importance of class, gender and 'race' or ethnicity as influences on our life-chances.
- The importance of these divisions in relation to our identities.
- The significance of other social divisions.
- Whether or not the social structure is becoming increasingly fragmented.

And, finally,

- Whether we need to recognize the possibility of resistance and negotiation in relation to these divisions.

As we said at the start, these questions are not easy and there was no expectation that, having completed the activities, you would be able to arrive at clear answers. But we hope that at least the work you have just done has enabled you to think about them more clearly.

We shall take each question in turn and, in the process, conclude our discussion of the interacting dynamics of class, 'race'/ethnicity and gender.

1　As we have seen in the last two units, social theorists often disagree over which social division to take as their starting-point. While marxists prioritize class, other theorists prefer to focus upon 'race'/ethnicity or gender. Despite this disagreement, there is increasing recognition among social scientists that class, 'race'/ethnicity and gender constitute distinct social divisions, that they are interrelated and that the relative priority of each varies. As Stuart Hall puts it in Unit 6, 'The "privileging" of (i.e. the granting of special explanatory importance to) class is now being contested; many social scientists are moving towards a more "interactive" model of social divisions, where each is considered to have an impact on the other.' We came across an example of such a model in Section 3, when we referred to a study of the clothing industry in the West Midlands. Here, some Asian male workers responded to unemployment by setting up a labour-intensive industry, which involved employing Asian women as a cheap labour force. Gender divisions were in the process used by this ethnic group to overcome class and 'racial' disadvantage. However, the adoption of an interactive model does not, of course, mean that theorists are no longer willing to privilege one of the divisions. Our first reading, in fact, argued that class rather than 'race'/ethnicity (or gender) was central to an understanding of riots in the 1980s and 1990s. On other issues, such as racial attacks or domestic violence, 'race'/ethnicity or gender may be prioritized.

2   The work we did on the Deech article indicated that we each have a range of cultural identities, including ones based on class, ethnicity and gender. How we see ourselves will vary, depending on the context. We may see ourselves as working class while labouring on the assembly line; or Indian while hearing the latest cricket score between England and India; or as a woman while preparing the evening meal. We must not, however, forget the wider context which can mean — as the reference to Jewishness in the 1930s in Nazi Germany indicated — that one identity becomes of overriding significance. The faith marxists had in social class becoming the 'master identity', however, has been eroded as the institutions which foster such an identity have weakened and new social movements, such as feminism and anti-racism, have come to the fore.

3   We have been preoccupied in the last two units with those social divisions where, as Stuart Hall put it in Unit 6, 'power and inequality are very strongly linked'. It is important to recognize, however, that there are other important lines of division in our society, including those of age, sexual orientation and whether or not one is disabled. Reference has been made to age in our discussion of each of the three extracts. Young's rioters were young; Field's underclass included the elderly; and Deech was middle-aged. We must note, however, that the significance of age is mediated through class, 'race'/ethnicity and gender. Thus, the young people involved in rioting were unemployed and male and the elderly people who formed part of an underclass were those who had been employed in poorly paid jobs during their working lives.

4   All the material you have just been looking at raised significant questions about fragmentation. Article 1 suggested that the working class is fragmenting with the increase in long-term unemployment. The work we did around Article 2 indicated that the experience of minority ethnic groups is not identical. In the discussion of Article 3 we saw that there are differences in the experience of black and white women. To point to fragmentation does not mean that we are questioning the significance of the structures earlier identified (viz. capitalism, racism and patriarchy). Rather, we are recognizing that the effects of these structures are not uniform. An appreciation of the complex ways in which social divisions have an impact on each other and the fact that those who share a common class, 'racial'/ethnic or gender position do not share identical life-chances, enables us to understand better how the range of competing cultural identities we referred to earlier cross-cut each other.

5   In the course of this half-unit, we have sought to show that people are not simply 'determined' by the constraints arising from their position in the social structure. They interpret these constraints, react to them, even resist them. Stuart Hall points out in Unit 6 that, 'The different social classes, the different gender groups (men and women) and the different "racial" groups (black and white) all have different degrees of power, influence and authority in the society.' The word 'degrees' is important here. For even subordinate groups have some power and will use whatever resources they have to resist domination. Some may, as we have seen, use ethnic resources to avoid the consequences of racism; others may join social movements, such as the women's movement, to resist patriarchy; and yet others may feel that given their class position they might join a trade union or that their class marginalization is so severe that the only resort is to riot.

Where, then, does this leave us? Are there major divisions in our society which impact seriously on our lives? And if this is the case, can we identify one of these divisions as the most fundamental, as the starting-point for any analysis?

Our own response to these questions would be that, in spite of the evidence of fragmentation, of the importance of a range of different divisions and of processes of negotiation and resistance, what these activities have shown is that Britain *is* still a fundamentally divided society and that inequalities of class, gender and 'race'/ethnicity structure the life-chances of all of us.

Questions of which – if any – divide is the most important are more difficult to answer. We believe that what is crucial is the interrelationship between the divisions and that, moreover, the way they interrelate may vary from one context to another. However, this does not rule out the identification of one particular division as being the most important one. Here we simply have to acknowledge the possibility of disagreement. As you have seen from the last two units, we can identify different theoretical positions according to whether they take class or gender or 'race'/ethnicity as their starting-point. Choosing between them involves those processes of assessment that we have already done some work on and which will be taken up again in Unit 9.

REFERENCES

Abercrombie, N. and Warde, A. (1988) *Contemporary British Society*, Cambridge, Polity Press.

Amin, K. and Oppenheim, C. (1992) *Poverty in Black and White*, London, Child Poverty Action Group with the Runnymede Trust.

Anthias, F. and Yuval-Davis, N. (1992) 'Contextualizing families: gender, ethnic and class dimensions', in L. McDowell and R. Pringle (eds) *Defining Women: Social Institutions and Gender Divisions,* Cambridge, Polity Press/The Open University.

Benyon, J. (1987) 'The roots of urban unrest', in J. Benyon and J. Solomos (eds) *The Roots of Urban Unrest*, Oxford, Pergamon.

Field, F. (1989) *Losing Out*, Oxford, Blackwell.

Galbraith, J. (1992) *The Culture of Contentment*, London, Sinclair Stevenson.

Gallie, D. (1988) 'Employment, unemployment and social stratification' in D. Gallie (ed.) *Employment in Britain*, Oxford, Pergamon.

Green, H. (1988) *Informal Carers*, General Household Survey Supplement, London, HMSO.

Halsey, A. (1989) 'Social polarization and the inner city' in M. Bulmer *et al.* (ed.) *The Goals of Social Policy*, London, Unwin Hyman.

Hughes, G. (1991) 'Taking crime seriously: a critical analysis of New Left realism', *Sociology Review*, vol.1(2).

Kelly, L. and Radford, J. (1987) 'The problem of men: feminist perspectives on sexual violence' in P. Scraton (ed.) *Law, Order and the Authoritarian State*, Buckingham, Open University Press.

Lea, J. and Young, J. (1982) 'The riots in Britain 1981: urban violence and political marginalization' in D. Cowell, T. Jones and J. Young (eds) *Policing the Riots*, London, Junction Books.

Lewis, O. (1968) *La Vida,* Harmondsworth, Penguin Books.

Lister, R. (1990) 'Concepts of poverty', *Social Studies Review*, vol.6(5).

LWT (1991) *Breadline Britain 1990s*, London, London Weekend Television.

Mann, K. (1992) *The Making of an English 'Underclass'?*, Buckingham, Open University Press.

Miles, R. (1982) *Racism and Migrant Labour*, London, Routledge.

Murray, C. (1990) *The Emerging British Underclass*, London, Institute for Economic Affairs.

Phizacklea, A. (1992) 'Jobs for the girls: the productions of women's outerwear in the UK' in M. Cross (ed.) *Ethnic Minorities and Industrial Change in Europe and North America,* Cambridge, Cambridge University Press.

Pilkington, A. (1992) 'Is there a British underclass?', *Sociology Review,* vol.1(3).

Rex, J. and Tomlinson, S. (1979) *Colonial Immigrants in a British City,* London, Routledge.

Robinson, V. (1990) 'Roots to mobility; the social mobility of Britain's black population, 1971–1987', *Ethnic and Racial Studies,* vol.13(2).

Walker, A. (1990) 'A poor idea of poverty', *Times Higher Education Supplement,* 17 August.

STUDY SKILLS SECTION: USES AND ABUSES OF STATISTICS

Prepared for the Course Team by Norma Sherratt

This is not the first time in the course that you have done any work with statistics. You have already read a section on statistics in *The Good Study Guide* and a number of the activities you have just done on 'race'/ethnicity and gender divisions were based on interpretation of information in tables and diagrams. In Block I, too, there were plenty of opportunities for you to work with numbers and not just the written word. This is the first time, however, apart from in the *Preparatory Pack*, that we have addressed working with numbers as a study skill in the actual course materials; and, if the statistics you have been looking at so far have caused you any worries, this is the time to try to sort them out.

This section *is* about help and reassurance to some extent. But it is also about seeing how working with numbers can be interesting and challenging. It also contains a warning about being over-enthusiastic about the usefulness of statistics. So let's take each of these in turn.

1   If you are one of those people who is worried about figure work, who skips quickly past any table or diagram, then work your way through this section fairly slowly, using the relevant parts of *The Good Study Guide* as additional support. (I will identify these as we go along.) Don't expect to become a fluent reader of numbers overnight. Remember that reading numbers is a skill just like other forms of reading and the more you practise the easier you will find it.

2   Perhaps your response to numbers is not so much worry as lack of interest. It may be based on a conviction that all the really interesting work and arguments is presented through words not numbers, or that social science is about ideas and that, whilst you will happily work through any numbers you are given, the real challenge lies elsewhere. I certainly have a lot of sympathy with parts of this position. Social science *is* about far more than gathering numerical data. But what I hope you will see from this section is that working on a table or diagram will lead you into all kinds of questions about definitions, meanings, power, communication. Working with numbers involves more than simply reading off what they say.

3   Leading on from this we come to the final aim. If you are somebody who feels that 'hard concrete evidence' is what the social sciences should be looking at and that the more of this there is the better, then I hope this section will show you that statistics are not necessarily always accurate, and that they are never value-free nor unproblematic. They always need to be studied critically and questioningly.

The rest of this section is divided into a number of activities. We will start by looking at some tables, then move on to other ways of presenting numbers. The examples I am using here will stay with the issue of gender, but in a slightly different way in that we will be looking at either European statistics or, in one case, statistics which show regional differences within the UK. For the final section you will do some work yourself on changing words into numbers.

Before we start, however, you may find it useful to look again at Sections 1 and 2 of Chapter 4 in *The Good Study Guide* — just to remind yourselves of some very basic points about statistics.

——————————— ACTIVITY I ———————————

The two tables below were taken from 'The roles of men and women in tomorrow's Europe' (*Employment Gazette* Special Feature, 1992).

1   Look at each table in turn and try to summarize each one in not more than 100 words.

2   Make a note of any problems you had in reading them or any difficulties in interpreting them.

Table I   Male and female activity rates, and percentages of male and female employees who work part-time and full-time (percentages)

| | Activity rate | | Per cent of employees | | | |
| | | | Part-time | | Full-time | |
	Male	Female	Male	Female	Male	Female
Europe 12	68	42	3	29	97	71
Belgium	61	36	2	28	98	72
Denmark	74	60	10	41	90	59
Germany	70	42	2	30	98	70
Greece	66	35	2	7	98	93
Spain	64	31	1	11	99	89
France	65	46	3	24	97	76
Ireland	69	34	3	15	97	85
Italy	65	35	3	10	98	90
Luxembourg	68	34	2	16	98	84
Netherlands	69	42	15	58	85	42
Portugal	71	47	1	8	99	92
United Kingdom	73	51	5	44	95	57

Source: *Employment Gazette*, October 1992; data from 1989 Labour Force Surveys

Table 2   Percentage having equal confidence in both sexes for various occupations, by country, in 1987

	Bus or train driver	Surgeon	Barrister	MP	Average of 4
EC 12 Total	63	64	63	67	64
Denmark	86	85	82	86	84
Netherlands	75	83	75	79	78
France	77	70	70	68	70
United Kingdom	61	70	66	75	68
Belgium	67	66	64	67	66
Spain	56	55	69	67	64
Portugal	52	67	65	63	61
West Germany	57	55	59	64	58
Luxembourg	47	58	60	62	56
Greece	52	58	61	58	56
Italy	54	56	55	59	56
Ireland	43	51	50	61	51

Source: *Employment Gazette*, October 1992

My summaries are as follows:

Table 1 shows the difference between male and female activity rates across the 12 EC countries. Overall, the percentage for men is higher than that for women (68 per cent and 42 per cent respectively), but there are variations across countries with the smallest difference in Denmark (14 per cent) and the greatest in Ireland. There are also gender divisions in terms of part-time/full-time work. In nearly every society the majority of men and of women are in full-time employment. The exception is the Netherlands where there is a higher percentage of women in part-time than in full-time employment.

Table 2 shows that across all 12 EC countries between 43 and 67 per cent of respondents had confidence in both sexes for the occupations named. There seemed to be a slight difference between occupations in that the least confidence in most countries was shown in women bus or train drivers. But the most marked finding was the difference between societies, with 84 per cent of respondents in Denmark showing confidence compared with Ireland's 51 per cent.

Turning now to any difficulties you may have had with the two tables, let's start from the beginning. Neither of these tables was as complex as some you may have come across. But, even so, here is a mass of numbers you have to make sense of. The advice given in *The Good Study Guide* (Section 3.2) is to look for:

(a) patterns — a row of figures which are all the same or which seem to change in a very clear way;

(b) some clear differences or contrasts; or

(c) 'blips'.

and in each case here this works nicely – look, for example, at the figures for male full-time workers in all societies in Table 1.

So far, then, you have read off from these tables what they are saying. But are we sure it is as straightforward as it seems from my summaries? Is there any way in which these tables could be inadequate or misleading?

Here are four further points I would want to ask about the data we have just looked at – though you may well be able to think of more:

• Table 1 does make it clear that the figures relate to employees only. So we have to remember that what we are not seeing here are any figures for people working within some family concerns. (For example, would the female activity rate for Spain be higher if the category used had been different?)

• It is also the case as well, of course, that the Table 1 categories are very broad. We can assume, looking at the percentages, that they relate to people of working age. But within these there is no breakdown in terms of class or ethnicity or region. As you know from the work you have done on Unit 8, these differences are very important as far as women are concerned.

• Looking at Table 2, it would be useful to know who were the respondents. Within the UK, for example, we could expect different responses according to age, class, gender and region. Has this been taken into consideration? Can we be sure that the samples used corresponded in each society?

• Finally, still with Table 2, what would also be useful to know would be how these figures compared with responses of, say, ten years ago. Taking just one time-period like this has limited usefulness.

————————————— ACTIVITY 2 —————————————

Figure 1 also comes from 'The roles of men and women in tomorrow's Europe'. Look at this diagram and see what information you can extract from it. Then answer the following questions:

1 How easy did you find it to read?

2 Is there any other way of presenting the material that you think might be more effective?

(You can refer to *The Good Study Guide*, Chapter 4, Section 4 to help you here.)

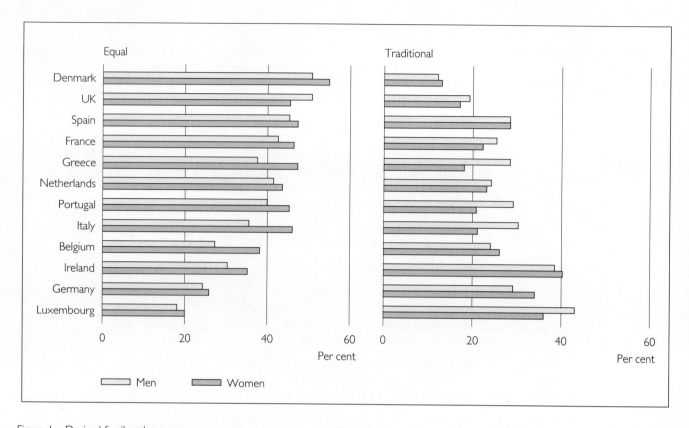

Figure 1   Desired family roles

Source: *Employment Gazette*, October 1992; data from *Men and Women in Europe 1987, Women in Europe.* Supplement No. 26, Commission of the European Communities

One obvious point to make, of course, is that without knowing what is meant by 'equal' and 'traditional' roles the diagram means very little. In fact, in this case, the diagram is accompanying a text which does make clear the meanings: 'Equal' (or egalitarian) is defined as a family in which the household tasks and looking after the children are shared equally between husband and wife, 'Traditional' as a family in which only the husband works and the wife runs the home. (There is also a middle option, in which the wife takes on more of the household tasks and looking after the children, for which figures are not shown here directly but which are 'hidden' in the diagram. Did you notice that the percentages did not add up to 100 per cent?) In this case it was very obvious that you needed to ask questions about the categories. But the lesson is the same even in relation to figures which *look* clear and 'scientific'. Always be sure that you know exactly what the categories refer to.

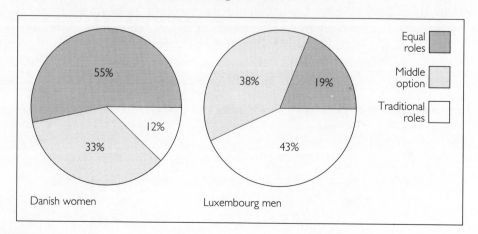

Figure 2

Once these definitions are clear, the figure is not difficult to understand. I can work out from it, for example, that it is Danish women who are the most likely to prefer equal roles and men from Luxembourg the least likely. Also from the diagram I get a clear impression that it is equal roles rather than traditional roles that are most preferred. But certainly, if I were trying to make a strong impact, I would not have presented the data in this way. My preferred alternative is shown as Figure 2. What do you think?

──────────── ACTIVITY 3 ────────────

Now look at the graph in Figure 3. (We are staying with the local/global theme but this time the local is the different UK regions.)
Just as a quick check for yourselves, jot down answers to the following questions:

1   Which region had the smallest percentage of women in the labour force in 1901?

2   When did the percentage of women in the labour force in all regions start to rise steeply?

3   How great were regional differences in 1981?

4   Can you *explain* these patterns from the graph?

5   How could you change the way the graph is presented to underplay the regional differences?

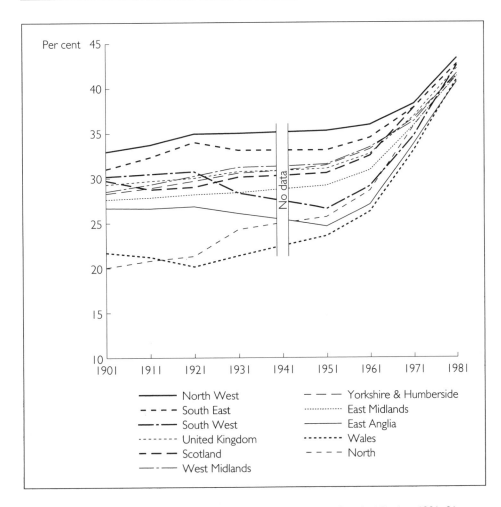

Figure 3   Female employees as a percentage of total employees by Standard Region, 1901–81

Source: Women and Geography Study Group of the IBG, 1984, p.72

The answers to Questions 1, 2 and 3 are, respectively, the North, 1961 and very small.

There were big regional differences right through the first half of this century (though note that the low numbers overall are probably an underestimation reflecting the underestimation of the numbers of women employed as governesses or servants at the start of the century). Since 1961, however, the differences have almost totally disappeared because, although the percentage of women in all regions increased, it increased most sharply in those where the employment rates for women had previously been the lowest.

Turning to Question 4, from the information on the graph, can we explain this information? Well, in a way, yes: we can make informed guesses if we already have some knowledge of the employment structure of the UK and the way it has changed. For example, the low figures for Wales and the North at the start of the period are possibly due to the concentration in these two regions of heavy industry/coal-mining (although I'm a little wary of putting together the whole of Wales); whereas the high figures for the North West are probably due to the dominance of the textile industry in which women have traditionally worked in high numbers. The post-1960 increase can be understood in terms of the expansion of a different area of employment — the service industries — which were more uniform in the opportunities they offered. *But* the graph itself does not tell us these things directly. Only if we had alongside it a number of others showing these changing structures would we be able to suggest explanations from the numerical information we have here.

Finally, Question 5. This is referring again to the way social trends or patterns can seem to convey different messages according to how they are presented. My suggestion is shown as Figure 4. By reducing the scale on the vertical axis, I have made the trends in all the regions appear much more similar.

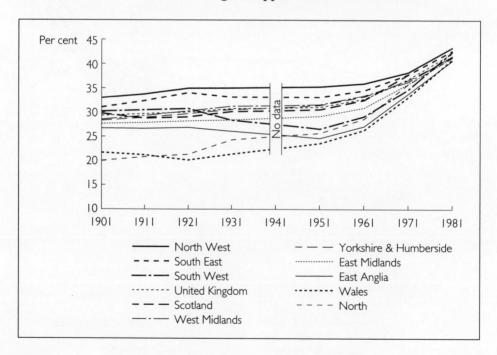

Figure 4

--- ACTIVITY 4 ---

One final exercise for you now. Below is an account of recent changes in levels of pay. Take the sections that have been highlighted and present them as a set of numbers — in the form of tables, graphs, bar charts or pie diagrams — rather than words. I have done the exercise myself so that, when you have done yours, you can compare what you have done with my response below (Figures 5a and 5b). There are, of course, a number of possible ways of doing this, so don't worry if yours is different. My aim is simply to give you the chance to think some more about the processes involved in presenting information as a set of numbers and to give you some more practice in doing this.

Women cut pay gap to earn 70% of male wages

By Martin Whitfield Labour Correspondent

Women are slowly narrowing the pay gap, although average weekly earnings are still only 70 per cent of those of male workers, according to official figures released yesterday.

Higher pay rises for women of 8.4 per cent, compared with men at 6.6 per cent, reinforced a trend seen since figures on the breakdown of the sexes began to be compiled in 1970.

Statistics from the Government's New Earnings Survey also show that the gap between the highest and lowest paid is at its widest for more than 20 years.

The highest-paid 10 per cent of workers — earning more than £489 a week — receive more than 3.3 times the lowest 10 per cent. In 1970 the ratio was 2.5 times.

Excluding overtime, women's full-time hourly rates are 79 per cent of men's, compared with 63.1 per cent in 1970. At the beginning of 1980 they had risen to 73.5 per cent.

Average weekly pay for women in the survey was £241, compared with £340 for men. The average weekly wage for all workers topped £300 for the first time, at £305 or £15,860 a year.

Pay rates increased generally by 7 per cent over the year but were lower for manual workers at 6.2 per cent.

The Equal Opportunites Commission welcomed the im-provement in women's relative position. But Frank Spencer, its pay specialist, said full-time rates were not the only factor: "We need to look at what is happening in industrial sectors dominated by women and part-time workers," he said.

The Department of Employment said that women's wages were lower than those of men because they tended to be in lower-paid occupations and worked shorter hours.

Men, on average, worked 41.4 hours a week compared to the female average of 37.3 hours.

Male manual workers had the longest week at 44.5 hours, while female non-manual employees worked an average of 36.8 hours.

The figures also show that public-sector workers received bigger pay increases for the second year in succession. Over the past two years, private-sector staff have seen salaries rise by 14 per cent, compared with 21 per cent in public service.

On average, public-sector workers receive £307.80 a week compared to £303.30 in the private sector. Overtime, shift pay and bonus rates made up 11 per cent of all employees' gross wages.

The survey shows that male medical practitioners are the highest-paid group of workers with an average annual salary of £39,291, followed by treasurers and company financial mangers on £38,537 and male solicitors on £32,427.

Female medical practitioners topped the women's pay league on £31,985, representing 81 per cent of the male grade. Women solicitors had an average of £23,883, 73 per cent of men's pay.

At the bottom of the scale, male workers in pubs and bars were the lowest-paid men on £8,767 a year, while female bar staff were paid an average of £5,922.

New Earnings Survey 1992 Part A; HMSO; £11.50.

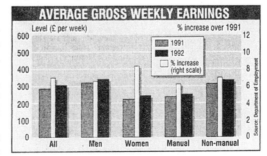

Source: *The Independent*, 25 September 1992

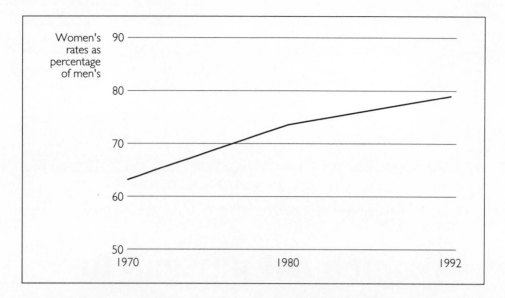

Figure 5a   Women's full-time hourly rates, 1970–92

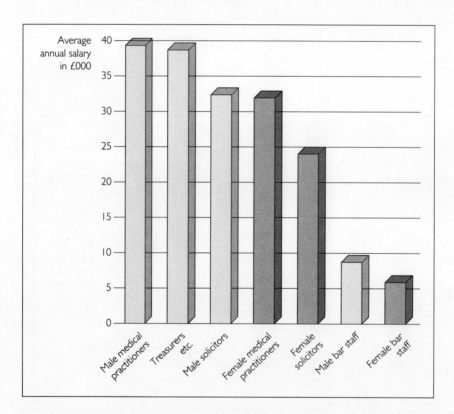

Figure 5b   Comparison of male and female annual salaries: examples of highest and lowest paid jobs

SUMMARY

1 Numbers need to be taken slowly. There are skills involved in reading them and the more you practise, the easier it will become.

2 Always think about:

- How and when was the information collected?
- Who were the respondents?
- What was the size of the sample?
- Are the figures too old to be useful?
- What were the assumptions underlying the categories of the researchers?
- What has been left out – is it only a partial account and, if so, why is this?

3 Think, too, about how the information has been presented:

- Are there unintended ambiguities in presentation?
- What do certain terms mean?
- Are the categories valid? Do they need breaking down further?
- Has there been deliberate manipulation to give an impression the figures do not substantiate?
- Have the trends been distorted by cutting short time-periods?
- Has relevant information been left out?

4 Following on from Questions 2 and 3, ask yourself:

- Why were these data being collected?
- What perspective or theories were directing the collection of information?

And, finally …

5 Whatever set of numbers you are looking at, be prepared to recognize their limitations for your purposes — that the categories used may not be the ones you really need, that the time-spans could usefully have been shorter or longer or that you can't make the comparisons you would wish to.

REFERENCE

Women and Geography Study Group of the Institute of British Geographers (1984) *Geography and Gender: An Introduction to Feminist Geography*, London, Hutchinson in association with the Explorations in Feminism Collective.

ACKNOWLEDGEMENTS

Grateful acknowledgement is made to the following sources for permission to reproduce material in this unit:

Text

'Most mothers reject home role to go back to work', *The Independent*, 23 September 1992; Clement, B. (1992), 'Small rise in jobs after recession" to favour women"', *The Independent*, 12 November 1992; 'Minister attacks slow progress for women', *The Guardian*, 18 November 1992; 'Impoverished queens of the mountain kingdom' and 'Third class citizens', *The Guardian*, 5 November 1992; Young, J. (1992), 'Riotous rage of the have-nots', © Jock Young, Centre for Criminology, Middlesex University, London; 'Racism is not the reason', *Sunday Times*, 3 May 1992, © Times Newspapers 1992; Goodkin, J. (1992), 'In a class of her own', *The Guardian*, 22 July 1992; Clement, B. and Macintyre, D. (1993), 'Employers prepare to ditch equal opportunities at work', *The Independent on Sunday*, 14 February 1993; Whitfield M. (1992), 'Women cut pay gap to earn 70% of male wages', *The Independent*, 25 September 1992.

Figures

Figures 1, 2: Department of Employment (1992), *Employment Gazette*, September 1992, © Crown Copyright, reproduced with the permission of the Controller of Her Majesty's Stationery Office; *Figure 3*: Office of Population, Censuses and Surveys (1988), *General Household Survey Report*, © Crown Copyright, reproduced with the permission of the Controller of Her Majesty's Stationery Office.

Study Skills Section: *Figure 1*: CEC (1987), *Men and Women in Europe, Supplement No. 26*, Commission of the European Communities, Women's Information Unit.

Tables

Table 1: Department of Employment (1991), *Employment Gazette*, February 1991, © Crown Copyright, reproduced with the permission of the Controller of Her Majesty's Stationery Office; *Table 2*: from the *Employment Gazette*, September 1992, © Crown Copyright, reproduced with the permission of the Controller of Her Majesty's Stationery Office; *Table 3*: from *The Guardian*, 11 February 1992; *Tables 3 and 4*: Amin, K. and Oppenheim, C. (1992), *Poverty in Black and White*, © Child Poverty Action Group, 1992.

Study Skills Section: *Table 1*: Eurostat (1989), *Labour Force Survey Results*, Office for Official Publications of the European Communities; *Table 2*: Department of Employment (1992), *Employment Gazette*, October 1992 © Crown Copyright, reproduced with the permission of the Controller of Her Majesty's Stationery Office.

Photographs

p.113: Bucks Free Press; *p.131*: Madeleine Bunting/The Guardian; *p.133*: photograph by Stephen Berkhauer, © Crown Copyright; *p.135*: The City of Edinburgh District Council; *p.150*: Edward Hamilton-West/The Guardian.

UNIT 9   THE ROLE OF CONCEPTS IN SOCIAL SCIENCE THINKING

Prepared for the Course Team by Gregor McLennan and Norma Sherratt

CONTENTS

1   INTRODUCTION

This half-unit has a slightly different focus from the preceding three units. Unlike the rest of Block II, this unit will *not* convey any further information about social processes; nor will it discuss any new theories of social divisions. In a sense, you could say that, for the moment anyway, everything we want to know about modern society has been satisfactorily covered already. Instead, we want to turn our attention away from society as such and place it more upon social scientists themselves. Or rather on the nature of social science *thinking* about society. In so doing, Unit 9 connects directly back to Unit 4 in Block I, which posed the question: What are social scientists doing when they attempt to 'make sense' of society? Here, we will be approaching that same question but this time around with the concerns and debates of Block II very much in mind. You should note that subsequent blocks of D103 contain a similar closing half-unit, whose purpose is to take a particular aspect of social science thinking in general, and discuss it with the concerns of their particular block in mind. These end half-units not only help to summarize and review key issues in their respective blocks but also form a *sequence* amongst themselves, a sequence which cumulatively builds up a picture of what we might call the 'cycle' of social science enquiry.

The different aspects or phases of this cycle of enquiry were introduced to you in Unit 4. There it was discussed how the social scientific investigation of a concrete topic — *any* topic — begins with a certain amount of *conceptualization*. These initial concepts are then 'worked up' into *classification* systems and theoretical *models*. Theories and models in turn help to provide *explanations* of social phenomena. The value of such explanations depends partly on how they deal with the factual *evidence*, and partly on their relative advantages over other theoretical explanations. Once the nature and value of a theoretical explanation have been provisionally assessed, the initial problem or topic can then be returned to anew, and reclarified in the light of that whole process of research and debate. This is what I mean by speaking of a 'cycle' of enquiry.

Now, Unit 4 only *introduced* you to the component parts of this cycle. You were not expected then, and you are not expected now, to be *fully* conversant with the array of terms involved. This is because asking questions about the nature of social science thinking — sometimes called *the philosophy of the social sciences* — can appear rather difficult and abstract on first acquaintance. So the end half-units of each block have been designed to overlap with, and build upon, one another. Each examines one or two key aspects of social science thinking, connects them to the issues of the block in which it is located, and then leaves some 'trailers' for the end half-unit of the *next* block to develop.

Thus, taking off from Unit 4's overview of the whole cycle of social science enquiry, the sequence is continued in this unit by concentrating on the nature of concepts and *conceptualization*, with some introductory remarks on theoretical *explanations* and how theories built on different concepts can be assessed. Unit 13 follows this by going on to look at the construction of *models* in social science. Then, in Unit 18, the relation between theory and factual *evidence* is considered. Unit 22, for its part, looks at various research methods which social scientists use to produce different sorts of evidence. Unit 26 deals more fully with how we should assess specific *theories*, and Unit 30 with assessing general explanatory frameworks, especially the four 'Traditions' introduced in Unit 5.

Unit	Block	Aspects of social thinking dealt with:
9	II	Conceptualization, explanation
13	III	Constructing models
18	IV	Evidence and theory
22	V	Research methods and principles
26	VI	Assessing theories
30	VII	Assessing explanatory frameworks

SUMMARY

——————————— ACTIVITY 1 ———————————

It is important that you begin your tour of the sequence of end half-units by familiarizing yourselves again with some of the terms used to label the various parts of the 'cycle' of social science enquiry. To that end, you should now briefly re-read Section 1.1 of Unit 4. Remember that at this stage you do *not* need to have a crystal-clear understanding of such terms as 'abstraction', 'conceptualization', 'explanation' and so on; they will become more familiar to you as you go along, but such terminology should at least strike a chord with you before going on.

2   THE NECESSITY OF CONCEPTS

One of the chief 'messages' of Unit 4 which has been amply reinforced in this block was the necessity of using *concepts* in trying to 'make sense' of society. In order to understand and analyse the social world, which is the main business of the social sciences, we must first develop appropriate concepts. From the last three units we know that we can use concepts of class, for example, to analyse social inequality. We can use the concepts of sex and gender to explain relationships between men and women. We can use the concepts of ethnicity and 'race' to comprehend multi-cultural interaction. Such concepts enable us to analyse, to explain and to understand.

Indeed, the general importance of conceptualization is such that the units in this block have had in effect a *two-fold* objective. On the one hand, they conveyed essential information about some of the key divisions at work in modern society, notably those concerning class, 'race'/ethnicity and gender. But, secondly, each in its own way demonstrated that the very activity of enquiring into central social processes requires social scientists to be as *explicit* as possible about the sort of concepts they are using to guide such enquiries. Thus, Unit 6 argued that the very idea of society itself, 'the social', only gets off the ground as a concept by being contrasted with apparently opposite concepts such as 'the individual' and 'the natural'. In Unit 7 we saw that it was not possible to get very far with exploring either class divisions or divisions of 'race'/ethnicity until we had really clarified what we meant by these terms. In Unit 8 Part I we needed to be clear about, not only the meaning, but the origins of patriarchy; and in Part II the concept of the 'underclass' had to be explored thoroughly before we could move any further in our discussion of the relations between the different divisions.

So, in a sense one of the major lessons of Block II is that what we think society is all about, what we believe makes it 'tick', depends greatly on the sort of concepts we use in processing information about it. That is why the debates around class, gender and 'race'/ethnicity appear to be as much about the meaning and relevance of *the concepts themselves* as about the concrete social situations to which they apply, whether these be our lives at home, at work, or in other public spheres. Block II thus builds on Unit 4's proposition that concepts are indispensable, not optional, in social science, and that concepts are the 'building blocks' of more developed theoretical models and explanations.

─────────────── ACTIVITY 2 ───────────────

Cast your mind back over Units 6, 7 and 8. Obviously the concepts of class, 'race'/ethnicity and gender cropped up regularly in the discussion of social processes and social divisions. But now try for a few minutes to make a list of some *other* relevant concepts which made an appearance in the block. What types of phenomena or information were these concepts intended to illuminate?

To get you started on this, here are some possibilities which occurred to us:

1   In Unit 6, Section 1.4, the concept of 'the body' was developed as a way of understanding smoking habits (especially those of women) and as a way of connecting people's personal motives for smoking to more general statistics about the state of health in our society. It was argued that we cannot really understand such data, or even individual testimonies, without first thinking about how an apparently very physical thing, i.e the body, is also socially constructed as a concept, according to certain social values, expectations and habits.

2   In Part I of Unit 7 Ken Thompson introduced you to the Weberian concept of 'status groups'. According to Weber, differences in prestige give rise to groups distinguished in terms of status or prestige; and the importance of the concept of 'status groups' lies not only in the way it introduces another structural component of stratification but also in the way it alerts us to how people enjoying the same privileges and prestige are more likely to *see* themselves as a group and act in their common interests. In particular, it alerts us to the way pursuit of group interests can result in practices of group closure either by exclusion or by usurpation.

3   In Unit 8 Part I a distinction was made between production and reproduction. Now, like 'the body', the idea of reproduction is not something which is completely strange to us. But in social science we try to be more precise about such terms than in ordinary language. Thus, the concept of 'reproduction' becomes not only a way of referring to the physical renewal of the human species. It also refers to the range of processes which reproduce a particular *form* of society. The processes in which we were particularly interested in Unit 8 were those located in the private sphere of the home — all the activities whereby the future and existing workforce is maintained. The concept 'reproduction' served to highlight the significance of women's work in the home, and the relationship of this work to the production processes of society. It enabled us to explore further the differences between women's lives and those of men in terms of the contribution each made to the continuity of a capitalist system of production.

4   Finally, in Unit 8 Part II we have an extended discussion of the concept of an 'underclass'. We will return later to the way in which the meaning of 'underclass' is contested. For the moment, however, you need to note simply how the concept of 'underclass' has alerted us to the possible existence of a group which

is cut off economically from the rest of the working class and effectively excluded from the citizenship rights enjoyed by the bulk of the population. It points out a possible new division which, arguably, has emerged during the last decade between what Galbraith (1992) refers to as the 'contented majority' and the rest of the population. At the same time, of course, it also raises questions about the extent to which the 'underclass' is a black phenomenon and questions about whether such a group really is characterized by distinctive attitudes and behaviour, different from those of the rest of the working class.

Other concepts you might have named include: meritocracy, proletarianization, technicians, automation, citizenship, welfare state from Unit 7 Part I; colony, slavery, reserve army of labour, migrant labour, black, from Unit 7 Part II; work, feminization, community care, family wage, cultural control from Unit 8 Part I. And many more!

3 CONCEPTS IN SOCIAL SCIENCE AND CONCEPTS IN EVERYDAY LIFE

Concepts, it has been argued, are necessary and valuable: they are the essential 'tools' that we need to analyse and understand society. However, you will have noticed that our examples in Activity 2 involved a rather more specialized meaning than these words usually carry in everyday conversation. Indeed, some people even say that inventing fancy conceptual jargon for what everyone knows is 'common sense' is both the hallmark and the bane of the social sciences! The implication here is that the very *abstractness* of concepts is something that has been invented by social scientists but which is wholly unnecessary, because in common sense and everyday life we can get on quite well enough without introducing off-putting conceptual jargon.

Such a reaction is understandable, but it is mistaken in a number of important respects. There are, as we shall see shortly, significant differences between the way concepts are used in social science and in the way they are used in everyday life, but there is no doubt that we resort to conceptual labels in *both* spheres of life all the time. Indeed, the use of any kind of *language* whatsoever, necessarily involves conceptualization. We simply cannot communicate with one another at any level, we cannot say anything about what is going on around us, without abstracting, that is, *generalizing* from experience and trying to convey what is *typical* about a situation. Concepts are no more, and no less, than the terms we use to convey what we believe to be general and typical. Inevitably, this means that they are also to a certain extent abstract.

When we speak, for example, of 'catching a bus', we are not normally trying to indicate a unique individual vehicle. Rather, we are indicating a general *type* of mobility which is used to fulfil an overall type of activity (getting to a venue). Similarly, instead of compiling an endless list of things called Rover, Rex, Sheba, that barking thing over there and the other one yonder, etc., to refer to all manner of canine quadrupeds, we simply use a word or label which *generalizes* and *typifies* the phenomena we have in mind, namely we use the term 'dog'. Now, although the everyday terms 'dog' and 'bus' do not look as though they are anything so grand as concepts, that is precisely what they are. And we don't think of these concepts as 'jargon' for the sole and simple reason that we have become thoroughly accustomed to them. So, as far as the constant use and necessity of concepts goes, there is no difference at all between social science and everyday language, since in both areas we resort to concepts all the time. (If you remember, this was exactly the brunt of the 'going fishing' and 'going shopping' scenarios that were sketched in Unit 4.)

The impression, then, that social science is *abstract*, whilst common sense is essentially *practical*, with little intelligent reflection going on, is a serious exaggeration. Some people believe it is because social science concepts are so much more *complex* than those in everyday life that makes some people shy away from conceptual abstraction. This belief, however, is also something of a myth. In fact, the way we use language in everyday life is often a good deal *more* complex than is social scientific discourse. Everyday understanding and speech actually manage to express a remarkable range of conceptual nuances and distinctions. And, as it happens, often these conceptual distinctions are precisely about the subject matter of social science.

Take social class, for example. Before we even think about the social scientific concept of class, we already know quite a bit about the kind of thing that 'class' refers to. And what we know *already* involves (a) the use of concepts and (b) quite a complex process of understanding. Moreover, these features can already be seen at work in much of the language we ordinarily use. At the drop of a hat, most of you would be able to cite class-type distinctions from your own background and experience. Alan Bennett, the playwright, made a TV film along these lines in 1988. The film was set in Harrogate and drew on his own upbringing. Early on in the film, there is a scene where Bennett is sitting in the lobby of the Crown Hotel, watching the Yorkshire middle class drift in and out. And he says: 'My mother's scheme of things admitted of much finer distinctions than are allowed by the sociologists. She'd talk of people being "better class", "well off", "nicely spoken", "refined", "educated", "genuine", "ordinary" and — the ultimate condemnation — "common".'

Each of Bennett's mother's terms here is a *concept* of sorts, in the sense that it abstracts, generalizes and typifies from a range of further particulars. The range of concepts is carefully graded, each notch in the vocabulary reflecting the complex reality of the observed society as the observer sees it. Bennett is right: his mother's gradation of class position is at least as complex as any to be found in social science.

How, then, *does* scientific, and especially social scientific conceptualization differ from ordinary discourse? Perhaps the most obvious general difference is simply that social scientists tend to be that bit more *conscious*, more aware than ordinary speakers, that they are using analytic concepts, and that the particular concepts they use have an important bearing on the nature of the assertions they make about the social world. As mentioned a little earlier, social scientists aim to be *precise* about their concepts, and they seek to establish fairly systematically what sort of phenomenon comes under that conceptual heading.

The need for definitional clarity in social scientific analysis is something that has been noted in several places in the course so far. Everyday speech is certainly very rich in suggestion and nuance, but it is also typically rather vague and impressionistic. This feature often makes it good for story-telling and for conveying the *atmosphere* of a social situation, but by the same token it makes it hard for us to identify precisely the nature of that situation. Alan Bennett's mother, for example, used a whole number of suggestive descriptive terms to register what social scientists would call 'indicators of class differences'. But we do not know from this admittedly very atmospheric account whether she is taking the concept of class to refer to the amount of wealth people have, or to their level of income, or to their educational attainment, or to their own sense of social status and self-esteem. Yet every single one of these criteria *could* be defended as the essence of the class concept, as was discussed in Section 4.4 of Unit 6. More likely, perhaps, Mrs Bennett had a *combination* of such criteria in mind. However, we cannot really tell what

Alan Bennett and Mum: 'respectable' working class?

that *combination* is, since even though such language is analytically suggestive, it is just not analytically precise *enough* for the purposes of the social sciences.

Similarly, whereas the term 'race' is used frequently in everyday speech, social scientists have consistently made clear the problematic nature of the concept; the need to recognize that what many people are referring to when they use the term is in fact a minority ethnic group, i.e. a group distinguished in terms of cultural not biological characteristics. However, as social scientists we also need to be aware that, although there is no scientific evidence to prove the existence of 'races', definitions of people in 'racial' terms are still a part of the reality of our society. Classifying people in racial terms has real effects.

At this point it can be firmly asserted that social scientific conceptualization is actually *simpler and more abstract* than everyday discourse and that this is one of its great *virtues*. This is because all the sciences attempt to get down to the 'bare bones' of the phenomena with which they deal. And in order to attempt this systematically, their key concepts need to be both economical and rigorous. In a sense, social reality needs to be conceptually *oversimplified* in the models of social science if those models are to produce fresh insights. (The role of models in social science conceptualization is extensively developed in Unit 13.)

The second aspect of concepts that social scientists are particularly conscious of is their empirical scope, that is, the range of things, times and places that various concepts 'cover'. Patriarchy, for example, as used by radical feminists is a concept having very great empirical scope since it is seen to apply to most societies throughout history as we know it. Accordingly, any theory prioritizing this concept will be making very big claims about all known gender relations. Such claims will certainly be very challenging just because of this extended scope of the concept. But, equally, a vast range of empirical considerations will have a bearing on the theory, drawn from research right across human society. And it may be that such a theory is more vulnerable to detailed objections as a result.

Concepts of class are rather less broad in scope, applying mainly to modern industrial societies, and in some theories applying only to *capitalist* societies. The concept of 'the working class' is obviously even narrower in scope, referring to just one type of class formation within industrial societies. The point, then, is that social scientists are not only concerned with conceptual definitions, but also with their varying empirical coverage or scope. (The relationship between theories, factual evidence and the research process is further developed in Units 18 and 22.)

Another major characteristic of social science thinking is that social scientists are often ready to acknowledge that many of the concepts they develop are 'essentially contested' or 'essentially contestable'. This means that even at the level of offering a *definition* of a concept, someone else might well try to challenge that definition as being inappropriate. Take 'class', for example, as expounded in Unit 7 Part I. Here the same *word*, class, can be given very different 'essential' characteristics by different social theorists, for example by marxists and Weberians. Marxists understand class in terms of ownership and control of capital (or lack of such ownership and control), whereas Weberians see class position as determined by market situation — what people can offer in order to gain an income.

Similarly, as you saw in Part II of Unit 8, whilst there is an area of agreement over the broad meaning of 'underclass', the agreement does not extend to an analysis of the causes of the formation of an underclass. Whereas those writing from a broadly liberal or conservative tradition emphasize cultural factors and see the emergence of an underclass as stemming from the adoption of deviant values and corresponding patterns of deviant behaviour, those writing from a broadly reformist or marxist perspective see it as a product of structural factors (increasing poverty, the growth of long-term unemployment). The underclass thesis, then, can take radically different forms; and this is, of course, reflected in what are seen as the essential defining characteristics of the concept itself.

Now whilst there will be much serious and persuasive argument about which of these interpretations — of class or of underclass — is the more 'valid' and which is 'the right one', in a sense there can *never* be a wholly 'correct', foolproof interpretation. This is because the 'essence' or content of such concepts as class or underclass is from the outset stipulated differently from within each of the competing theoretical perspectives. Understandably, the most notable 'contested' concepts are those which generate strong political and moral allegiances amongst social scientists, and 'class' and 'underclass' are clearly two of these. Other examples would include such concepts as poverty, equality, freedom, justice, oppression, and so on.

It is sometimes thought that an appeal to the 'facts' of the matter can decide between the contested definitions offered by different conceptual frameworks. However, appealing to the facts, surprisingly perhaps, does not usually resolve anything. For example, it was indicated in Unit 7 Part I how marxists and Weberians have each tried to make perfectly good sense of 'factual' evidence of changes and fragmentation amongst the modern working class. Weberians may see this as support for the 'group closure' concept arising out of the activities of status groups, whereas marxists prefer to understand occupational and status fragmentation as a process taking place *within* the broad working class, brought about by capitalism's great capacity to introduce new ways of dividing all workers. In other words, there is still a major contest between these theorists about what the essential meaning of class is, whatever the state of the facts about class composition.

SUMMARY

- Concepts are essential in social science analysis.
- Social scientific and everyday conceptualization do overlap to some extent.
- Social science is neither as abstract nor as complex as it sometimes appears.
- Everyday thinking has its own storehouse of abstract concepts.
- Social science can, however, be differentiated from everyday thinking by its concern for definitional precision, and by its concern to establish the empirical scope and significance of concepts.
- Many of the key concepts in social science are 'essentially contested' and social scientists are generally aware of this.

4   MORE TO PERCEPTION THAN MEETS THE EYE

So far we have argued that we cannot 'make sense' of society (whether in social science or everyday life) without the extensive and explicit use of abstract concepts. Some people, however, take a lot of persuading on this basic point. Such sceptics include those students who get a little frustrated with the abstract stuff and want to get down straight away to the nitty-gritty of real-life situations. The sceptics also include some philosophers (known as 'empiricists') who believe that the commonsense suspicion of conceptual abstraction is to an extent justified. Empiricist philosophers down the years have tended to argue as follows:

> OK, yes, let's agree that concepts are unavoidable at some point. But let's not get hung up on them. Life is not that complicated. Concepts should be derived as far as possible directly from our perception, that is from our sensory experience of things and events. In the end, only the evidence of our sense perception (eyes, ears, noses etc.) is reliable.

What the empiricist philosopher and the frustrated social science student share is a belief in the primacy of perception or observation over conceptualization or theory. They both want to say 'why can't we just *observe* what's going on; why not just *look and see* without much resort to concepts at all?' In the end, however, such an attitude is short-sighted. Both philosophical empiricism and the commonsense distaste for concepts that tends to go with it need to be firmly rejected because they seriously underestimate how vital the role of concepts and theory are in human understanding. Over the years, non-empiricist philosophers and psychologists have developed quite a formidable range of experiments and arguments which do severely undermine faith in the primacy of perception. The general motto here is: there is always more to observation than meets the eye. Or, to put it another way, there is no such thing as pure observation or perception. As was noted in Section 8.3 of Unit 8, our direct observations are always *patterned*, shaped or organized by the concepts and theories at our disposal. What we *see* is, moreover, strongly conditioned by our general cultural stock of beliefs, values and expectations.

To grasp this point, consider the following picture.

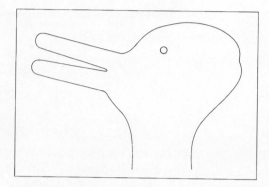

Figure 1

What do you see? Is the drawing a representation of a duck or a rabbit? Perhaps some of you saw only one sort of animal at first, then later (after reading this, perhaps) realized that it could be taken for the other sort as well. However, now that you have realized that both images are possible, you would probably agree that it could be taken *either* as a duck or a rabbit. What we see in the image is a duck, a rabbit, or both. The image itself cannot magically tell us what it *really* represents. What the image 'really' is depends on the *way* we happen to see it. This is a first indication that what we see depends not so much on our perception as on our conception.

Now imagine that we do not have any experience of 'rabbithood' in our culture. The image would then be completely unambiguous and we would see a duck. If on the other hand we lived in a rabbity culture which boasted no ducks, we would see a rabbit, with no argument. Imagine further, if you will, that our culture did not have the concept of a *picture* at all. The same sensory image that we now happen to see as a duck–rabbit would then be little more than one long squiggly line and a dot. We would not 'see' anything which made sense at all. You might think this train of thought is becoming a little far-fetched. Whatever else it is, you might say, it is definitely a picture of some sort. But you would be rash to think so.

What do you think of this next image?

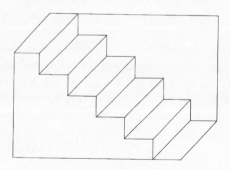

Figure 2

Like the duck–rabbit, after a while this second image makes sense to us as being similarly ambiguous. You could see it as a staircase with the *upper* surface showing, or you could see it as one with the *under* surface visible. Or each in succession. Above all, we would again probably see it first of all as a drawing, a pictorial representation. But in fact, this image was shown to a number of African communities whose cultures do *not* include the custom of representing three-dimensional objects in this two-dimensional way. What they 'saw' was simply a two-dimensional array of lines. Seeing such lines as a 'picture' of any kind thus involves many conceptual assumptions about the aesthetics and technology of our culture and society.

These examples show firstly that perceptions and observations are dependent upon concepts and, secondly, that concepts are embedded within particular cultures and societies. What we 'see' literally depends on these conceptual interpretations and cultural expectations. Modern research in developmental psychology has in fact come round to supporting the eighteenth-century philosopher Immanuel Kant's original argument that even space and time themselves are concepts of a sort, and not 'raw' data out there in the universe. It follows that perceiving such things as staircase images as if 'from below' or 'from above' is itself a 'trained' activity, one which is very much mediated by concepts relative to a particular intellectual universe. It was Kant, by the way, who originated the excellent shorthand phrase 'concepts without perception are empty, perception without concepts is blind'. That can usefully serve as our conclusion at this stage in the discussion.

—————————————— ACTIVITY 3 ——————————————

Here is yet another ambiguous diagram:

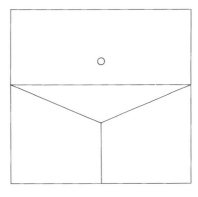

Figure 3

This time it is perhaps less clear what the 'double vision' represents. For many of us, it may strike us initially as little more than some lines and a dot. However, it *could* be seen as either an olive dropping into a cocktail glass or (part of) someone in a bathing suit. Now try to think through for yourselves:

(a) What *concepts* are involved in regarding the image in each of these ways?

(b) What *cultural norms* are involved? (For example, norms concerning the use of leisure, the consumption of alcohol, and the idea of 'the body' as a social construction [remember Unit 6, Section 1.4].)

ACTIVITY 4

In our discussion of observation, we have been considering figurative *diagrams* only. Think, therefore, how much more difficult it is to observe a complex *social* process or event without the use of a whole number of concepts to guide and shape our understanding. Imagine, for example, that you had seen the arrival of the first ship bringing Afro-Caribbeans to Britain (after the passing of the British Nationality Act of 1948). In what sense could this 'event' be usefully described from observation alone?

Try to describe this event without using terms which imply more general social concepts.

How did you get on with that? When we tried' we only managed to come up with: 'In 1948, some Afro-Caribbeans arrived in Britain.' Now, since that is a meaningful sentence, maybe after all it is possible to deduce *something* from 'pure' observation. But not much. We found ourselves having to continually stop and start again, progressively eliminating all the interesting conceptual terms we have encountered in Block II, such as 'black', 'workers', 'capitalism', 'migrant labour' and so on. Even a phrase like 'arrived in Britain' carries implications about immigration which by no means stem spontaneously from perceptions. And hold on: even place names (such as 'Great Britain') and terms like 'Afro-Caribbean' are concepts of sorts, with a rich history of cultural assumptions and conflict behind them. So really, what is simply there to be observed and described is virtually nothing — it is a bit like being left with the bare lines in the earlier diagrams once the conceptual interpretation has been artificially 'removed'.

SUMMARY

- Observation is strongly guided by the concepts we use.
- Concepts are drawn from a wider stock of cultural values.

---

5 CONCEPTS AND REALITY

So far we have argued that conceptualization is the principal element in all human knowledge, whether in social science or in everyday life. The most obvious alternative, and the only possible escape route from the labours of conceptualization, was the idea that we can make perfectly good sense of the world through direct observation alone. However, we think the points made in the last section effectively close off that escape route: there is no such thing as 'pure' perception, independent of concepts.

At this point we want to return to a very basic question, one that we have certainly been tackling in a number of ways, but which we have not so far taken head-on, namely: what exactly are these concepts that we appear to be stuck with? One reason for delaying this question until now is that often the simple-sounding questions turn out to be the most difficult ones to answer clearly! Much philosophical effort is, then, required just to get the discussion under way. However, we have enough under our belts by now to have a go at this deceptively basic question.

Figure 4   Concepts as representations

Perhaps the key thing to note about concepts is that they have a *dual* character. On the one hand, they are mental or linguistic representations of reality. On the other hand, they are the means by which people effectively communicate with each other in language. Let us call the first point the *representational* aspects of concepts and the second the *communicative* aspect.

As indicated earlier, concepts enable us to 'pick out' (i.e. select or abstract) various features of reality by giving those features a general label. If you think about it, 'reality', and our experience of it, contain an infinite number of things, qualities and processes. It would be literally impossible to 'capture' in thought each element of life and experience *without* using concepts to generalize and typify. So one role of concepts is to try to 'cut the world up' in various ways so as to identify its component parts and the range of species that it contains. You should note here that by 'species' we not only refer to natural species such as dogs, plants and planets. Concepts also enable us to cut the *social* world up into parts and species, such as classes, or occupations, or status groups. So the first main aspect of concepts is that they serve to 'represent' in thought the structures and processes of reality itself. Concepts are all those signs, ideas, words and labels (= representations) which help to provide a 'map' of reality for us.

But it is very important to see that although concepts are certainly attempted representations of reality, they cannot possibly be *replicas* of it. In other words, concepts no more *resemble* reality than the map of a mountainous area *is* a mountainous area. Similarly, the concept 'dog' (unlike the real thing) does not bark! Concepts, like maps and words, are best seen not as mirror images of reality (as in Figure 4) but rather as shorthand *codes* which enable people to establish common understandings of reality. Such shared codes are essential if human beings are to communicate successfully with each other, and in a sense this is a crucial aspect of the use of concepts whether or not the concepts in question 'accurately' reflect the nature of reality or not. Language is, after all, a definitively social phenomenon, and we develop concepts not so that we can construct absolutely accurate pictures of reality as such, but, in the first instance, so that we can effectively communicate with one another.

Figure 5   Concepts as vehicles of communication

The point here is that whilst concepts are certainly attempted representations of reality, they can never be *copies* of reality. Moreover we can never check *exactly* how good our concepts are as representations of reality, since this would require an omniscient 'God's eye view' of things, a view which is simply unattainable. So without denying that our concepts do often seek to be adequate representations which can then be regarded as more or less valid encapsulations of reality, concepts are very much *provisional* representations, and moreover are themselves the products of culture and history. The representational aspect of concepts is thus always *embedded* within their wider communicative dimension. It follows that whilst we use concepts to try to capture something 'objective' about reality, the reality and the conceptual representations alike are liable to debate and *change*. Moreover, we have to constantly bear in mind that the 'objects' of social scientific thinking are far

Figure 6   Concepts as representations of society

less open to straightforward pictorial representation than the dogs and planets of the natural sciences. of the natural sciences.

In Unit 6 Section 2.4, for example, it was shown how our notion of the *individual* would have appeared strange and somewhat 'unnatural' prior to the onset of 'bourgeois' civilization in the eighteenth century. Similarly, Marx did not sit down one day and think: 'Class. Now there's a fine concept. Let us define it in the abstract then see how it applies to modern society.' Ideas simply do not get plucked out of thin air in this way. Raymond Williams' book *Keywords* (1976) was cited in Unit 6 to contextualize the rise of the concept of the individual. In the same way, Williams goes on to tell us, for example, about how the concept of class only gradually became prominent in the early nineteenth century, emerging out of a cluster of more common terms used in journalistic social commentaries to indicate social distinctions. These were words such as 'rank', 'order' and 'estate'. And 'class' only became the preferred analytical term amongst that verbal cluster through the process of the industrial revolution in Britain and the establishment of capitalistic economic organization. Karl Marx's genius was thus not to *invent* the concept of class, but to refine it theoretically and to turn it to political uses which fundamentally challenged the capitalist context which gave birth to concepts of class.

We have emphasized the dual nature of concepts because for around two thousand years there has been a philosophical battle going on as to which aspect of conceptualization is most important. Some thinkers have tried to argue that in spite of the culturally specific contexts in which concepts are developed, we *can* and must in the end decide whether some concepts are really more representative of reality than others. This firm position (often called 'realism') thus very much highlights the representational aspect of concepts. Other thinkers have argued that since all attempts to represent reality in thought are culturally specific, we might as well get rid of the misleading idea of an independent objective reality, out there, which our ideas more or less accurately reflect. This position (known as 'cultural relativism') is thus much keener to emphasize the communicative role of concepts, and the way concepts *construct* our sense of what reality is.

You will be pleased to learn that we are not proposing to resolve two thousand years of philosophical dispute in this half-unit! We would merely advise that whilst there is undoubtedly an element of tension between these two views of the primary aspect of conceptualization, it is probably better for our purposes to think of concepts as having a *dual* character. Sometimes we might want to emphasize the representational aspect, but sometimes we might want to highlight the communicative aspect. Rather than see 'realism' and 'relativism' as locked in mortal combat, it is possible to see them as forming a spectrum of different *emphases*, a spectrum that we should perhaps feel free to draw upon in different ways, depending upon the task in hand.

SUMMARY

- Partly, concepts are attempts to *represent* the world in thought.
- The representational aspect of concepts is always embedded in their *communicative* aspect.
- There remains a fascinating and still unresolved debate between 'realists' and 'relativists'.

6 CONCEPTS AND THEORIES

It would be convenient in a way to leave off the discussion of concepts at this point where their fascinating but problematic relationship with 'reality' has been aired. However, there is another relationship which cannot be left entirely to later units (though it arises there too) and that is the relationship between concepts and *theories* or theoretical models. The reason we cannot omit reference to theories is quite simple. Social scientists, as we have mentioned, are very much interested in the precision of conceptual definitions and in establishing the empirical scope of concepts. It may be readily accepted that concepts interestingly pattern observations and enable us to generalize from experience. All that is true enough. But even so, it is very unlikely that social scientists would be greatly bothered by these aspects of concepts, or that they would be interested in choosing between a range of contested concepts, if the use of concepts was not strongly and intimately connected to the search for good *explanations* of social phenomena.

Now, as it happens, concepts, taken individually and in isolation, do not really provide explanations of anything. It is theories and models, not concepts, which provide explanations of society. However, concepts are the building blocks of theories, and theories can be thought of as coherent 'packages' of related concepts. So concepts *are* of explanatory importance, but only because they form part of a wider theoretical framework.

6.1 CONCEPTS AND CLASSIFICATION

One major contribution that concepts make to the development of theoretical explanations is to facilitate distinct systems of classification, that is classification of both people and of data.

A good example of this process can be found in Table 4 of Unit 8 Part II which looks at employment patterns in Great Britain. Here we have three types of classification system at work:

1 Classification by ethnic origin in which the key concepts are white, West Indian/Guyanese, Indian and Pakistani/Bangladeshi.

2 Classification by gender in which the key concepts are men and women.

3 Classification by type of occupation in which the key concepts include non-manual, managerial and professional, clerical etc.

Each classification system depends on the key concepts which organize it. It is these key concepts which determine exactly how the data are presented to us — which pick up particular patterns and not others. So in this case we have four categories of ethnic origin which lead us to see, for example, that Indian men are more likely to be in non-manual than in manual employment, and that this is not the case for men of other ethnic origin. It would, of course, be possible to use other concepts to denote ethnic origin (you have an example in Table 7 of Unit 7 Part II), and you may actually be querying the usefulness of some of the categories used here. But the essential point in this instance is that any concepts based on ethnic origin will show how people from different ethnic groups have different experiences of employment.

Working now from a different starting-point, classification by occupation also alerts us to certain patterns. In particular the concepts manual and non-manual work alert us to the fact that women overall are far more likely to be in non-manual work than in manual work whereas for men (except Indian men) it is the reverse. But a different system of classification built on, for example, part-time/full-time work or work in service/non-service industries would possibly have given a different kind of description.

6.2 CONCEPTS AND THEORETICAL EXPLANATIONS

The use of concepts in social science theorizing does not stop with the way they enable us to make classifications. Concepts are also important because together they build up into theoretical explanations. These provide answers to *why* society is to be classified one way rather than another. They try to establish arguments and evidence about the underlying causes and dynamics of particular social relations.

Let's look at this in a series of stages.

First of all, most social scientists would argue that social science is important because it can to some extent offer explanations of events, patterns or processes in a society. Social science is not *only* about explanations; nor are social scientists the only ones who offer explanations for whatever is most exercising us as members of society at any one time. But the social scientist will claim that his or her explanation is different from others in that it is more rigorous and more scientific. (You may want to remind yourself of what James Anderson had to say about this in Section 1.2 of Unit 4.)

The reasons for this claim brings us back to concepts. A theoretical explanation in social science consists of a network of concepts each of which has been carefully defined. For example, a marxist attempting to understand 'racial' divisions would build a theory around the concepts of migrant labour, capitalism, colonialism, profit. So, a marxist explanation of, for example, high unemployment rates amongst young black people in the UK would come from within a very clear conceptual framework in which what is happening to the workforce today is to be understood in terms of the needs of capitalism both in the past and today.

A second example: a radical feminist theory of gender divisions would be built around the key concepts of patriarchy, power, cultural control. A radical feminist explanation of, for example, the very small number of women judges would come from within a conceptual framework in which this lack of representation would be seen as just another example of the way men occupy all the positions of power in a society, and are able to maintain that power through a variety of mechanisms ranging from direct discrimination to more indirect forms of control.

However, as you know from the work you have just done in this block, there is always more than one theoretical explanation on offer for whatever aspect of society we are looking at. For each of the divisions you have just studied there have been at least two theories put forward; each consisting of a different combination of concepts. The key concepts in marxist explanation of class divisions (capitalism, relations of production, class conflict) are different from those prioritized in a Weberian explanation of class (market situation, hierarchy, competition). Each theory privileges certain key concepts over others. It deems certain concepts to be especially important, more important than others, in understanding the phenomena in focus.

SUMMARY

- Concepts are the building blocks of theories.
- Concepts enable us to classify social relationships in different ways.
- Concepts also help us to explain; a theoretical explanation consists of a network of concepts.
- Different theories privilege different key concepts.

6.3   ASSESSING THEORETICAL EXPLANATIONS

This brings us to a second reason for asserting that social science can actually take us beyond 'commonsense' explanations. Not only is social science able to offer a number of different kinds of explanations; it is also able to provide guidelines on how to go about deciding which explanation is the most useful one. Assessment of different theories, that is, is an important part of doing social science.

As you worked through Block II looking at social divisions and the way they can be explained, we asked you at certain points to do some preliminary work thinking about the strengths and weaknesses of different theories. So, for example, in Part I of Unit 8 you were asked to look at both marxist feminism and radical feminism in terms of a number of questions:

- Can the theory explain some of the patterns already identified earlier in the unit?

- Can the theory explain changes in gender divisions?

- Can the theory account for those aspects of gender divisions which you are most aware of?

- Is it an explanation which is applicable to *all* women in *all* societies?

In the commentary following the activity it was pointed out that, for example, marxist feminism seemed to have some advantages over radical feminism because it enabled us to see how the experiences of contemporary women could be understood in the context of the division between the public and the private which was created by capitalism. On the other hand, however, radical feminism seemed to be stronger in the way it was able to explain issues such as violence against women in *both* capitalist and non-capitalist societies by the use of the concept of patriarchy. This issue does not seem to be so easily understood through a theory in which the key concepts all relate to production and reproduction, i.e. marxist feminism.

So assessment is about 'strengths and weaknesses'; and about exploring these systematically in a way which does not mean falling back on a simple individual preference for one theory over another. We could quite easily leave you at this point until you are much further into the course. Certainly you have done enough work on assessing theories in this block to have an understanding of what is required of you when you are asked as part of a TMA question to make a comparison between different theories and to come to some decisions about their strengths and weaknesses.

However, we are going to take you one step further because you may well be feeling at this stage that, although you understand what is meant by assessment of theories, you are not sure that you would actually know where to start without some guidelines on what to look for. It is these guidelines which we are just going to introduce briefly now. (They will be explained to you more fully in the half-unit at the end of Block VI — Unit 26.)

If you think back to all the questions we were asking as we worked through the different explanations of class, gender and 'racial'/ethnic divisions, you can probably see that they fell into three main groupings:

1   How good was the *reasoning* of the explanation? That is, did all the steps fit together into a logical, clear and coherent argument?

In addition, was it able to account for what seemed to be important evidence?

So, for example, in Unit 7 Part I, Ken Thompson points out the way in which a marxist theory starting from the conflict inherent in the relations of production can move step by step to an understanding of the processes of deskilling in the

UK in the 1990s. Marxist analysis provides a carefully reasoned, systematic explanation of one of the key issues of contemporary economic life.

He also goes on, however, to point out that Weberian theory also has strengths as far as reasoning is concerned, if by reasoning we mean the way in which a theory can account for the evidence. Weberian theory seems to be very useful for the light it throws on what he calls the 'dynamics of coalition and sub-division of class fractions'. Starting from the concepts of market situation and work situation Weberian theory seems to do a good job of accounting for the complexities of the British class structure, the very important distinctions between, for example, skilled and unskilled manual work, or between different kinds of non-manual work. It, too, is strong on reasoning though in a different way from marxist theory.

2 How wide was the *scope* of the theory?

How much was it able to account for, both in terms of looking back and looking outwards? Could it be used to explain what was happening in the UK 500 years ago? Or what is happening today in societies other than the UK? What did it leave unexplained?

For example, one criticism offered of marxist feminist theories was that they could only explain the experience of women in capitalist societies whilst radical feminist theories had a broader reach, claiming to be able to account for all inequalities in all known societies past and present.

Conversely, of course, in Unit 7 Part II, Andrew Pilkington noted that one of the strengths of a marxist approach to understanding 'racial' divisions was its comprehensive scope, the way it accounted for 'a wide range of apparently unrelated facts (colonialism, migration, racism etc.)' and could also account for similarities between Britain and other Western societies.

(Don't let this worry you ... the message is simply that the scope, or reach, of a theory can be defined in different ways.)

3 Did the theory lead us to believe that it had the *ability to adapt*?

That is, did it have the flexibility to take on board any changes that occurred in the divisions we have been looking at? Did it seem as if the basic concepts could be built on to provide explanations of changing circumstances? Was the theory showing itself able to respond to points raised about its weaknesses?

So, for example, whilst it is clear that marxist analysis can work very well to explain class issues involving conflicts between the major classes, critics have argued that it is not able to explain the range of issues to do with the rise of the middle classes. We saw in Unit 7 Part I, however, that marxists have responded by developing the theory using the concept of 'contradictory class locations' — a concept which can then be built on as circumstances change.

Openness of another kind is demonstrated by radical feminist theory as those working from this perspective have turned their attention to what is happening in the workplace. The continued inequalities experienced by women even in times of rapid change (and changes of a kind which might be expected to benefit them) can be understood, as we saw in Unit 8 Part I, in terms of the continued supremacy of men's definitions of what counts as skilled and essential work.

In Unit 26 these three sets of questions are referred to respectively as: questions involving *explanatory power*; questions involving *explanatory reach*; and questions involving *explanatory openness*. At that point there will be much more detailed discussion of what each one entails. You might try, however, to use these kinds of guidelines each time you are faced with exploring the strengths and weaknesses of a theory, so that by the end of the course you will find it coming much more easily.

6.4   THEORIES IN COMPETITION

What, though is to prevent you, having explored the strengths and weaknesses of a number of theories, each looking at the same issue, from combining them to get a 'complete' explanation?

As we have seen from both TV04 and the ethnographic material in Part II of Unit 8, the lived experience of any one individual or group will reflect a range of different influences. This half-unit has made it clear that single theories do omit important factors and experiences, leaving gaps which may be filled by other available theories. Isn't there a case, then, for sometimes combining them?

This is a difficult question and part of an ongoing debate in social science. Certainly at one level theories can be combined. In Unit 7 Part II, for example, the point is made that the third explanation of 'racial' divisions, the one centred on globalization and cultural identity seems to accept both marxist premises (that it is capitalism which is the important concept) and Weberian premises (that economic factors are overlaid by other significant ones). In Unit 8 Part I we showed how a more complete understanding of women's experiences at work is achieved by combining the concepts of marxist feminists and radical feminists, as in the work of Heidi Hartmann.

However, some social scientists would argue that there may come a point at which a choice has to be made. This is the point when we have to decide whether it is class or 'race'/ethnicity or gender which is to be the key concept in any explanation. After all, the 'autonomy' of each main concept, and its full theoretical force, has traditionally only been established by theorists of one perspective or another insisting that in the end, it is *their* concepts and classifications, and not the others, which must be given analytic primacy in properly explaining the dynamics of social processes.

Feminist explanations, for example, particularly radical feminist ones, did not make their impact simply by pointing out that 'the gender question' was somewhat underplayed in other available perspectives. On the contrary, it was generally argued by such feminists that for many key areas, gender must take a clear analytical and political *priority* over other factors. Similarly, marxism has often been accused of trying to 'reduce' issues of gender and 'race' to those of *class*. As mentioned in Unit 7 Part I, serious attempts have been made, within marxism, to try to avoid this tendency towards 'class reductionism' — i.e. the inclination to see *class* issues as being the real hidden meaning of all sorts of apparently *non-class* issues (such as 'race', gender, age, nationality etc.). And yet, if marxists did *not* somehow assert class factors as primary over other social influences — however important those others might be — then ironically the very insight which gives marxist analysis its unique distinctiveness would simply evaporate.

So the combination of different key concepts at the level of descriptive classification is certainly possible and even desirable. But, having said that, there is an ongoing debate in the social sciences as to whether, at the 'deepest' level of explanation, key theoretical concepts logically *can* have equal weight, even where such a combination is considered eminently desirable.

6.5 THEORIES AND VALUES — A POSTSCRIPT

The final step in this initial exploration of theories we are going to leave until later. James Anderson alerted you to the role of values in social science at the end of Block I and certainly your own values will, ultimately, be part of your assessment of a theory. You will have more opportunity to explore this in Block VII.

SUMMARY

- Assessment of theories is an important part of social science.
- Theories can be assessed in terms of:
  - (a) their reasoning;
  - (b) their scope;
  - (c) their adaptability.
- There is an ongoing debate in social science about the extent to which theories can be combined.

---

7 CONCLUSION

In the first four sections of this half-unit we were concerned to establish in various ways the centrality of conceptualization to social science understanding — partly by showing how pervasive concepts are in everyday life as well as in social science, and partly by ruling out the possibility of understanding through pure observation. The conclusion of those parts was very clear: the explicit introduction of organizing concepts is something to be encouraged in social science; their precise definition is to be welcomed; and a sense of the proper empirical scope of concepts is indispensable. In addition, the 'essentially contested' nature of concepts enjoins us to be *critical* where necessary in our approach to all concepts and to any research reports which follow their guidelines. (Incidentally, all these strictures apply every bit as much to your own student TMAs as they do to advanced scholarly theses!)

In Section 5 we were less concerned to establish firm conclusions than to introduce you to two profound debates about the nature of social science thinking. One of these debates concerned the relationship of concepts to the 'reality' they are supposed to represent. Sometimes this issue is presented as an outright alternative: *either* concepts reflect reality or they actually *construct* reality for us. However, our own view here was that whilst there was much room for open debate here, since there is indeed a certain *tension* between the representational and communicative aspects of conceptualization, *both* aspects should in the end be seen as essential and complementary.

Then we touched on another important relationship: that between concepts and theories. Concepts are in the end interesting for social scientists in so far as they enable insightful *explanations* of social phenomena. But it is only as part of more elaborate *theories* that concepts do manage to generate such insights. How we finally choose — and whether we *have* to choose — between the insights that are offered by different conceptual frameworks or theories are, however, questions which can only be raised not resolved at this stage. The short review half-units in later blocks take these issues further.

REFERENCES

Galbraith, J.K. (1992) *The Culture of Contentment*, London, Sinclair Stevenson.

Williams, R. (1976) *Keywords*, London, Fontana.

ACKNOWLEDGEMENT

Grateful acknowledgement is made to the following source for permission to reproduce material in this unit:

p. 173: Alan Bennett/Peters Fraser and Dunlop Ltd.